POPULATION AND DEVELOPMENT: OLD DEBATES, NEW CONCLUSIONS

POPULATION AND DEVELOPMENT: OLD DEBATES, NEW CONCLUSIONS

■

Robert Cassen and contributors:

Dennis A. Ahlburg
Lisa M. Bates
Nancy Birdsall
Schuyler Frautschi
Lynn Freedman
Kaval Gulhati
Allen C. Kelley
Cynthia B. Lloyd
Deborah Maine
William Paul McGreevey
Thomas W. Merrick
Theodore Panayotou
Farida Shaheed
Sharon Stanton Russell
Michael S. Teitelbaum

 Transaction Publishers
New Brunswick (USA) and Oxford (UK)

60111490

Library of Congress Cataloging-in-Publication Data

Cassen, Robert.
        Population and development: old debates, new conclusions/Robert Cassen and contributors.

(U.S.-Third World Policy Perspectives: No. 19)
        1. Developing countries—Population—Economic aspects. 2. Population—Economic aspects. I. Cassen, Robert. II. Series.

HB884.P6624 1994   304.6′09172′6—dc20   94-11399 CIP

ISBN: 1-56000-165-8 (cloth)
ISBN: 1-56000-740-0 (paper)
Printed in the United States of America

Director of Publications: Christine E. Contee
Publications Editor: Jacqueline Edlund-Braun
Edited by Rosemarie Philips
Cover design: Snorek Design Group
Book design: Tim Kenney Design Partners, Inc.

Contents

Foreword

Few development issues have aroused as much dissension—politically and academically—as the relations among population growth, economic growth, and human welfare. The first international population conference in 1974 was dominated by North-South debates over the importance of population relative to other development concerns. Developing countries rejected U.S. and other donor assertions that rapid population growth was a serious impediment to development. By 1984, at the second world population conference, the reverse was true. Developing countries were now convinced of the urgent importance of dealing with population growth, but the United States asserted that population growth was not inherently good or bad for development. The infamous "Mexico City" policy, which led to the withdrawal of U.S. support for the International Planned Parenthood Federation and the United Nation's Fund for Population Activities, was motivated primarily by domestic political considerations. At the time, however, there was also a school of thought emerging in academic circles which argued that the economic environment of a given country largely determined the consequences of population growth. An example of this line of thinking was a 1986 National Academy of Sciences study which concluded that while "slower population growth would be beneficial for most developing countries," it was not the most important factor in development. The report further suggested that population growth itself could induce the technological and policy change necessary to accommodate growing numbers.

It was against this backdrop, and in anticipation of the third international population conference in Cairo in 1994, that ODC was asked by the World Bank and The Rockefeller Foundation to undertake an analysis of current research on the relationship between population and development. The result, *Population and Development: Old Debates, New Conclusions,* represents the current best assessment of what is known about the consequences for development of rapid population growth. The authors address the complex issues that currently face both developed- and developing-country governments in the area of population: the relationship between population and economic growth; the relations of family planning and fertility reduction to women's reproductive health and women's rights; population growth consequences, at the family and societal level, for investments in human resource development; the impact of population growth on local ecosystems; and the rationale for population assistance programs.

We were delighted to enlist as director of this project Robert Cassen, a professor of development economics at the International Development Centre at Oxford University and one of the world's experts on the interrelationship between population and development. He previously held a variety of academic posts, acted as an economic advisor to the British aid program in India, and served on the staff of the World Bank and the Brandt Commission Secretariat. He also directed and coauthored the seminal study, *Does Aid Work?*

This project was made possible by grants from The William and Flora Hewlett Foundation, The John D. and Catherine T. MacArthur Foundation, The Andrew W. Mellon Foundation, The Pew Global Stewardship Initiative, and The Rockefeller Foundation. The support of The Ford Foundation and The Rockefeller Foundation is crucial for the Council's overall program.

John W. Sewell
President
July 1994

Part I
Overview

Population and Development: Old Debates, New Conclusions

Robert Cassen

The "old debates" about population and development started, famously or infamously, with Thomas Robert Malthus. His first grim views of the relationship between them, enormously influential in his own time and since, were based on a mistake. While food production could only grow at a rate of simple interest, he thought, population would grow at a compound rate and would always outpace the growth in food supplies, until famine and death put food and population back in balance. In fact, the world's food output has consistently grown faster than the world's population, and can probably continue to do so for a long time to come, although in the future not without economic and environmental problems.[1] Malthus later revised many of his views, but his writings gave rise to punitive social philosophies in the nineteenth century and beyond: there was no point, according to his followers, in helping the poor—they would only "breed" further, until they were cut down by war, hunger, or disease.

Malthus' legacy is possibly one reason why the population and development debate has been so heated. Anyone who suggested in recent years that population growth had negative effects on development, for whatever reason, could be labeled "Malthusian" or "neo-Malthusian," and thus immediately classified with some fairly obnoxious thinkers. Because Marx had attacked Malthus, many radical thinkers put alleged Malthusians into the imperialist, or neo-colonialist camp, at least as far as the debate between developed and developing countries was concerned.[2] "Population control" was a northern idea, dressed up as an aid to development and the reduction of poverty; in the South, underdevelopment was often considered to result from northern domination of the world economy, if not from capitalism itself, but certainly not from excessive population growth.

In addition to the Malthusian connection, population issues have been controversial for three reasons. First, there is a widespread lack of clarity about the aspects of development that population growth is claimed to affect. Second, the available evidence from empirical studies does not clearly show that population growth exerts a negative influence on development. And third, difficulties arise from ethical perspectives and in policy issues: especially the North-South debate, issues concerning sexuality, reproduction, relationships between men and women, and questions relating to family planning itself.

The debate in the research community has been paralleled and amplified in the media, where in addition to these already difficult legitimate issues, much uglier ones have been raised. These include what has been termed the "race suicide" theme: the idea that differential fertility of various population sub-groups, or particular migratory flows, poses a threat to the dominant group. The possibility of social conflict and of extreme or even lurid consequences for the environment and the quality of life arising from population growth have also made their appearance.[3] The present volume does not discuss such issues, but it is important to recognize the heat that population matters—or matters assumed to be connected with population growth—can generate in some quarters.

THE INTERNATIONAL DEBATE

The divisions between developed and developing countries are part of the background to the international debate on population. As Kaval Gulhati and Lisa Bates note, the 1974 World Population Conference in Bucharest was dominated by North-South divisions; it produced such memorable lines as, "development is the best contraceptive" from the Indian Health Minister and "the future of mankind is bright" from a Chinese delegate. Although South and North were by no means monolithic, one can characterize the northern view at that time as strongly concerned about rapid population growth, with the United States in the lead calling for tough, targeted, family planning initiatives. Developing countries in general resisted the idea that their lack of development had to do with population growth, which they did not wish to address separately from larger social and economic development issues.

Ironically, by the time of the 1984 World Population Conference in Mexico City, developing-country views had changed considerably; the African delegations in particular had lost their earlier optimism that their continent's large land mass and abundant natural resources could indefinitely sustain growth of population. China, too, did a complete *volte face*, describing and justifying its new population-control policies. The United States retreated from its earlier leadership; responding to anti-abortion (and even anti-family planning) factions, as well as neo-conservative and libertarian thinking, the Reagan administration took the line that population was a neutral or even positive factor, provided the desirable economic system was in place.[4]

Today numerous developing countries have active family planning programs; interestingly, almost all their official positions are based on concerns for the individual, stressing the health of women and children, access to contraception, and women's rights. They also speak of the difficulties of providing education, health, and employment to rapidly growing numbers. There is an increasing international consensus surrounding the idea of sustainable development, although divisive issues remain.

Some of the divisions have been sharpened by nongovernmental organizations (NGOs), which have become active in the debate. Religious groups and women's groups have vociferously debated abortion and other issues, with the debate between "rights to life" and "rights over one's own body" having an international as well as a domestic dimension. Women's organizations have campaigned against individual contraceptive methods that they consider unsafe, as well as against family planning programs that rely too heavily on specific methods (e.g., female sterilization), or that put demographic targets over the needs and rights of women and mothers. Environmental groups, too, have increasingly made themselves felt, some of them claiming extremely negative impacts of population growth on the environment.

In the developed as well as the developing world, few development issues have aroused as much dissension—politically and academically—as the relations among population growth, economic growth, and human welfare. It should be a simple issue: Can countries which are already poor raise the living standards of their people if those people are fast increasing in numbers? The answer *is* simple—they not only can, they have mostly done so. But the follow-up questions are not so simple: Could they have done better if their populations were growing more slowly? And if so, what should be done about it?

It is obvious that population growth cannot continue indefinitely—there are *some* limits to the number of people our planet can accommodate. But what about quality of life? Are there advantages to slowing population growth well before the limits of the earth's "carrying capacity" are reached? Does not the *scale* of population size in relation to resources matter, as well as the rate of growth of living standards?[5]

On the whole, rates of population growth are declining. One effect of economic development is first to reduce mortality, which increases population growth, and then, usually with a time lag, to reduce fertility, eventually to the point where it barely exceeds mortality and population growth slows to a minimum—the process known as the "demographic transition." Since this can be expected to happen everywhere, the question really boils down to how important it is that the transition be accelerated, and why.

Part of the motivation for the present volume was provided by the National Academy of Sciences study of 1986.[6] This accepted a "qualitative conclusion" that "slower population growth would be beneficial for most developing countries"; but it did so in a very low-keyed and non-urgent tone. It laid particular stress on the capacity of population growth itself to induce appropriate technological change and policy modification—matters on which it is possible to be quite skeptical, in the light of many instances where this has not happened, whether it be in the management of common property resources, agricultural pricing policies, environmental controls, or urban development. And, as the study noted, population growth is not *necessary* to induce such change.

Our own conclusions can be summarized very briefly: the clearest evidence of negative effects of population growth under high fertility are at the individual and household levels. Mothers exposed to large numbers of pregnancies have a high risk of dying; many of these deaths are from unsafe abortions. Children with large numbers of brothers and sisters will be more likely to be deprived in various ways. Girls suffer in particular; and once they fail to be educated, the scene is set for intergenerational transmission of poverty and high fertility.

The macroeconomic evidence is much more equivocal. Statistical analysis across developing countries examining the effect of population growth on income per head and other variables yields no firm results. Examination of individual countries, however, shows that there are certainly near-term problems for several countries, especially the poorer of them, in providing remunerative employment, adequate schooling, and health services. There are particular problems where agriculture is already at the margin of rewarding production.

Looking at other issues such as poverty, environment, and migration, we find that the influence of population is mediated by a range of other factors, and the influence of population growth depends very much on how those other factors behave or are managed. Population growth can affect some of these mediating factors; it also serves as a long-term contributory element itself. Institutional capacity to set the right policies and incentives in place is critical in determining whether or not population growth will be accommodated without major negative consequences; unfortunately it is often the same poor countries in which this capacity is lacking. For such countries, it seems quite clear that slower population growth will prove beneficial.

THE DEMOGRAPHIC FUTURE

Thomas Merrick outlines what the demographic future is likely to be, and the difference that could be made by active health and population policies. Most of the world's population growth is going to occur in developing countries. Rates of population growth in these countries have already begun to diminish, from a peak average level of more than 2.5 percent per year in the 1970s. But one effect of past high fertility is a young age structure, which means that even after replacement fertility is reached (some 2.1 children per couple), populations will continue to grow considerably—what demographers call "population momentum." Most countries are still some way from replacement fertility. The average for developing countries is 3.6 children per couple, which is down from 6.2 in 1950, but it ranges from nearly 6 in Africa to just over 3 in Asia and Latin America.[7]

Projections vary mainly according to assumptions about future fertility trends. The World Bank's standard projection yields a world population of 8.3 billion in the year 2025. Almost 7 billion people (five-sixths of the planet's population) will live in the developing world, and one-sixth in the developed world, compared with two-thirds and one-third, respectively, in 1950. Assuming replacement fertility is reached somewhere around 2030, with some variation among individual countries, the developing countries' population should stabilize at just over 10 billion by the end of the twenty-first century, with India and China each reaching 1.9 billion.

Various factors can affect these numbers. Mortality may not behave as expected, mainly because of the uncertainty about AIDS; even under pessimistic projections, however, AIDS-related deaths will at most keep mortality rates from falling as far as they otherwise would. (Only one or two epidemiologists suggest AIDS could generate actual population decline in the countries of greatest prevalence; their views are not widely shared.) To a large extent, future population growth depends on the pace of fertility decline—whether individual couples will choose to limit the number of children they have sooner rather than later. Fertility decline can be accelerated in two complementary ways. First, access to contraception can be improved for those who already wish to limit their fertility. More than 100 million couples (some 15 percent of couples with wives of reproductive age) are thought to be in this position. Second, social and economic change can help to induce desires for smaller families among those who still want large ones. Such change includes later marriage and longer intervals between births; these delays are part of the process of fertility decline, and they can also reduce population momentum after replacement fertility is attained.

Merrick notes that debate about the determinants of fertility has moved beyond the simplistic opposition of "supply" versus "demand." In the past, some argued that merely making family planning services available would assist the reduction of fertility; others argued that generating "demand" for services is what mattered. Once people *wanted* to limit their fertility—primarily a result of socioeconomic change—they would do so. Merrick regards the supply versus demand debate as insufficient for policy guidance. Attention needs to be given to both. He does, though, note widespread evidence of the important role of family planning services today in assisting fertility decline, even in adverse social settings.

A HISTORICAL PERSPECTIVE

Allen Kelley and William McGreevey provide a historical perspective of the macroeconomic debate. They cite studies showing that, for long periods in the history of some industrial countries, significant increases in population growth applied downward pressure on wages and, in the short run, could shift income away from labor. The impact on economic growth in the long run, however, is not clear, either theoretically or historically. At some point these negative effects of population growth diminished, arguably the result of improving markets and technology, which made it easier to take advantage of a growing labor force. A key factor in the industrial countries' accommodation of population growth was increasing agricultural productivity (which permitted movement of labor into manufacturing) and increasing rural prosperity.

The authors contrast this experience with that of the developing countries, where, in many cases, populations are growing considerably faster than was ever the case in today's industrialized countries.

Moreover, questionable government policies—such as price controls and a bias against agriculture—often undermine incentives to introduce new technology and to help rural economies adapt to growing populations. Poor policies and several other factors can also keep families from finding it advantageous to have fewer children. Wasteful resource allocations emanating from poor policies can be amplified by rapid population growth. But if policy failures are not rectified, economic growth can languish even with slower population growth. The 1990s will see increasing liberalization in trade and factor flows, markets, and fiscal policies; the authors predict that these trends will soften the potential adverse consequences of rapid population growth—although in the poorest countries, those consequences will probably still be negative.

Kelley and McGreevey illustrate an alternative method of looking at the population problem—the so-called "revisionist" approach. Instead of examining only short-run impacts of one or two elements of the situation, the revisionist examines longer time-periods and takes into account the many processes by which society can adjust—or fail to adjust—to growing numbers. Only where specific binding constraints cannot be compensated for by human ingenuity do economies encounter effective limits to growth.

THE NOT–SO–SIMPLE ARITHMETIC OF POPULATION AND DEVELOPMENT

What is referred to when we talk about the influence of population growth on development? Development could be taken to mean the growth of the economy, as measured by the gross national product (GNP). If that were the index of development, we could probably say that population is a positive factor, at least on the GNP as conventionally measured. Although some studies have disputed this, they are not much believed today.[8] There is, though, a major problem with the conventional measurement of GNP: it does not take adequate account of the environment.

If a country's scarce natural resources are used up in the process of growth, or if air, water, and soils are contaminated, the year-to-year changes in GNP as conventionally measured are little affected. Economists talk of the NNP, the net national product, or national income. This differs from the GNP in accounting for utilization of *man-made* capital, but it still does not account for the utilization of natural capital. If population growth were associated with strongly negative natural resource effects, the beneficial effect of population on GNP growth would be called into question.

What about the effect of population growth on *per capita* income? Suppose population growth does contribute positively to GNP growth, even natural-resource-adjusted GNP growth, what is its effect on GNP per person? Here simple economics suggests that the effect is probably negative. Unless population exerts a strong positive influence on capital formation—and the suggestion that it does is a minority opinion—the more people there are, and the less capital there is per person; as a result, even though total output may be larger with a bigger population, output per person is smaller.[9] There are however three possible arguments against this: larger populations may generate *economies of scale*; they may induce *favorable technological change*; and when population is growing, the *average age of the labor force will be younger*, which may have beneficial productivity effects.

Each of these three arguments is plausible, but their quantitative significance is unclear. Although a bigger population might enjoy economies of scale not available to a smaller one, there is a question of what happens to the economy while it is acquiring the larger population. If the initial costs of population growth are heavy, the later advantages could be canceled out. Economies of scale in tradeable goods are in any case available through trade and do not require a large population at home. Moreover, economists have not been successful in measuring scale effects.

Whether or not population growth induces favorable technological change is also unclear. When first put forward, this argument was applied to agrarian societies over the long sweep of history; as population density increased, new measures of intensive agricultural cultivation were introduced, leaving people richer than before.[10] Today, however, quite apart from the environmental problems of intensifying agriculture, there is much evidence of population growth *failing* to lead to beneficial change—from recent studies of the causes of decline of the ancient Incan civilization, to much of rural Africa in the last 30 years.

In the late twentieth century, technological change is not to any great extent a function of population growth. Where countries are far from the frontier of existing technical knowledge, population growth is not needed to "induce" the creation of technology, which is, in any case, usually the product of intensive research rather than social forces. One of the supposed benefits of being a "late developer" is the opportunity to take advantage of technology that others have created. And as we shall see, rapid population growth in poor countries may hinder rather than help the adoption of new technology.

Questions about the effect of the average age of the labor force on economic growth and development go beyond the relatively simple capital-driven economic model we have implicitly been discussing thus far. Indeed, exciting new work on growth theory in current economics gives much more credit than older economic theories to the role of human knowedge and human resources.[11] But the issue is not whether more people are an advantage, but more healthy, educated, and employed people. Where population is growing rapidly, what is the country's capacity to bring those benefits to its growing numbers?

Failure to ask this question led to a fallacy in Julian Simon's influential book, *The Ultimate Resource*.[12] Simon argued that the more people are born, the more geniuses there are, who in turn provide immeasurable benefits to society. While this is perhaps true of genius, or more prosaically, inventors and scientists, using this as an argument in favor of population growth regardless of other consequences verges on the absurd. Simon ignored the fact that where population growth hinders governments from offering decent health and education services to their people, millions are born and die without ever realizing their potential. Commonly in his models, everyone is productively employed, and social overhead capital is free. The truth in poor developing countries is very different.

THE EVIDENCE

The two main sides in the population debate both cite evidence based on international comparisons. In particular, the "unconcern" or "optimistic" school relies heavily on the fact that there seems to be little correlation between developing countries' population growth and growth in per capita income, or indeed between population growth and most other variables of potential interest. If you belong to the "concern" school, you should expect, other things being equal, that the higher a country's rate of population growth, the lower would be its rate of per capita income.[13] Or should you? Certainly the correlations do not show anything very consistently.

Of the large numbers of such studies that have attempted to examine the relationship between population growth and growth in per capita income, some conclude that there is a positive, some that there is a negative, and some that there is no relationship. In all cases, the effects are small; some are, and some are not, statistically significant. Questions have been raised about every aspect of these studies: Are the data reliable? Do the models take into account all the appropriate variables? Do they include the possibility that while population influences development, development may be influencing population?[14] Most studies to date looked at the relationships in the 1960s and 1970s. More recently, it has been found that, in the 1980s, there appears to have been a negative relationship. But this conclusion is awkward for both "concern" and "unconcern" views. Those who rejected the earlier non-correlation findings as unreliable cannot now uncritically accept the new findings; and those who argued that non-correlation meant that population was not a negative factor must explain the new data.[15]

It is likely that all of these studies are too unreliable for significant inferences to be made, except perhaps for two: 1) that population is not a *dominant* effect—if it were, the studies would produce more unequivocal results, whatever the statistical weaknesses of the exercise; and 2) that no analyses have yet been conducted that fully meet contemporary econometric standards. This in turn implies that if research gold is to be found in this particular vein, it has to be explored again but with improved technique. It is quite possible, however, that there is in fact little gold to be found in inter-country statistical exercises; population is a slow-acting phenomenon, changing little from year to year, while economies are much more volatile, and influenced by a huge variety of factors.

Looking at individual countries, or groups of countries that are similar in relevant respects, over longer periods of time may well be more revealing. The fact that "no association" (the term employed by Kelley and McGreevey in this volume) is found across all countries does not imply that population is necessarily insignificant in each country; research should refine the issue by seeking to establish in greater detail the conditions under which population growth may be a favorable or unfavorable factor. It should be noted that when economists say—as some do—that there is "no evidence" of a negative relationship between population growth and growth in per capita income, the average relationships resulting from inter-country statistical comparisons are normally the *only* evidence they have in mind. Other evidence should be examined as well, as is done in this volume.[16]

Altogether, simple economics may seem to suggest that countries with faster population growth will in the long run end up with lower per capita income. But once the economic model is complicated to allow for the effects of economies of scale, induced technological progress, and labor-force age effects, there are then too many empirical uncertainties to reach a clear conclusion—certainly not one that could be valid for all countries in all circumstances. Neither the direction nor the magnitude of these possible effects are known with any certainty. It seems likely that, in a poor country—with large existing deficiencies of infrastructure, productive capacity, and employment, and poor provision of health and education—a growth rate that doubles the population in 20 or 30 years would harm the rate of improvement in living standards. But neither theory nor econometrics has so far been able to demonstrate this relationship beyond doubt.

Some Case Examples

It is possible to contrast recent "success stories" with unfavorable cases. The rapidly growing East Asian economies owe their success principally to the rapid growth in manufactured exports, which they have pursued as a matter of high national priority. This has produced rapid employment growth, which in turn has generated high returns to investments in education and training. All the successful East Asian countries had active family planning programs and population growth that declined rapidly, which helped families to afford these human resource investments. The whole process has been referred to as a "virtuous circle."[17] By contrast, in Africa and Asia, high population growth rates have forced some of the poorest countries to continue investing heavily in increasingly costly agriculture, thereby reducing the resources available for manufacturing investment;[18] others have neglected agricultural investment, with equally serious consequences.

These poorest countries have not been able to participate significantly in the rapid growth of developing-country manufacturing, and so employment and the returns to human investment have not grown quickly. Improvements in education, so important to successful economies, have generally not occurred, even though school enrollments have grown faster than population. Educational expenditures are determined mainly by demography and the macroeconomy: population growth under high fertility raises the number of children who must be educated both absolutely and relative to the working population that is taxed to pay for them; and economic growth or policies to raise the share of GNP going to education provide additional resources. While numerous developing countries have been able to raise per pupil expenditures as their populations were growing, improvements have most typically occurred in the better-off countries where fertility has been declining. In many poorer countries, school populations have grown rapidly, economic growth has been modest, and the share of GNP devoted to education has not risen. In such circumstances, the quality of education has frequently failed to improve, or has even worsened. In part because of inadequate investment in human resources, these countries have had the greatest difficulty in raising living standards and achieving international competitiveness.

Malawi is an example of a low-income country with fast growing population and high fertility. In 1990, its labor force was 3.4 million; by 2010, the labor force will double to about 6.8 million. Only a quarter are currently employed in the formal sector or the urban informal sector; even at optimistic rates of economic growth, those sectors will employ only a third of the labor force projected for 2010. The remaining 4.5 million workers will presumably have to be absorbed in small-holder agriculture. But each small-holder already cultivates just two-thirds of a hectare—barely enough to support a family. To absorb increased agricultural labor, additional land will need to be brought under cultivation, but since the best land is already in use, much of the new land will be marginal. Malawi has had a good record of increasing agricultural productivity in the last two decades, but very large investments and levels of modern agricultural inputs will be needed to maintain crop yields and prevent a decline in farm incomes. At the same time, Malawi is finding it difficult to improve present educational standards and will continue to do so as long as its population is doubling every two decades.

Even if fertility declines soon in Malawi, the declines will have little impact on employment problems in the near term; most of the labor force of 2010 is already born. However, projections of labor force growth to 2045 illustrate that near-term fertility declines could make a large difference. With no fertility decline, the working age population would number 37 million in 2045; with moderate fertility declines, it would reach 22 million; and with rapid declines, only 15 million. Without declines in fertility it seems unlikely that Malawi will be able to increase the amount of capital per worker enough to produce significant improvements in productivity, wages, and living standards in the foreseeable future.[19] One cannot exclude the possibility of improvements on an individual basis in Malawi even under the high population growth scenario. But such improvements have been fairly exiguous in the last 20 years, and the challenges ahead seem enormous in the absence of significant fertility decline. The case illustrates many of the themes of this volume.[20]

Korea provides a contrasting example. If Korea had maintained its 1960 fertility level until 1980, the number of primary school children would have been one-third larger, and expenditure on primary education (at the same cost per pupil) would have been higher by 1 percent of GDP.[21] In fact, however, Korea effectively promoted fertility decline through publicly funded family planning programs at the same time that socioeconomic change made smaller families attractive. It was thus able to improve both the extent and the quality of education, helping to lay the foundations for its manufacturing success.[22] Its rapid growth in exports provided rapidly growing employment outside agriculture, enabling Korea to resolve many of its development problems—an example of the "virtuous circle" at work.

These particular cases capture important aspects of the relationship between population and economic growth and development. But the relationships they characterize are not necessarily universally true; nor has research yet demonstrated that they are inevitable. Certainly there is no evidence of a "trap" from which countries cannot escape, even when there are mutually reinforcing effects that make it harder for countries to make progress.[23] But as economic research continues, it is likely that the role of human resources in development—and therefore countries' capacities to ensure high standards of health and education for their populations—will come to seem increasingly important for productivity. In this sense, rapid population growth may turn out to be more disadvantageous than we currently know.

Two new concerns may ultimately refocus attention on the macro case against population growth: 1) the human resources issue— how well can countries meet the health and educational needs of their population? and 2) the food versus manufacturing issue—can countries make the necessary investments in nonagricultural production or must they continually focus on producing enough food for their growing populations? If further explored and measured, these connections could show population growth to have negative macroeconomic effects. But the size of the effects cannot yet be established, and the circumstances that might magnify or mitigate them cannot be defined.

FROM MACRO TO MICRO ASSESSMENTS

For the present, therefore, the population debate focuses not on macroeconomic arguments, but on more microlevel questions. These include such issues as the influence of population growth on poverty, the role of women, health, the development of human resources, the environment, and migration.

The authors in this volume examine these issues and have come to conclusions that mostly support the view that rapid population growth in poor countries under conditions of high fertility is inimical to many development goals. (Notice the details of this sentence: *mostly* support the view; *rapid* population growth, which one might take to be in excess of 2 percent annually; *poor* countries; conditions of *high fertility*, women having four or more children; and *many development goals*). This does not mean that population growth at all rates, at all times, and independently of the wealth of countries and the size of their populations, necessarily has negative consequences for all aspects of development.[24] But, in general, the authors conclude that many goals of development are better served by low fertility and slow population growth than by high fertility and rapid population growth.

Population and Poverty

Dennis Ahlburg examines the relationship between population growth and poverty. To the limited extent that empirical estimates are reliable, there does not appear to be any correlation between the rate of population growth across countries and the extent of poverty in them. This should not be surprising; the large range of factors that contribute to poverty—from government policies to all the conditions that influence economic growth and the distribution of income—cannot all be taken into account in econometric modeling. One of the few studies that looks at a single country over time—among different states in India—does find population growth contributing to poverty, but not very powerfully. At a minimum, the findings suggest that population is not a dominant factor in explaining poverty. (There *does* appear to be a negative relationship between population growth and a country's score on the United Nations Development Programme's Human Development Index, which incorporates education and longevity as well as income; but the usual cautions about correlation findings apply.) On the whole, most developing countries have, at least until recently, managed to reduce the *proportion* if not the number of people living in poverty, even when their populations are growing.

The relationship between population and poverty is traced through intermediate variables such as education and other assets, family size, gender, race, ethnicity, age, wages and earnings, and components of income derived from common property resources such as forest products or grazing land—all related to poverty. Where the influence on these factors of high fertility or population growth can be traced, it is often, but not always, found to be negative, and generally not very large. A number of policies could both reduce the negative consequences of population growth and improve the income and assets of the poor. There are certainly many ways to combat poverty directly; such measures are likely to have stronger effects at least in the short run than anything that can be accomplished by family planning alone. As in many other population-related areas, population is only a contributing factor to poverty, not its prime cause. But addressing poverty and population concerns requires many of the same policies that are mutually reinforcing.

Population and the Environment

For many people, the impact of population on the environment is perhaps the most crucial issue in the debate. But as in other areas, the pure effect of population on the environment is hard to discern, mediated as it is by many other influences. A number of false impressions have been created by the oversimple I = PCT formula and its equivalents: environmental impact is the product of the number of people (P) times their consumption and the technology employed (C and T), that is, environmental impact results from the impact each person makes times the number of people.[25] This approach fails to allow for all-important trade-offs. It is well accepted that most destruction of the global environment thus far has stemmed not from developing countries, where population is growing rapidly, but from the high-income industrial countries, where population has grown relatively little in recent decades. If the macroeconomic "concern school" is right—that is, if population grew more slowly, incomes would grow more rapidly—which case would have the greater effect on the environment?[26] The I = PCT formula does not even allow this question to be framed. To clarify the effects of population on the environment, one must look at effects that are strongly population driven: that is where the difference will be made.

Theodore Panayotou defines the problems as a matter of adaptation or failure to adapt. Many local environmental problems are due to the presence of "open access resources"—common property such as forests, water supplies, and fish and animal populations. Where these are not subject to defined property rights or systems of management or regulation, the resources in question effectively have no "price"; they are taken by what the author calls "capture." In such circumstances, growing population will have a destructive effect; indeed, the incentive structure may encourage families to have additional children who will add to the household's capture-capacity.

Statistical studies show that a considerable proportion of deforestation, marine pollution, and other adverse environmental effects is associated with population growth. But this happens most commonly in situations of open access, or where destructive behavior carries no price to the actor in question. The cost of environmental destruction must be internalized, so that those carrying out destructive activities pay a penalty for doing so. In some situations of greatly increasing population density, conditions have prevented any ecological deterioration, or even led to improvements. Where markets, management, and regulation are in place, the impact of population growth will be more modest. Adverse impacts are compounded by poor policies in other areas; if policies affecting employment are distorted, households will lack alternatives and be forced to rely on capturing common property resources.

Within existing technologies, there is ample scope for increasing efficiency in the use of resources. Once limits to efficient sustainable use are reached, appropriate prices and policies will provide the incentives for the development of substitutes in consumption and production. Sustainable growth requires this process to work smoothly; it also requires technology to continue to overcome resource constraints. There are no guarantees, however, that adequate technology will come on stream; if incentives are not in place, it will not.

Policies and institutions are often slow to change, and where they do not favor good environmental management, population growth will exacerbate environmental problems. But even if population growth slows, the problems will continue. Reducing fertility can help to mitigate environmental problems, but all the conditions that mediate the impact of population on local ecology must improve too—those that affect the environment directly such as the pricing and regulation of resource use, and those that affect employment opportunities, consumption, production, and trade.

In the context of this volume—which addresses the consequences of population growth *within* developing countries where most of that growth will take place—Panayotou was asked to discuss local rather than global problems. But there clearly are relationships between population growth and such wider issues as global warming and other sources of climate change, the ozone layer, acid rain, and pressure on renewable resources beyond national borders. Developing countries, especially as they grow more affluent, will contribute to and suffer from these consequences. Accounts of these problems vary in their optimism about what will happen. Most agree, however, that the difficulties *can* be managed; the question is whether they will be. Population growth will exacerbate the difficulties, particularly if policies and incentives are not put in place nationally and internationally to prevent environmental damage.

In the end, some of the most important questions about population and the environment are beyond the scope of economics: they are ethical issues, about the kind of world people will wish to live in, the kind of world each generation should bequeath to its successors.[27] Given limited capacities for global management, it will obviously help if aggravating factors are mitigated. Environmental arguments certainly give strong support to the case for development and population policies that will lead to slower population growth; but, while slower population growth may lessen a range of threats to the environment, it will not eliminate them.

Women, Children, and Households

Two chapters in this volume concentrate on the effects of population growth and high fertility at the household and individual level. Cynthia Lloyd explores the consequences for children of having a large number of siblings and finds that 1) such children are more likely to be malnourished, especially if they are the parents' later children; and 2) since health is related to educational performance, both nutritional effects and limitations on parents' capacity to pay affect the educational attainments of children in large families. When opportunities beyond the household are restricted, parents have relatively little incentive to limit the number of their children. As opportunities improve, much depends on how parents act, since they are the gatekeepers to their children's access to public and private resources. In today's poorer developing countries with very high rates of past fertility and large numbers in the young age groups, especially in countries that have had to pare down social sector budgets in recent years, public resources for education and health are limited, and costs to parents have risen. In a harsh economic climate, rapid population growth and high fertility can have "extremely negative" implications for family resources and overall investment in children.

The results are not gender-neutral. Lloyd shows that in larger and more traditional families, households are more likely to be male-dominated and less child-oriented in their spending; parents' time and resources are limited; and female children suffer most. When girls do not get educated, they will grow up with fewer marketable skills, know less about family planning, and be more dependent on the support of *their* children. These and other equity effects within the family create a tendency for a self-reinforcing cycle of intergenerational transmission of high fertility and poverty; female education is the most powerful force that can interrupt the cycle.

The consequences of high fertility and rapid population growth for women are explored by Deborah Maine, Lynn Freedman, Farida Shaheed, and Schuyler Frautschi. They set their findings in the perspective of human rights, which encourages acknowledgment that at many points value choices are being made, even in the use of data, and that as a matter of human rights, women must be consulted and their choices recognized.

Death rates from complications of pregnancy and childbirth, including unsafe abortion, are much higher in developing countries than in the industrial world. Modern contraception, although having its own health risks, reduces mortality by reducing exposure to pregnancy; it does not, however, reduce the risks associated with pregnancy and childbirth themselves; this requires good maternal health programs and emergency obstetric care. Family planning is often justified in terms of maternal health, which it can indeed improve; but the authors argue that if family planning programs are driven, as they frequently have been, mainly by demographic goals, they will often fail to address women's reproductive health problems and actually diminish the prospects of the demographic goals' being achieved.

Reproductive health requires a range of services that include, but are not limited to, contraception. These services must be provided in ways that are sensitive to women's real needs, which include balancing the risks of having and not having children. Health services must also recognize dangers from sexually transmitted diseases—an issue that is currently under-researched and inadequately addressed. Women have their own views of what contributes to their well-being. Their attitudes vary according to their circumstances and their culture, as do their health problems. Wrongly targeted family planning programs, which ignore these realities and misuse health data to justify narrow population-control objectives, ride roughshod over women's rights and health requirements. Women need information, contraceptive choice, and access to services that respect their view of their health needs and respond to the variety of conditions that affect them. Oriented by such principles, family planning programs are far more likely to be successful.

Migration and Population Growth

The last two chapters deal with somewhat broader questions. Michael Teitelbaum and Sharon Russell show the complexity of the relationship between migration and population growth. Migrants today tend to be young adults from countries with past high fertility and rapid population growth. But this is far from simple cause and effect. Of the estimated 100 million migrants in the world living outside their countries of citizenship or birth, more than half have moved from one developing country to another. While saturated or stagnant labor markets in countries of origin and the hope of economic improvement in receiving countries have been significant causes, the movement of migrants has been motivated by a host of other conditions as well: hunger; persecution; human rights violations; political instability in the countries of out-migration; and policies, economic opportunities, and social conditions in the receiving countries. Some countries have encouraged out-migration, and some have encouraged immigrants, but such policies can change, often quite quickly.

Migration flows are volatile and unpredictable, as are their costs and benefits to receiving and sending countries. Recently the well-publicized acts of hostility toward migrants in a number of European countries have helped to put international migration high on the list of foreign policy concerns in the industrial world. But stemming population growth would not make a major difference to migratory flows—certainly not in the short run, as the young adults who will be the migrants of two decades from now are already born. At most, population growth increases the pool from which migrants come; if catastrophes occur, or economic development fails, larger numbers of people will be affected. But whether or not they migrate depends on many other things. The existence of 100 million migrants out of the world's population of 5.5 billion suggests that the vast majority of people either cannot or do not want to move. Economic development, employment creation, and the observance of human rights are the most important factors that will encourage people to stay at home, although in the short run, economic development may sometimes increase emigration by providing people with the resources to move.

The Role of Government

Nancy Birdsall addresses the role of government in population activities. Many have argued that government has no role in this area—that the number of children a family has is its own affair. Yet what individuals see as desirable may not coincide with what is socially desirable. Three potentially damaging social effects can accrue from individuals' collectively contributing to rapid population growth: they could slow the increase of living standards, put pressure on fragile environments, and worsen poverty and the distribution of income.

This chapter persuasively argues that even if these social effects were not to occur, the policies they would require are desirable in their own right—hence the "win-win tale" of the chapter's title. The interventions that are justified by what are believed to be discrepancies between the public and the private good are justified on grounds of individual welfare. These interventions include education and other social programs that improve individual opportunities, and thereby raise the cost of having children; adjusting the price of contraception to overcome the factors that prevent couples wishing to limit their fertility from adopting it; and improving the flow of information relevant to the choice of family size. At the same time, governments must adopt principles of economic management that promote broad-based growth benefiting all social groups. Poor economic policies penalize the poor and encourage high fertility, as does poverty itself. Parents will look on children as their best assets against economic insecurity and will want more of them than may be otherwise desirable until the economy delivers better opportunities and assets.

CONCLUSIONS

What are the "new conclusions" to be drawn from all this? It seems fairly clear that population growth is not the overwhelming affliction for developing countries that some have claimed, and certainly not the prime cause of difficulties of development; but it also should not be regarded with equanimity. The degree of hindrance to the improvement of individual living standards that rapid population growth is likely to afford is hard to establish. It has not been helped by economists' models, which give the same result whether a country has a hundred or a hundred million people; whether the population is growing fast or slowly; whether the country is well-off or poor; and whether or not it has good government with sensible economic policies, equitable income distribution, well-functioning markets and institutions, and efficient agriculture with scope for expansion.

But the balance of the assessments in this volume is that there are clear negative effects—at the individual and household level—of population growth under conditions of high fertility. These effects include impacts on the health and education of children and mothers' health and life opportunities. Women of all generations tend to be disadvantaged in these circumstances. The household level effects will be compounded when rapid population growth puts pressure on public resources for health and education.

At the macroeconomic level, matters are less definitive; much depends on circumstances. Several countries have shown considerable ability to accommodate population growth successfully. The principal benefit of population growth and high fertility is a labor force with a young average age. Countries in a position to take advantage of this will be mainly those which are able to educate, train, and employ their young people while keeping them well nourished and healthy; these are likely to be relatively well-off countries, and ones where fertility is declining from previously high levels. For poor countries with large-scale unemployment or underemployment and with low levels of school enrollment and quality of education, rapid increases in the population of labor force age will exert downward pressure on wages and further squeeze limited public resources. Efforts to raise the quantity and quality of education will thus be severely hindered, even when countries can increase the efficiency of educational spending within existing budgets. The current emphasis on human resources in explaining economic growth may well revitalize the macroeconomic argument against population growth.

Much also depends on agricultural conditions, because growing populations need increasing supplies of food. Countries successful at exporting either agricultural or manufactured products can import food; large developing countries, however, typically must produce the major share of their food needs, for strategic or security reasons among others. If they can expand food production without increasing economic and environmental costs, countries can more easily accommodate growing populations. But if pressure on existing land is already intense, and increasing food output comes at increasing cost, there will be problems. Countries in these circumstances will have to invest heavily in agriculture and will find it more difficult to move into manufacturing and manufactures exports, which has been the path to rapid growth in several countries. There is a distinct possibility of a growing divide between economically successful developing countries, in which population growth is declining to modest levels, and countries struggling with economic difficulties compounded by rapid population growth.

This is not to say that some countries are permanently "trapped" at a low economic level. The conditions studied in this volume are often mutually reinforcing, but they are not inescapable. Countries that develop start out less developed; they also go through a demographic transition, from high to low levels of fertility and mortality. Korea was considered a hopeless case in the 1950s but is now a successful example of the "Asian model" of development, with human resource investments, economic growth, and fertility decline reinforcing each other. The question is how the transition will be accomplished in countries where it is still to happen—how the complex interactions of economy, society, and population will unfold.

The most difficult part of this assessment is the effects of rapid population growth on the environment. Initially, global environmental problems were an industrial-country concern. More recently, individual developing countries are increasingly aware of their own ecological and environmental problems: as fuelwood supplies diminish, communities have to send their members further and further to gather cooking fuel; intensifying agriculture and the increased use of agricultural chemicals have resulted in deforestation, soil deterioration, and water pollution; and rapid urban growth and pressure on wildlife habitats, fish populations, and water supplies are increasingly problematic.

Some countries that were land-rich only two or three decades ago now suffer from land scarcity.

Not all of these effects are equally population-driven, but people and governments everywhere increasingly recognize that population growth is contributing to their difficulties, however much they can be mitigated by improvements in the operation of markets, the definition of property rights, and government policies and regulatory mechanisms. Such improvements can help to share common property and exhaustible resources equitably and ensure their use on a sustainable basis; but they generally cannot expand the volume of such resources. The challenge is to provide alternative resources and livelihoods in a pattern of growth that will help the poor and permit the costs of conservation and sustainability to be met.

Policy Implications

This book is about consequences, not about what should be done.[29] Nevertheless, it is worth reflecting on the policy implications of our findings. Two complementary types of interventions are needed when development is looked at from a population point of view: family planning measures for those who already desire to limit their families, and socioeconomic development that will encourage that desire. Such policies—beneficial to the poor and to women—are justified in terms of individual welfare. In the past, macroeconomic justifications have been used both in favor of and against active population policies. Today, these justifications are not necessary.

The macroeconomic debate is of course not wholly immaterial; if population growth turns out to have major macroeconomic benefits, there might be a choice between individual needs and the collective good. But the opposite tends to be found. Population research generally has not found rapid population growth to have macroeconomic benefits in poor countries; it is more a question of uncertainty about the magnitude of disadvantages, and the conditions under which various costs or benefits may accrue. At the household level, parents—especially poor parents—may see advantages to themselves in large numbers of children; but they are commonly not advantages from the point of view of society as a whole—or, indeed, from their children's point of view.

This will not necessarily persuade hard-pressed finance ministries to devote resources to family planning or to accelerating female educational enrollment. But if they are not persuaded on the grounds of equity or the economic benefits of human resource investment, they could still find at least some such expenditures justified in terms of their own budgets. Studies have found, for example, that governments will typically more than recoup the costs of family planning programs, often over a relatively short period, through savings in health and education budgets.[28] In general, there are few if any contradictions between policies seen from a population point of view and those seen from the point of view of development more generally: on the contrary, they reinforce each other—provided that the goal of development is taken to be the improvement of individual well-being, in particular the well-being of the poor, especially poor women.

Another new conclusion is that population policies have a high likelihood of success. Much has been learned in the last decade about family planning. Where family planning services have not succeeded— and there have been numerous examples of clinics without clients—it has often turned out to be the result of poor services, i.e., low quality services offering little variety, insufficiently attentive to women's rights and needs, overly targeted at quantitative goals, and driven by misplaced ambitions of population "control." Similarly, much of the analysis of the economics of family size has assumed that all fertility was desired fertility; it is now known that in many cases, it is not. Some 50 percent of couples in the developing world already practice contraception; another 15 percent want it and do not have access. In a number of settings, people are adopting contraception who a decade ago would not have been thought likely clients for family planning, including poor and uneducated people. At the same time, as household level studies bear out, a variety of social and economic factors that alter opportunities for individuals and their sense of economic security have a major part to play in changing attitudes to fertility. Reducing population growth requires the right kind of development and the right kind of family planning.

Populations will continue to grow for some time. The analysis presented here indicates that the extent to which population growth inhibits development depends on incentives, which in turn depend on markets and governments. A large variety of policies could help economies adjust to growing numbers: allocations between and within health and educational sectors could make health and education expenditures more efficient; pricing, investment, and trade policies could create more employment; a range of measures could enhance women's roles in development; institutional change, regulatory policy, and pricing could far better protect the environment. Many of these policies would also have the effect of changing desires and incentives for larger families. This volume's final message is that virtually everything that needs doing from a population point of view needs doing anyway.

Notes

The author is grateful to his co-authors in this volume, and also to Paul Demeny, Adrienne Germain, Catherine Gwin, Geoff McNicoll, and Steven Sinding, for helpful comments. Invaluable assistance has also been provided by George Mavrotas. Despite all the good advice the author has received, he has undoubtedly persisted stubbornly in his own views on several points—for any faults thus remaining, he alone is responsible.

[1] There are modern Malthusians, even on the food-population issue; see, for example, Paul Ehrlich and Anne Ehrlich, *The Population Explosion* (New York: Simon and Schuster, 1990). They are probably misreading global trends in cereal production, which have experienced downturns (some of them as the result of deliberate policy); world food production as a whole has not. Lester Brown (ed.), *State of the World 1994* (Washington, DC: Worldwatch Institute, 1994) is more balanced, but still pessimistic. For an antidote, see Tim Dyson, "Population Growth and Food Production: Recent Global and Regional Trends," Department of Population Studies, London School of Economics, unpublished paper, 1993.

[2] Marx also made several errors in his counterblast to Malthus, as was pointed out by other Marxists such as Kautsky. See Michael Teitelbaum, "Demographic Change Through the Lenses of Science and Politics," *Proceedings of the American Philosophical Society*, Vol. 132, No. 2 (1988), p. 182.

[3] The media debate in the United States has been well surveyed by John R. Wilmoth and Patricia Ball, "The Population Debate in American Popular Magazines," *Population and Development Review*, Vol. 18, No. 4 (December 1992).

[4] See Michael Teitelbaum, "The Population Threat," *Foreign Affairs*, Vol. 71, No. 5 (Winter 1992-93). The title of this article was chosen by the journal, not the author.

[5] Several aspects of "scale" are covered by the authors in H.E. Daly and K.N. Townsend (eds.), *Valuing the Earth: Economics, Ecology, Ethics* (Cambridge, MA: Massachusetts Institute of Technology Press, 1993).

[6] National Research Council (National Academy of Sciences), *Population Growth and Economic Development: Policy Questions* (Washington, DC: National Academy Press, 1986), p. 90.

[7] Of course, fertility rates within regions differ from country to country. In China, the fertility rate is close to replacement, at 2.4 children; in Pakistan, it is still at levels comparable to those in Africa; in India, it is in between, at 3.9. Data in this chapter, unless otherwise indicated, are from World Bank, *World Development Report 1993: Investing in Health* (New York: Oxford University Press, 1993).

[8] In an influential book, Coale and Hoover argued that population had a negative influence on savings and therefore on the rate of capital formation. With this assumption, their economic model, where growth was mainly driven by the accumulation of capital, implied that the faster population grew, the slower GNP would grow. Ansley J. Coale and Edgar M. Hoover, *Population Growth and Economic Development in Low-Income Countries* (Princeton, NJ: Princeton University Press, 1958). The jury is still out on whether in fact population growth does reduce savings; most observers think it does not. Even if it does, the effect may be quite small. If there are no other negative effects, it is likely that more labor will mean more output—although whether there is more output *per person* is another matter.

[9] Strictly, we should be talking of output per *worker*; it is possible that output per worker declines and output per person rises, if the proportion of workers in the population increases sufficiently to compensate. The argument here assumes the proportion stays constant.

[10] Ester Boserup, *The Conditions of Agricultural Growth* (London: Allen and Unwin, 1965).

[11] See, for example, Robert J. Barro, "Economic Growth in a Cross Section of Countries," *Quarterly Journal of Economics*, Vol. 106 (1991); Robert E. Lucas, "On the Mechanics of Economic Development," *Journal of Monetary Economics*, Vol. 22 (1988); Paul M. Romer, "Increasing Returns and Long-Run Growth," *Journal of Political Economy*, Vol. 99 (1986).

[12] Julian Simon, *The Ultimate Resource* (Princeton, NJ: Princeton University Press, 1982).

[13] By the "unconcern school," we mean writers such as Julian Simon (ibid.) or (some of) the authors of the 1986 National Academy of Sciences study (op. cit.). Perhaps one should call them optimists, those who think that population growth confers either positive benefits on balance, or that negative consequences are relatively modest and can be taken care of at low cost. The "concern school," on the other hand, are those authors who believe that population consequences at least in some settings are sufficiently negative to justify active population policies, although of a voluntaristic nature. They do not necessarily believe in the views of Malthus and indeed have often published criticism of his arguments. The present author would place himself in this school. There are also what one might term "population alarmists," who ascribe extreme consequences to population growth. Their arguments often are somewhat Malthusian, if in modern dress, and in some cases, they would claim the situation justifies population control measures going beyond the purely voluntary. (An example of alarmist writing is cited in note 23 below). Extremist views on analysis of population consequences tend to go hand-in-hand with extremist views on policies, just as the "unconcern" school tends to take a relaxed view on policy.

[14] In the language of econometrics, many studies have possibly omitted variable bias and simultaneity bias; few have been subjected to mis-specification tests or incorporate lags to permit dynamic adjustment. Mostly the population variable employed is the average annual rate of growth of population over the decades examined. Normally, no distinction is made between high and low fertility and mortality countries: the same rate of population growth may occur with different combinations of the two variables. This is a criticism made by Ansley Coale, "Population Trends and Economic Development," in J. Menkin (ed.), *World Population and U.S. Policy: The Choices Ahead* (New York: W.W. Norton, 1986). It has to be said, though, that the few studies that employ a fertility measure do not produce significantly different results.

[15] See Didier Blanchet, "On Interpreting Observed Relationships Between Population Growth and Economic Growth: A Graphical Exposition," *Population and Development Review*, Vol. 17, No. 1 (March 1991); and Didier Blanchet, "Reversal of the Effects of Population Growth on Economic Growth Since the End of the 1970s: Reality or Artefact?" paper presented to the U.N. Expert Group Meeting on Population Growth and Demographic Structure, Paris, 16-20 November 1992.

[16] Even if the relationship were well established by correlation studies, it is incorrect to make an inference from aggregate relationships across countries to what would happen in an individual country over time. These studies also fail to answer the (counterfactual and therefore difficult) question of what would have happened if population had grown more slowly.

[17] For an account of some of the factors behind this success, see World Bank, *The East Asian Miracle: Economic Growth and Public Policy* (New York: Oxford University Press, 1993).

[18] For evidence of rising costs of agricultural intensification, see, for instance, K.N. Ninan and H. Chandrashekhar, "The Green Revolution, Dryland Agriculture and Sustainability: Evidence from India," in George H. Peters and Bernard F. Stanton (eds.), *Sustainable Agricultural Development*, Proceedings of the 21st International Conference of Agricultural Economists (Aldershot, UK/Brookfield, VT: Dartmouth Publishing Company, 1992); Christopher L. Delgado and Per Pinstrup-Andersen, "Agricultural Productivity in the Third World: Patterns and Strategic Issues," paper to the American Agricultural Economics Association/International Food Policy Research Institute Workshop, Orlando, Florida, July 1993, especially pp. 20-21.

[19] Figures from World Bank, *Malawi: Human Resource Development Study*, Report No. 7854-MAI (Washington, DC: World Bank, 1989). The World Bank has conducted a number of such country studies. For example, see *Rapid Population Growth in Pakistan: Concerns and Consequences*, Report No. 7522-PAK (Washington, DC: World Bank, March 1989); *Zimbabwe Population Sector Report*, Report No. 7703-ZIM (Washington, DC: World Bank, October 1989).

[20] In Malawi, economically cultivable land is already scarce and population density relative to land high; countries with good land still not under the plow face less difficulty.

[21] See World Bank, *World Development Report 1984* (New York: Oxford University Press, 1984). Another calculation is presented by Jee-Peng Tan and Alain Mingat, *Education in Asia* (Washington, DC: World Bank, 1992), pp. 19-20 and 108; this volume gives data for the fiscal burden of education per adult as it is affected by the dependency ratio. Korea had the lowest ratio of countries in the study: "If Korea had had Lao PDR's dependency ratio, other things being equal, Korea would have had to spend 70 percent more than it did in 1985 to achieve its education system's coverage in that year."

[22] On the role of education in Korea and other Asian countries, see Naohiro Ogawa, Gavin W. Jones, and Jeffrey G. Williamson (eds.), *Human Resources in Development Along the Asia-Pacific Rim* (New York: Oxford University Press, 1993); and Nancy Birdsall and Richard Sabot, *Virtuous Circles: Human Capital, Growth and Equity in East Asia*, Policy Research Department, World Bank (Washington, DC: World Bank, 1994).

[23] An egregious example of a "trap" argument is Maurice King, "Health Is a Sustainable State," *The Lancet*, Vol. 336, No. 8716 (15 September 1990). He actually argues that because population growth is so damaging, it is mistaken to try to save lives until fertility has declined. This flies in the face of all the evidence that in very many settings the improved survival of children has been virtually a *precondition* for fertility to fall.

[24] Compare this statement with that of the 1986 National Academy of Sciences study commented on by Kelley and McGreevey in Chapter 3 of this volume.

[25] See, for example, Ehrlich and Ehrlich, *Population, Resources, Environment*, op. cit.

[26] The answer to this question depends in part on who receives the additional income. If it accrues to the poor, especially to poor women, it could have beneficial effects on the environment because it reduces poor people's need to live off the environment. But if the rich get richer, consumption patterns and technology could change in environmentally unfriendly directions.

[27] An up-to-date survey of the technical, economic, and (some of the) ethical issues is provided by David Pearce and Jeremy Warford, *World Without End: Economics, Environment and Sustainable Development* (Oxford: Oxford University Press, 1993).

[28] See, for example, James Tarvid, Dennis Chao, and Mary Rice, "FamPlan Application for the Philippine Population/Family Planning Evaluation," Research Triangle Institute, Research Triangle Park, NC (April 1992), mimeo; Mary Scott and James Kocher, *A Cost-Benefit Analysis of the Family Planning Programme in Jamaica, 1970-2000: Final Report* (Research Triangle Park, NC: Research Triangle Institute, May 1992).

[29] The policy implications of population and development are further explained in Robert Cassen, *Population Policy: A New Consensus*, Policy Essay No. 12 (Washington, DC: Overseas Development Council, 1994) forthcoming.

Part II
Chapter
Summaries

Chapter Summaries

Developing Countries and the International Population Debate: Politics and Pragmatism

Kaval Gulhati and Lisa M. Bates

The seriousness of the problem of rapid population growth has been increasingly recognized by many governments in Latin America, Africa, and Asia. Many have formulated national population policies and implemented programs that provide access to family planning services. The adoption of such policies and programs, with an emphasis on slowing down the rate of population growth, is remarkable in view of early developing-country positions on the issue.

Historically, developing countries' perspectives on population have been guided more by national political and socioeconomic interests than by concern about overwhelming numbers. At the 1974 U.N. population conference in Bucharest, most governments in the developing world argued that the crux of the development problem was not high fertility, but poverty and the inequitable distribution of resources between North and South. But confronted with the enormous pressure of rapid population growth on already strained economic and social conditions, many developing countries began to express concern about high fertility rates; by the time of the next U.N. population conference in 1984, many countries eagerly sought international assistance for family planning and related efforts.

Despite waning interest in population activities in the 1980s on the part of the United States, the largest population assistance donor, developing countries have maintained their commitment to population and family planning efforts. As preparations for the 1994 population conference in Cairo have demonstrated, there is a widespread consensus within the developing world on the importance of population factors in sustainable development and on the need for comprehensive strategies to lower fertility. Furthermore, a number of developing-country concerns have been reflected in the preparatory process leading up to Cairo. Conference documents and individual country statements show an interest in integrating population activities with other aspects of social and economic development; and they also show a willingness to address unsustainable patterns of consumption in industrialized countries. There is widespread agreement on the need to invest in women's health and socioeconomic advancement and to stress the role of men as responsible partners in family planning.

Yet international controversy over population issues is not entirely resolved; developing countries are engaged in a number of debates. The various "sides" of the debates, however, are characterized less by traditional North-South divisions than by alliances of individual countries around transnational issues of shared concern. Several developing countries are debating what the Vatican and others consider ethical issues, for example, abortion and reproductive rights, adolescent versus parental rights, and the various forms of "the family" (female-headed households, etc.). Others are drawing attention to anti-migration trends in developed countries and encouraging the international community to respond to migratory pressures by addressing their root causes rather than by closing borders.

Many developing countries are also concerned about protecting their right to develop without being unfairly burdened by the costs and constraints of environmental protection. They believe that the industrialized countries should take greater responsibility for their own role in environmental degradation, as well as provide tangible support to developing nations for the economic growth and development needed both to lower fertility and to enable sustainable resource use. Developing countries recognize the importance of domestic expenditures for social sector programs such as health and education; they will continue to call on the international community to provide additional resources not only for family planning measures but also for the aspects of social development that are now widely recognized as central to population efforts.

Population Dynamics in Developing Countries

Thomas W. Merrick

The surge of population growth in developing countries, which began when death rates declined earlier and faster than birth rates, has begun to abate, as many countries experience the transition to lower fertility. Even with slower growth rates, however, developing countries continue to experience large absolute increases in population. In fact, their populations are expected to increase by more during the 1990s than during any previous decade. The reason for this added surge in population is the combination of still-high fertility rates and youthful age structures, which generate large numbers of births and relatively small numbers of deaths and could add several billion more people to developing-country populations. How large those populations will be depends mainly on the speed of transitions to low fertility. This is a key demographic issue, not only for poor countries but also for the world at large.

Demography is not destiny, however. Population projections, especially longer-term forecasts, are based on extrapolations of trends in vital rates that may turn out to be myopic. The main value of long-term projections is that they demonstrate the long-lasting effect of population momentum. This, in turn, points to the importance of actions to reduce fertility. John Bongaarts at the Population Council has examined possible strategies to reduce the long-term effect of population momentum and to achieve a total developing-country population below the 10.2 billion now projected for 2100. Two of the strategies address the reproductive behavior of the growing numbers of women of reproductive age; they would, if fully implemented, theoretically reduce the rate of fertility to replacement level. The third looks at the possibility of offsetting population momentum by delaying marriage and increasing the average age of childbearing.

The first strategy requires expanding high-quality family planning services to those who have indicated a desire to delay or limit births but are not doing so for one reason or another; eliminating this unwanted fertility could reduce total developing-country population in 2100 from 10.2 to 8.3 billion. Motivating additional couples to have smaller families through information campaigns, increased education, and other social policy initiatives could trim a billion from the projected total (bringing it to 7.3 billion); and if these same efforts could delay the age of childbearing, the final total could be reduced by another billion.

Can population growth be restrained through such measures? Experience with family planning and reproductive health programs has shown that couples will use high-quality services when available. Social research on reproductive behavior also shows that motivation to use these services is related to increased education, particularly for girls, and that education can also raise the median age at marriage and the median age of childbearing. Thus a comprehensive strategy to expand family planning/reproductive health services, expand educational opportunities, and bridge the gender gap in education, combined with efforts to improve the status of women, could further accelerate fertility decline in developing countries and significantly reduce the long-term effect of population momentum.

Population and Development in Historical Perspective

Allen C. Kelley and William Paul McGreevey

History offers perspective in assessing both the debates about and the consequences of rapid population growth. Since 1950, most economists specializing in population issues have held the view that somewhat slower population growth from current high levels would facilitate economic development in most low-income countries. In contrast, many scientists and policy analysts have held a more alarmist, Malthusian view that rapid population growth represents an absolute impediment to economic development. On one hand, the economists' somewhat tempered perspective has emphasized the longer run in which positive "feedbacks"—induced by population growth and facilitated by markets, governments, and social mechanisms—counter the negative short-run effects of population growth. Non-economists, on the other hand, have focused on the short-run costs, which stem from the need to finance youth-related social services and from diminishing returns to the expansion of one or more factors of production.

When and under what circumstances are feedbacks large or small? They are small—and thus the population problem is large—when governments, social institutions, and markets "fail," i.e., when allocation mechanisms do not respond, with reasonable speed or sensibly, to economic scarcities in the face of rapid demographic change. Yet feedbacks are often quite large, and they can compensate for diminishing returns. Empirical studies now tend to downplay the traditional concerns about 1) running out of nonrenewable resources; 2) pressures on saving; and 3) poor allocation of investment funds due to population pressures. However, in the case of renewable resources for which institutions and markets often fail (e.g., rain forests and fishing grounds), overuse occurs. Poor countries, still largely dependent on agriculture, are those most likely to suffer from market and government policy failures; they are, therefore, the least likely to be able to absorb rapid population growth.

In the future, as institutions and markets develop, as international economic integration advances, and as domestic policies become more liberalized, the feedback mechanisms could become increasingly effective in attenuating the shorter-run impacts of population growth. At the same time, population growth in the poorest countries is likely to continue to come down from present high levels, thereby also contributing to economic development. Population policies should complement other actions that aim to advance national economic goals.

The post-1950 pace of demographic change in today's developing countries is far faster than that experienced in Europe before 1800; in the five or six centuries prior to that, any significant acceleration of the population growth rate shifted income away from the poor to the better-off landowners. Only after the shift to cities and the development of more efficient markets were nineteenth-century Europeans (and later, Japanese) able to absorb population growth without reductions in labor's share of income.

In today's developing countries, government policies too frequently both deter agricultural productivity increases and encourage high fertility. Prices of agricultural outputs and inputs are often controlled to the detriment of farmers, a distortion that substantially accounts for poor agricultural performance. Persistent population pressures amplify these policy (and indirectly, market) failures. The *vicious circle* of population pressure and institutional failure is difficult to break. While policy should be primarily directed at the *causes* of these failures, population policies, even though slow to act, can complement effective development policies.

There is no inevitable Malthusian barrier to economic progress. *Virtuous circles*—in which institutions send signals that facilitate agricultural productivity increase and simultaneously lower the value of large families—are possible, as is evident from the experience of the East Asian success stories. The key is the development of markets and institutions, and facilitating government policies—factors as important today as they were in Europe two centuries ago when modern economic growth began.

Population Growth and Poverty

Dennis A. Ahlburg

More than one billion people, a third of the population of the developing world, live in poverty. All countries for which data are available show declines in the percentage of the population in poverty from the mid-1960s to the mid-1980s, although some of these gains were eroded in the late 1980s.

Rapid population growth may affect poverty by affecting the correlates of poverty: low wages, lack of human capital such as education and health, and lack of income-earning assets such as land; income inequality and loss of economic growth; and gender, and sometimes, race and ethnicity.

The empirical evidence on whether population growth has a negative impact on the correlates of poverty, or on poverty itself, is mixed. Despite unprecedented population growth, developing countries generally have been able to absorb the increases in labor supply at higher productivity and higher income per head by shifting labor toward more productive employment. Historically, the exceptions to this have been principally in Africa and Latin America. In the future, however, prospects for such accommodation appear bleak in many regions of the world. There is some evidence that population growth has decreased access to the common property resources that are particularly important in the livelihood of the poor, such as wild fruit and animals, firewood, building and thatching materials, water from tanks, streams, and ponds, free-ranging of poultry, and grazing for livestock. not accounted for in GDP

At the level of the household, it appears that on average additional children reduce the education and health of other children in the family, but estimates of the size of these effects vary considerably. At the national level, rapid population growth reduces expenditure per child, but it is not clear whether this results in lower educational attainment.

Population growth has important negative and positive impacts on economic development, but on balance it appears that slower population growth would be beneficial to economic development. Although it is widely believed that population growth worsens the distribution of income, theoretical and empirical evidence for this impact is ambiguous.

Thus, rapid population growth has negative impacts on some of the correlates of poverty, but the size of these impacts is undetermined. There is very little evidence available on the direct impact of population growth on poverty. Overall, many countries have been able to reduce poverty while population has been growing, but in many others, population has contributed to the difficulties of reducing poverty.

If a government seeks to improve the economic position of the poor, it is best to use the most direct policy instruments available. Among such instruments are policies to increase access of the poor to land, credit, public infrastructure, and services, particularly education and health. In regions where there is an insufficient resource base, policies to aid out-migration are also needed. Family planning programs may help reduce poverty, but the effects may be small and may take a long time to be felt; however these small effects may be cumulative and reinforcing. A family planning program that emphasizes health services to the poor may be more easily justified on the grounds that it directly redistributes health resources to the poor than on the grounds that lower fertility may decrease poverty.

Population, Environment, and Development Nexus

Theodore Panayotou

On the surface, rapid population growth appears to be correlated with deforestation, soil erosion, destruction of local ecosystems, and general environmental degradation. However, on closer examination, it turns out that how population behaves is more important than how population grows. The effects of population on the environment are not unequivocally positive or negative; rather, they depend on human actions, which in turn are contingent on the efficacy of markets and governments, as well as on the culture and the country's level of development. Responses to population growth include intensification of agriculture, increased savings and capital accumulation, diversification of sources of income, occupational change, migration, induced technological and institutional change, resource substitution, trade, and structural adjustment. When all avenues of response are blocked by market failures and misguided policies, the response to population growth takes environmentally destructive dimensions such as forest encroachment, deforestation, evasive agricultural practices, and squatting in crowded cities.

Analyzing how households, communities, and the national economy adjust in response to population growth and increasing scarcity under varying conditions suggests that growing population density in poor countries on balance has negative impacts on environmental conditions mainly because possibilities for helpful responses are muted, and because rapid population growth affects the speed of adjustment. The evidence for this conclusion is drawn from both case studies and formal empirical analysis, but it is not overwhelming. Within limits, population growth and rising density need not lead to depletion and environmental degradation. The relationship between population and negative impacts on the environment is neither immutable nor direct. It is mediated by mobility, access to markets, distribution of wealth, institutions, and government policies. Governments, therefore, should focus on policy reform, market development, and facilitation of the adjustment process, rather than simply on addressing population growth, which is as much a symptom of environmental degradation and poverty as it is a cause.

Population has its greatest impact on local ecosystems in poor agrarian societies with undeveloped or incomplete markets, poor governance, distortionary policies, barriers to mobility, skewed distribution of income and assets, and severely limited economic opportunities. To make local ecosystems sustainable as development proceeds, governments must pursue policy reforms that raise agricultural productivity and labor mobility (e.g., secure and transferable land titles, liberalized interest rates, and promotion of rural credit) while simultaneously encouraging off-farm employment by removing subsidies to capital-intensive industries, promoting rapid growth, and improving education and training, especially for women.

Investing in the Next Generation: The Implications of High Fertility at the Level of the Family

Cynthia B. Lloyd

The effects of high fertility and family size on children's welfare go well beyond the familiar ones of family resource dilution and mothers' nutritional depletion (from frequent pregnancy). Fertility and family size also have implications for children's access to opportunities beyond the home and their socialization into adult roles. Three effects that may be particularly important in the long term are: 1) the *opportunity effect*, the effect of fertility on the access that parents are willing to provide their children to public investment resources; 2) the *equity effect*, the effect of fertility on the distribution of family resources among siblings; and 3) the *intergenerational effect*, the effect of fertility on assumption of nontraditional roles and transmission of opportunities across generations.

In many parts of the world, children growing up with many siblings are increasingly at a disadvantage. In larger, more traditional families, the authority structure within the household is more likely to be male-dominated and less child-oriented in its expenditure patterns. Parental time and resources are also more constrained, limiting the resources available for investments in each child and reducing parents' ability to assist their children in taking advantage of new opportunities as they come along. In addition, differentiation and specialization among children is more prevalent when parents have many children; children with fewer siblings tend to receive more equal treatment. While some children with many siblings are able to pursue their education to the extent of their abilities, this is usually at the expense of their mothers and other siblings who will work harder on their behalf.

There are important links between fertility, the wantedness of children, and child investments; environmental factors play an important role in determining the strength of these relationships. High fertility is likely to have its greatest negative impact on levels of child investment when children are unwanted, because of the lost opportunities such regret or disappointment implies. Unwanted fertility, in conjunction with prevalent levels of per-child investment, thus becomes a measure of the unrealized potential for parental investment in children within a particular socioeconomic and cultural context. Four key environmental features shape the family size-child investment relationship. They include 1) the level of socioeconomic development, 2) the role of the state, 3) the culture of the family, and 4) the phase of the demographic transition.

The implications of high fertility are not gender-neutral. In all societies, women's special reproductive function lies at the heart of sexual divisions of labor and socialization of children for adult roles. High fertility could not occur without a significant proportion of women's lives being devoted to childbearing, with all its attendant risks and responsibilities. Furthermore, the inequalities between children that result from high fertility are particularly acute between boys and girls. The consequences of these gender inequalities are long-term. Girls with many siblings are likely to grow up with little education, limited earning opportunities, and limited control over resource allocation decisions within their households, with the result that they will be likely to start families at an early age, bear many children, and have limited capacities to make investments in their own children.

In sum, a child with fewer siblings is more likely to be a wanted child, more likely to be granted access to public resources by his/her parents, more likely to receive equitable treatment in relation to his/her siblings, and more likely to take on nontraditional roles that will lead to lower fertility aspirations in the next generation.

Risk, Reproduction, and Rights: The Uses of Reproductive Health Data

Deborah Maine, Lynn Freedman, Farida Shaheed, and Schuyler Frautschi

Sex, pregnancy, and childbirth all entail risks. "Reproductive health" is, in part, about the management of those risks: what they are, how to assess them, how to control them, and who should have the authority to do so. Risk data are used to address reproductive health issues at four levels: the population level, the clinical level, the individual level, and the political level. Such data are important not just because they elucidate biological processes, but because they shape the way we think about health and disease, and because they guide choices about programs and policies. Risk data can inform choices about women's health, but they cannot provide a basis for weighing the risks they describe. For that, "reproductive rights" have a critical role to play.

The fundamental dignity of women as human beings requires that they be regarded not simply as childbearers and rearers, but as full individuals entitled to dominion over their own physical being, and as moral agents capable of understanding and making decisions about their own lives. Three specific guidelines can be derived from this basic human rights principle. First, if a woman is to be more than a means to reach some externally-defined goal (which she may or may not share), then reproductive health must be understood from her point of view. Second, the weight that a particular risk or benefit is to be accorded in decisionmaking should be determined primarily by the woman, based on her own understanding of her particular circumstances. Third, a woman's view of her reproductive health and the decisions she makes, are influenced by many factors—including the health system itself. Thus, the health system should give priority to creating conditions that give positive meaning and support to a woman's right to make informed decisions about her reproductive life.

These principles can help inform the program and policy decisions made on the basis of reproductive health data on maternal mortality and morbidity, contraceptive risks and benefits, and sexually transmitted diseases (STDs). For example, the discussion of maternal mortality in this chapter focuses on different "risk factors," including age and number of previous births of women, and the "wantedness" of current pregnancies.

Data such as these can be interpreted in different ways; how they are interpreted affects the program and policy conclusions drawn. Data from Matlab, Bangladesh illustrate this point. The "relative risk" of maternal death in Matlab is highest among women younger than 20 or older than 40; yet many more maternal deaths occur in low risk women between the ages of 20 and 40 (because so many women in this age range are bearing children). Thus relative risk is important to study causation, and to guide clinical practice. But from the standpoint of the individual woman, her own absolute risk—not her chances *compared to* other women—is most pertinent. From the standpoint of designing programs, it is important to reach the large number of low risk women between 20 and 40.

Whether or not a particular pregnancy is wanted is not usually included in the list of "risk factors" for maternal death. Yet where women do not have access to safe abortion services, this may be the most powerful "risk factor" of all. Improving access to modern contraception can reduce maternal mortality by decreasing the number of pregnancies in a population. But it will not reduce the risks to women who do become pregnant, nor will antenatal care substantially reduce maternal mortality. For this, access to emergency obstetric care must be improved.

Contraceptives pose some health hazards, but when considered within a risk-benefit framework at the population level, they generally prevent more illness, disability, and death than they cause. Unfortunately, such risk data have sometimes been used to justify family planning policies and programs that severely limit women's choices and the quality of services at the individual level, in violation of rights principles.

STDs pose staggering health risks to women, who nevertheless have experienced a combination of neglect and blame in this area. For example, the early characterization of HIV/AIDS as associated with high risk *groups* rather than high risk *behavior* led to a focus on prostitutes—on women who defy conventional norms of wifehood and motherhood. Consequently, the great majority of women who suffer from HIV/AIDS are either ignored or stigmatized.

Adequate diagnosis and treatment of STDs has been missing from most reproductive health programs, where the overwhelming emphasis has been on promoting family planning and delivering antenatal care. In part, this emphasis is due to the influence of policy agendas not directly related to women's health *per se*—most significantly, population reduction and child survival. Risk data have been used at the political level to demonstrate that such programs are also important for women's health; indeed, the data *do* show that family planning can improve women's health. But approached from the perspective of reproductive rights principles, the data support—even mandate—a different emphasis. The issue should not be whether a particular type of program improves women's health, but rather what kinds of programs will best address women's health problems.

Distinguishing among the different concepts of risk can help clarify which view of the data is most appropriate. Which point of view should govern decisionmaking is less a scientific question than it is a question of rights.

International Migration, Fertility, and Development

Michael S. Teitelbaum and Sharon Stanton Russell

The volume of human movement across national borders, especially among developing countries, has become very large. Moreover, it is increasingly volatile, unpredictable, and unwanted by many receiving countries. Current global economic and political conditions and trends imply high potential for continued increases in international migration.

It is difficult to generalize about reactions to real and perceived international migration trends, given the heavy impacts of context-specific circumstances. For many migrant-sending countries, emigration is viewed as a positive contributor to development, while in a number of migrant-receiving countries, negative responses can be triggered by unemployment, nationalism, and the rise of anti-immigration political parties and movements. Such negative responses are often sudden, sometimes overwrought (most recently in the developed countries of Europe), and usually full of dissonance, ambivalence, and political contention.

The greatest volume of international migration is between developing countries. Demographic differentials do little to explain these movements, since both origin and receiving countries are characterized by high fertility and youthful age structures. Demographic differentials are more likely to play a role in migration from developing to developed countries, and indeed, some argue that high fertility is a major cause of increasing international migration. However, linkages between the demographic forces of international migration and high fertility are more complex and indirect than such a view would imply; the potential linkages are perhaps best understood in terms of three demographic juxtapositions. The first is between high fertility in developing countries and low fertility in industrialized countries. The second, a demographic consequence of the first, is between the very "young" age structures of developing countries and the "older" age structures characterizing developed countries. Finally, in many developed countries, low (sometimes very low, as in Germany and Italy) domestic fertility is juxtaposed with high levels of migration from countries with higher prevailing fertility norms. However, these juxtapositions do not help to explain migration between the low fertility countries of Eastern and Western Europe.

Similar complexity and indirection characterize the links between international migration and economic development trends. The 1980s was a decade of rising economic differentials between developed and developing countries; although per capita economic growth was often slow and fitful in the former, it was frequently negative in the latter. Saturated labor markets along with economic and political instability in many developing regions produced a large number of international migrants, whose movement was facilitated by improvements in communication and transportation technologies.

International migration from developing countries, in turn, produced real if poorly understood impacts upon development in migrant-producing countries. Remittances sent home by expatriate workers became substantial, continued to increase, and represented an important element of net financial transfers from developed to developing countries. Nonetheless, their impacts have proved to be difficult to demonstrate, with different research methodologies producing disparate conclusions; in general, observable benefits tend to be local, short-term, and sector-specific, whereas national and long-term effects are more difficult to discern. In some cases, remittance flows have proved to be vulnerable to unpredictable and sometimes dramatic political and economic changes in the destination countries.

As to the future, proposed efforts to accelerate economic development so as to restrain the potential for outmigration may produce counter-intuitive results. While increasing economic growth is an important, and perhaps the only, effective means of moderating out-migration pressures over the very long term—i.e., two to three decades—there is consensus that over the short-to-immediate term of one to two decades, no such moderating effect should be expected, and indeed accelerating economic growth may increase the potential for outmigration.

Government, Population, and Poverty: A Win-Win Tale

Nancy Birdsall

The high rates of fertility that continue to characterize many developing countries tend to elicit three principal concerns: first, that rapid population growth reduces public and family investments in human capital, reducing an important input to (and thereby slowing down) economic growth; second, that increased population imposes greater stress on natural resources (at a local and national level as well as a global level), leading to rapid degradation of some of those resources; and third, that increased population reduces the incomes of certain groups (particularly the poor) relative to others and therefore exacerbates problems of poverty and income inequality. Each of these concerns is related to the existence of certain negative "externalities" associated with childbearing. This is to say that the costs of an additional child coming into the world are not fully borne by the parents and therefore parents may choose more children than is socially optimal.

These concerns and the market failures they represent imply that there is a need for certain public interventions. Yet interventions that aim solely to affect fertility by raising the private cost of a child to include its social cost may in fact decrease welfare because the costs are likely to hurt the poor disproportionately. The poor have many children in part because they are poor. An intervention, therefore, must not only raise the cost of having a child, thus lowering fertility, but simultaneously increase rather than diminish the welfare of the poor.

Four types of interventions meet this criterion. First, public investments in the human capital of the poor can raise the "cost" of children to parents but are also associated with greater family welfare and reduced fertility among the poor. Increased educational opportunities for girls, for example, increase the economic cost of children by raising a woman's productivity and therefore the value of her time.

Second, adjusting the price of contraceptives, both in terms of improving information and availability and eliminating inappropriate regulations that limit access to contraceptives, reduces the cost of controlling fertility, which implicitly raises the "cost" of having another child. It also minimizes unwanted fertility resulting from an "unmet need" for contraception. Third, increasing the access of the poor to information critical to fertility decisions (such as knowledge about increased returns to education and lower child mortality rates) enables poor couples, for whom information costs are particularly high, to make informed family planning decisions, improving the welfare of the poor, and thus directly encourages reduced fertility. Finally, good public management which ensures broad-based growth, that is, growth which raises the incomes of all groups including the poor, reduces poverty without impinging on their welfare.

Each of these interventions aimed at reducing fertility is justifiable; each meets the criterion of increasing the cost of children to the poor, so that the poor are forced to internalize more fully the social costs of having children, while at the same time improving the welfare of the poor. These interventions make society better off as a whole, and they are sound social programs with high social and economic returns in their own right.

Part III
Old Debates,
New Conclusions

Chapter One

Developing Countries and the International Population Debate: Politics and Pragmatism

Kaval Gulhati and Lisa M. Bates

The U.N. International Conference on Population and Development (ICPD), to be held in Cairo in September 1994, has the potential to be the first major intergovernmental population conference relatively free of fundamental disagreements between developed and developing countries over the importance of population issues. Since the 1974 U.N. World Population Conference through the 1992 U.N. Conference on Environment and Development (UNCED), developing countries have approached the population debate with varying degrees of ambivalence and political posturing in the international arena on the one hand, and growing concern and action at the national level on the other. Historically, the perspective of developing countries on population has been guided more by national political and socioeconomic interests than by concern about growing numbers of people. Developing countries have consistently sought to protect their interests and defend their sovereignty against intrusions by developed countries; now, however, they are increasingly concerned about the consequences of high fertility and interested in mobilizing greater international action to slow population growth.

Meanwhile, the developed world, particularly the United States, has moderated its approach, which many developing countries and outside experts considered too aggressive in the early stages of the debate. The domestic political preoccupations that dominated official U.S. thinking on population in the 1980s have subsided, and developed countries have addressed many developing-country concerns by, for example, integrating population programs with other development activities. As the 1994 conference approaches, there is widespread consensus within both the developing and industrialized worlds about the importance of population factors in sustainable development and the need for comprehensive strategies to lower fertility. Yet, while the most divisive North-South dimensions of the population debate have diminished, a number of unresolved issues remain.

This chapter discusses the evolution of developing-country approaches to population since the 1950s and leading up to Cairo. It describes evolving official positions at international fora and suggests the degree to which these at times have been inconsistent with national attention to population. It also outlines outstanding issues as represented by various nongovernmental constituencies that influence the policies and positions of both developing countries and donors. Actual policies and programmatic activity at the country level are illustrated with brief historical sketches of four countries—Brazil, Kenya, India, and China.

THE EVOLUTION OF DEVELOPING-COUNTRY VIEWS ON POPULATION

Developing-country positions on population can be broadly grouped into three phases. The first phase of *optimism and indifference* regarding population issues and the need for international attention covers the period from the 1950s up to the 1974 population conference. The second phase, a period of *growing concern* over the role of population in development, covers the intervening decade, culminating in the 1984 population conference in Mexico City. The third and current phase, leading up to the 1994 population conference in Cairo, is one of *emerging consensus* on population and sustainable development issues. The perspective of developing countries is not monolithic; it consists of many nuances and different attitudes held by various countries and regions. However, the collective perspective is useful for delineating broad differences in views between developed and developing countries, where they have existed, and for understanding the evolution of the debate over time.

Optimism and Indifference, 1950s to 1974

During the 1950s and early 1960s, the population and development debate was largely shaped by Western countries concerned that rapid population growth was an impediment to the development of the

"Third World" and socialist countries that rejected such "Malthusian" thinking, maintaining that population growth was a neutral phenomenon, with socialism providing the best answer to development problems. This East-West debate surfaced at the first two world population conferences, primarily technical meetings, in 1954 and 1965.[1] At the time, developing countries themselves gave little attention to population issues, although India adopted a population policy as early as 1951, and a few other countries offered basic family planning services through private agencies. Most developing-country governments, skeptical that population growth was a serious constraint on development, remained in the background of the debate.

Early U.S. thinking on population was driven primarily by foreign policy concerns. Although the U.S. government did not become formally engaged on the issue until the mid-1960s, a loose coalition of demographers, concerned prominent citizens, and members of the foreign policy community warned of the threat to U.S. strategic interests posed by "rampant population growth" in developing countries.[2] Such apocalyptic thinking was reinforced by ecologists, sounding the alarm about environmental degradation caused by the "population bomb."[3] This crisis mentality shaped the initial U.S. population program, which was justified on humanitarian grounds and the need to protect U.S. economic and security interests abroad. The program was heavily weighted toward demographic goals and the supply of contraceptives— often without the prerequisite demand in developing countries. Many developing countries, perceiving imperialist and even racist origins in U.S. concern, were suspicious of U.S. motives for assistance and resented the overzealous approach.

International concern about rapid population growth intensified in the late 1960s. In 1969, the United States, along with the Nordic countries (especially Sweden), led the effort to create the United Nations Fund for Population Activities (UNFPA) and became its largest contributor. Believing that both a population crisis and a consensus on the need for international action existed, the United States and other donors initiated the 1974 U.N. World Population Conference in Bucharest, the first international population conference at which governments were represented at the ministerial level. Delegates and observers from the United States expected unanimous endorsement of population programs in the developing world and sought full cooperation for an agenda endorsing active family planning measures, including time-bound targets for certain regions. Representatives from the United States and some countries in Western Europe and Asia worked to mobilize greater activity on the part of governments and international institutions and saw Bucharest as a forum to press for concerted global action. The draft World Population Plan of Action reflected these expectations by calling for population and related social and economic measures with a direct effect on fertility.[4]

Much of the U.S. optimism stemmed from the perception that earlier ideological and religious differences had subsided and that there was now widespread international agreement on the significance of population growth and the measures needed to slow it. A series of U.N. resolutions adopted in the 1960s and early 1970s had, among other things, established family planning as a human right and had legitimized government attention to and involvement in efforts to limit fertility.[5] Furthermore, just prior to the Bucharest conference, at the May 1974 Asia Region Preparatory Meeting, the U.N. Economic Commission for Asia and the Far East (ECAFE) gave its full-scale support for population/family planning programs.

Despite these official endorsements of family planning measures and the fact that many developing countries were themselves taking action to check population growth (by the late 1960s most Asian countries had adopted population policies), developing-country delegates expressed very different views from their Northern counterparts at the conference itself. Many developing countries felt that donor countries placed too much emphasis on fertility control and not enough on the underlying socioeconomic factors affecting fertility levels. They argued that population growth was a consequence, not a cause, of underdevelopment and could only be addressed as part of a comprehensive development strategy. This perspective was embodied in the assertion of the head of the Indian delegation that, "development is the best contraceptive." Led by Argentina and Algeria, the Group of 77 (the nonaligned bloc of developing countries, or G-77) sought to redraft the action plan to reflect the principles of the New International Economic Order (NIEO) adopted at a special session of the U.N. General Assembly just five months prior to the population conference. The NIEO stressed the need for socioeconomic development and called for the redistribution of economic resources between rich and poor countries.

The idea that population growth could not slow down without economic development was consistent with the widespread perception among many developing countries that family planning programs had failed.[6] It has been noted that the "redistribution" position also suited the political interests of developing countries in a number of ways. A unified Southern bloc rallying around one set of issues was an important show of solidarity against the industrialized world, particularly because of the widespread publicity surrounding the conference. Furthermore, it was good strategy to follow Algeria's lead and thus remain on good terms with the Organization of Petroleum Exporting Countries (OPEC), especially at a time when the cartel was flexing its newly found muscles.[7] The position also had an obvious ideological appeal for socialist countries such as China, which asserted at the conference that "population is not a problem under socialism" and that "the superpowers raise the false alarm of a 'population explosion'" (see Box 1).

The United States responded by pushing for a focus on population and dismissing calls for attention to the NIEO principles as "polemics and ideological statements" that merely "obscured the substance of the plan of action."[8] However, other industrialized countries did not react so insensitively and, in fact, sought to distance themselves from the U.S. position. The Nordic countries in particular, with their own tradition of social welfare, were much more responsive to the NIEO goals and did not see them as incompatible with efforts to reduce population growth.[9]

Criticisms of the heavy-handed U.S. population-control orientation also came from participants in the non-official "Population Tribune," a concurrent forum for representatives of nongovernmental organizations (NGOs), independent experts, and activists. Almost 1,500 individuals attended, approximately 300 of whom represented NGOs. Most of the influential organizations were from the North and virtually all the population NGOs were either international or U.S.-based.[10] Many of these groups were critical of the alarmist views expressed by several developed-country delegations and of efforts to promote population control. Support for the developing-country view even came from within the ranks of the U.S. population establishment; in an unexpected speech to the Population Tribune, John D. Rockefeller III noted the population-development link and stressed the importance of women in population policies and programs.[11]

The result of the Bucharest conference was a compromise embodied in a much debated redrafted World Population Plan of Action. The document was adopted by consensus, with the Vatican abstaining. Unlike the earlier draft, the final version eliminated any reference to fertility reduction targets and placed population growth as a problem within the context of social and economic development and the need for a restructured world economy. The document affirmed the right of couples to family planning (despite Vatican objections) but stressed the sovereign right of every nation to determine its own population policy and de-emphasized the need for government support of family planning programs. The revised plan of action, a significant victory for developing nations, generated considerable disappointment within the U.S. delegation and the supporting population community.

BOX 1. EXCERPTS FROM OFFICIAL COUNTRY STATEMENTS PREPARED FOR U.N. POPULATION CONFERENCES IN 1974 AND 1984

Brazil
....

1974 Conference

". . . Brazil will be able to absorb the foreseeable demographic increments and . . . this growth is even to be considered as a necessary element for economic development, for national security. . . . Birth control is a matter for decision by the family unit, which in this context is not subject to government interference; being able to resort to birth control measures should not be a privilege reserved for families that are well off, and therefore it is the responsibility of the state to provide the information and the means that may be required by families of limited income. . . ."

Source: Statement by the Head of the Brazilian Delegation to the III World Population Conference, Plenary Session, Bucharest, 26 August 1974.

1984 Conference

"The Brazilian government still considers as valid the basic principles of the Brazilian population policy, formulated in 1974. . . . Furthermore, the Government is aware of the fact that today the Brazilian people increasingly demand knowledge and adequate means for planning its reproduction . . . the planning of the number of offspring is one of the fundamental rights of the human being . . . . Governmental interference in birth control, which depends on each family's own decision, is . . . not to be found in Brazil."

Source: Statement by His Excellency Dr. Waldys Mendes Arcoverde, Minister of State for Health, Head of the Brazilian Delegation, Mexico City, August 1984.

Kenya
....

1974 Conference

"In the past family planning has been carried out on an ad hoc basis. There have been no targets set for attainment. This has resulted in family planning having no appreciable impact on the rate of population growth. The Government has decided to intensify family planning through a definite programme with set targets."

Source: Country Statement, Bucharest, August 1974.

1984 Conference

". . . since the 1974 Population Conference in Bucharest, Kenya has made progress towards implementing the recommendations of the Plan of Action. . . . In summary, Kenya has realized that rapid population growth frustrates her efforts to provide the population with the basic needs services of education, health, housing, food, and employment. For this reason we have given a lot of thought on how to mount an effective family planning programme while at the same time realizing that family planning is not the panacea of all population issues."

Source: Country Statement at Mexico City, August 1984.

India

··

1974 Conference

"The path to family planning in every country lies through the eradication of poverty, which in fact has historically been the main cause of over-population. . . . It has truly been said that the best contraceptive is development."

Source: Country Statement by Dr. Karan Singh, Minister of Health and Family Planning, India, August 1974.

1984 Conference

"Whatever the criticism on our shortfall, we have . . . averted 60 million births so far. Without a family planning effort India's [annual] growth rate would have exceeded 3 percent. As much as 94 percent of the expenditure on population programmes comes from our own resources. . . ."

Source: Country Statement by Babu Rao Shankarananda, India's Minister for Health and Family Welfare, Mexico City, August 1984.

China

··

1974 Conference

"The superpowers raise the false alarm of a "population explosion" and paint a depressing picture of the future of mankind. . . . The condition of the population of a country is determined by its social system and the political and economic conditions. . . . [Overpopulation] is mainly due to aggressive plunder and exploitation by the imperialists. . . . Our birth planning is not merely birth control as some people understand it to be, but comprises different measures for different circumstances. . . ."

Source: Statement by the Head of the Delegation of the People's Republic of China, Bucharest, August 1974.

1984 Conference

". . . family planning is a basic national policy of China. Since 1979, the Chinese Government has advocated the practice of 'one couple, one child'. . . . In seeking the solution in its population problem, China mainly relies upon its own efforts."

Source: Statement by Wang Wei, Chairman of the Delegation of the People's Republic of China, Mexico City, August 1984.

The significance of developing-country opposition to population control at Bucharest is somewhat mitigated by the attention given to population issues by many countries immediately following the conference. Indeed, less than two years later, the Government of India issued a statement identifying population as a national priority that required immediate action: ". . . To wait for education and economic development to bring about a drop in fertility is not a practical solution."[12] Similarly, by the late 1970s, the Chinese government had decided that "the very future of socialism depended upon limiting fertility within marriage to only one or two births" and initiated an aggressive population program.[13]

Growing Concern, 1974 to 1984

The period leading up to the 1984 International Conference on Population in Mexico City was characterized by increased attention to population issues among developing countries. By 1984, many countries had become convinced of the importance of population issues and the desirability of international assistance for fertility control efforts. Developing-country governments were still interested in advancing the principles of the NIEO, but they had begun to see population pressures as an impediment to development and were now prepared to endorse the expansion of family planning and related measures to limit fertility. At the same time, donors and international agencies took steps in the late 1970s and early 1980s to decentralize their population programs and link population activities to other development initiatives such as education, migration, and mortality, thereby reflecting the integrated, development-oriented approach to population sought by the G-77 at Bucharest.[14]

The shift in developing-country thinking witnessed at Mexico City was especially pronounced for the African delegations. At Bucharest, Africans had been optimistic about the continent's capacity to absorb growing numbers given its vast land mass and rich natural resources, but by 1984, many African governments, having witnessed first hand the social and economic problems associated with high fertility, began to express concern.[15] Other countries that had advocated the NIEO position at Bucharest, such as China, Brazil, and Algeria, also came to Mexico City with a commitment to addressing population issues and a greater interest in and acceptance of family planning measures.[16] The political issues and motivations that so overshadowed the population debate at Bucharest were relatively absent from the developing-country positions at Mexico City. Tensions between the North and the South had diminished considerably between 1974 and 1984, and OPEC was no longer in a position to wield as much influence with the industrialized countries. Also, by the end of the 1970s, sufficient differentiation among developing countries in terms of economic growth made it less desirable to pursue their objections with the North as a unified bloc; negotiating with the developed countries through bilateral or regional arrangements made more sense.[17]

In Mexico City, the infusion of politics came not from developing countries, but from the United States, the country that demonstrated the most dramatic reversal in thinking on population, both in its analysis of the demographic situation and in its policy prescriptions. Declaring that population was a "neutral" factor, the U.S. delegation asserted that the population activism of the 1960s and 1970s was a "demographic overreaction" and that the perceived crisis was really the result of "economic statism" and "too much governmental control."[18] It advocated "sound economic policies" based on free markets and individual initiative. The United States also announced that it would discontinue all funding for private organizations that offered abortion information and/or services—the now famous "Mexico City policy" that resulted in the withdrawal of U.S. support for the International Planned Parenthood Federation (IPPF). IPPF could guarantee that its national affiliates would not use U.S. contributions for abortion-related services (a stipulation that had already been in effect since the 1973 Helms Amendment to the Foreign Assistance Act), but the new policy extended this restriction to any agency providing abortion services or information or any institution funding or assisting such an agency—even if it used non-U.S. funds for such purposes. It also led to the de-funding of UNFPA in 1986 because of its support for China's family planning program (against which allegations of coercive practices had been made).

The turnabout in the U.S. position was a departure not only from its leadership role at Bucharest and in subsequent international population assistance efforts, but also from statements made as recently as January and March of 1984 at the two preparatory meetings for the conference. With a presidential election approaching and high media coverage of the conference, U.S. officials were responsive to the aggressive efforts of a conservative coalition of "pro-life" activists, libertarian "think tanks," administration officials, and Congressional members and staff to shape the constitution and position of the U.S. delegation. They succeeded in getting former Senator James Buckley, known for his hostility to overseas population assistance, to lead a delegation of mostly administration officials with dubious credentials in the population field.[19]

Despite the obvious anti-abortion agenda of the U.S. delegation, the United States encouraged the Vatican to take the lead in proposing language to disqualify abortion as an "acceptable" method of family planning.[20] The United States, however, did work to have a reference to *illegal* abortion deleted from the conference report, a move vehemently opposed by Sweden, which argued that it downplayed the important health consequences for women.[21] The final conference report accommodates other aspects of the U.S. position—mention of the role of the private sector in achieving population and development objectives, for example—but in general U.S. influence on the conference proceedings was minimal. The declaration and recommendations that came out of the conference strengthened and expanded the provisions of the World Population Plan of Action adopted at Bucharest, reaffirming the role of development in lowering fertility but recognizing that, even in the absence of development, family planning efforts can have a much needed impact on fertility. Unlike the U.S. policy statement, the final document also highlighted the links between women's social and economic status and high fertility, and stressed the importance of integrating women into the development process.[22]

Emerging Consensus, 1984 to the Present

Developing-country positions at Mexico City and the fact that, by 1988, 62 developing countries had adopted measures to slow population growth (compared to 42 in 1976)[23] demonstrate the commitment of developing countries to population activities and the extent to which disagreements about the role of population in development have subsided. However, the 1992 U.N. Conference on the Environment and Development in Rio demonstrated that the *politics* of population continue at some levels.

Most developing countries at Rio clearly recognized the importance of population issues—approximately 70 percent of conference country reports identified population as a critical issue in the environment and development debate. But they were reluctant to focus on population in the context of a discussion on the environment.[24] They feared that such a focus would imply that demographic factors in developing countries are responsible for global environmental problems rather than what they considered the real issue of excessive consumption patterns in the industrial world. Developing-country governments were also opposed to addressing population issues without guarantees of assistance from developed countries for the environment-friendly technologies needed to achieve sustainable development.[25]

At the final preparatory meeting for UNCED, the United States insisted on deleting language from Agenda 21—the action plan for national and international action prepared for and approved at UNCED—regarding quantitative targets for consumption reduction. Developing countries retaliated by watering down the chapter on population, substituting euphemistic language for explicit references to population issues. In later negotiations, developing countries retreated somewhat from this position, realizing that it carried little weight with a U.S. administration already indifferent, if not antagonistic, to family planning efforts. By that time, however, other interested parties, particularly the Vatican and women's groups, had succeeded in diluting much of the language dealing with demographic concerns. The final document identifies population as a "cross-cutting" issue but is weak both in making population-environment connections and in identifying measures, such as family planning, to reduce population pressures.[26]

Once again, however, the political considerations of developing-country governments evident in the international arena did not lessen their resolve in dealing with these issues on their own terms. Just three months after Rio, many developing countries seemed prepared to address environmental problems associated with rapid population growth. At the 1992 Summit Meeting of Heads of State or Government of Nonaligned Countries in Jakarta, officials expressed concern about unprecedented rates of population growth and, while restating the need to address "unsustainable production and consumption patterns" in the developed world, called for greater attention to the "interrelated issues of demographic pressures, protection of the environment, exhaustion of natural resources, and growth requirements."[27]

With the approach of the International Conference on Population and Development to be held in Cairo in September 1994, both developing and developed countries appear to be in agreement on 1) the consequences of rapid population growth and 2) the need for comprehensive strategies to address that growth. Population is recognized as a key ingredient in efforts to promote sustainable development. Both donors and recipients are stressing the need for family planning services for those who already desire to limit their families, as well as measures of social and economic development to generate such demand where it does not yet exist. Governments are also in agreement that women and gender issues must be central in the population debate.

In the preparatory meetings and regional conferences leading up to Cairo, developing-country governments have reiterated old concerns and articulated new priorities. Country statements show that most are concerned about the effects of population growth at the individual level—the impact on employment, food and land availability, women's health and status, and the provision of health and education services. Several emphasize the need to improve the status and well-being of women and to address male responsibilities and participation in population programs.

Most developing countries now indicate they strongly support the goals of sustainable development and are prepared to examine the role of population in environmental problems. Many, however, such as Brazil, India, and Kenya, maintain that population must be treated in

the context of social and economic development and not without attention to issues of consumption and lifestyle. Several developing-country
delegations to the third preparatory meeting of the Cairo conference
also made it clear that environmental considerations should not inter-
fere with their right to economic growth and that the ICPD should not
address environment issues beyond those agreed upon in Agenda 21.
Some governments also still draw attention to their place in the world
economy and to the link they perceive between poverty in the South
and economic policies in the North (e.g., the impact of external debt
and structural adjustment). They fully endorse active international
cooperation on population programs, but stress the importance of
national sovereignty.[28]

   The United States is not triggering controversy either; so far it
has played a constructive, leadership role. Departing radically from its
position in 1984 and 1992, the United States now emphasizes women's
rights and reproductive choice, including access to safe abortion, and,
along with other industrialized countries, is addressing consumption
issues.[29] The United States is also broadening the scope of what it
considers population activities to include reproductive health, female
education, HIV/AIDS, and infant mortality, among others.

   Indeed, the biggest "North-South" conflict of the Cairo conference will most likely be around resources. Developing countries are
stressing the need for *additional* financial resources to implement conference goals. They are pursuing donor commitments closer to levels
proposed at the International Forum on Population in the Twenty-First
Century, a gathering of ministers, senior government officials, and
population experts sponsored by the United Nations in 1989. At the
Forum, representatives from 79 developing and donor countries agreed
that the share of total development assistance spent on population-
related activities should be increased from 1.5 percent to 4 percent.[30]
Many donors appear prepared to allocate a greater proportion of aid
resources to population, but shrinking foreign assistance budgets in
some countries may result in little if any increases in terms of absolute
volume. Some donors, most notably the United States, Japan, and
Germany, have at least verbally pledged substantial increases in population funding but others, particularly European Union countries, are
holding back.[31] Developing countries are also seeking assurances from
donors that increases in aid for population will not come at the expense
of resources for other aspects of development. They have legitimate
reasons to be skeptical of donor intentions after the resource commitments made at UNCED failed to materialize.

Even the potentially volatile issue of migration has not emerged as a matter of contentious debate between developing and developed countries. The draft final document for the Cairo meeting stresses the need to maximize the benefits of migration to all concerned while addressing the root causes of "involuntary" movements. Most countries find this approach agreeable and any conflict so far has concerned the extent and nature of rights afforded to different groups of migrants, rather than more fundamental questions of sovereignty and bases for asylum.

The promising consensus surrounding the 1994 conference does not, however, diminish the urgency of what lies ahead over the next several years. Persistently high rates of population growth continue in some places, especially in Africa, where many countries also lag behind in a range of critical social and economic indicators. Furthermore, agreement today on the need to limit fertility at replacement level does nothing to slow the present growth in human numbers resulting from past inaction; efforts must be made to delay and space the childbearing of the present generation of reproductive age in order to slow population momentum. Developing countries and donors are also dealing with a greater number of complex issues related to population, among them: human rights; migration and urbanization; female education; sustainable development issues, including consumption; male responsibility; and reproductive rights and health, including abortion. Although they may agree on the need to address these issues, developing countries, along with the donor community, must work to develop the appropriate policy and programmatic responses.

Today, the population debate is largely shaped by such transnational concerns. Alliances are more likely to be formed around sets of key issues than along traditional North-South lines. Unresolved and frequently contentious issues such as abortion and reproductive rights, the extent to which reproductive health should be integrated with family planning, and whether family planning should be integrated with social development, continue to generate heated debate both within individual countries and in the international arena. Furthermore, not only have the issues evolved, but the actors have as well. NGOs from both developed and developing countries have had an unprecedented level of involvement in the U.N. preparatory process for the 1994 conference; and they are lobbying not just their own governments but those of other countries as well. More than ever, women, both as NGO participants and as country delegates, have also been a powerful and effective voice on a number of population-related issues.

NONGOVERNMENTAL INFLUENCES ON SOUTHERN PERSPECTIVES

The non-official actors that actively seek to influence positions and policies on population in both developing and developed countries can be loosely grouped into four coalitions or interest groups:

1) the population "community" or "establishment," consisting of lobbyists, research institutions, and foundations (in developed countries), members of the medical and scientific communities (in both developed and developing countries), and family planning providers (in developing countries) whose primary interest (real or perceived) in population activities derives from demographic concerns; because the views of this constituency are discussed implicitly throughout the chapter, they are not elaborated here.

2) institutions and organizations opposed to abortion and "artificial" methods of family planning based on moral or religious grounds;

3) the international women's movement, consisting of advocates for women's health, reproductive rights, and the improvement of women's social, legal, economic, and political status; and

4) the international environmental movement whose biologists and grassroots organizations are drawing attention to the environmental consequences of rapid population growth; this is a fairly new, but increasingly influential, coalition on the population scene.

Religious Influences

Religious "forces" that oppose population control efforts in developing countries include the Catholic Church, religious fundamentalists, and the transnational coalition of anti-abortion activists that call themselves "pro-life."[32] The interests of religious-based groups in population derive from, among other things, the desire to promote social justice and to protect the "dignity of the human person"; the need to maintain a social order where women and reproductive behavior are tightly controlled; and the desire to "save the unborn" through evangelical crusades. It is probable that, in general, formal religious dogma has less influence on *individual* fertility behavior than do traditional beliefs and customs. However, religious-based groups, as well as the Catholic Church as a politically active, hierarchical institution, have had a significant impact on population positions and policies at both the national and international levels. At both the 1974 and 1984 population conferences and at UNCED in 1992, the Vatican (which participates in U.N. international conferences as a permanent observer with voting rights) played down the importance of population issues and successfully deleted from conference documents explicit language pertaining to family planning and abortion. Leading up to the 1994 conference, the Vatican has mounted an aggressive lobbying campaign, aimed at heads of state, against several aspects of the Cairo draft document: the treatment of abortion, in particular, but also the definition of the family, the rights of adolescents and unmarried women to family planning, the meaning of reproductive rights, and others.

The Catholic Church has been vocal in its opposition to international population programs since their beginnings in the 1960s. But since 1978, under the leadership of Pope John Paul II, the Vatican has significantly increased its political activism in both developed and developing countries. The Pope has argued that contraceptive programs are to blame for "increased sexual permissiveness" and "irresponsible conduct" and has remained absolute in the Church's opposition to abortion.[33]

The International Women's Movement

Feminists have long questioned the motives of the population community and criticized an approach they see as too heavily dominated by demographic goals at the expense of individual welfare.[34] In many ways, the demands of women's groups have mirrored those of developing countries, calling for less attention to population issues and more to the underlying socioeconomic reasons for high fertility. An exclusive focus on women's reproductive capacity, many argue, downplays both the important productive roles women play[35] and the economic, social, and legal barriers they confront.

Demographic priorities have also resulted in a narrow focus within family planning and reproductive health programs. When guided by societal and demographic goals instead of women's self-identified needs, these programs often neglect important health problems such as sexually transmitted diseases and reproductive tract infections. Feminists argue that family planning, including abortion, should be offered as part of comprehensive reproductive health services that respect a woman's analysis of her health needs and facilitate her ability to make informed decisions about her reproductive life (see Chapter 7 in this volume). The case for access to safe and affordable abortion is based both on the right of women to control their own fertility and on the negative health consequences of illegal or unsafe abortion. Feminists also make the point that women need quality services not just to avoid pregnancy but to ensure safe childbirth as well.

Feminists criticize the bias in family planning programs toward sterilization and surgical or hormonal methods such as the intrauterine device (IUD), Norplant, and Depo Provera, because these are not user-controlled—once a woman undergoes the procedure she cannot easily (or in the case of sterilization, ever) reverse it without medical assistance. These methods are also considered by many, not only women's groups, to have significant potential for abuse; the risks and side effects they entail are often not fully explained and they can be used coercively on targeted populations.[36] Some advocates who see the potential virtues of methods that do not require daily vigilance nor depend on male cooperation take a reformist position, arguing that improvements must be made in the provision of services, namely, full information and proper follow-up care. Other, more radical critics, reject these methods entirely.[37]

Women's groups and many consumer advocates are also concerned about what they consider a double standard for safety: contraceptive methods that fail to pass regulatory standards in industrialized countries are "dumped" on women in developing countries. Furthermore, many complain that drug companies use developing countries as "laboratories" for contraceptive research to avoid the stricter guidelines that prevail in developed countries; in many settings the meaning of "informed consent" is often negotiable.[38] Nonetheless, research is needed in the socioeconomic and cultural settings of developing countries to avoid the import of inappropriate methods or approaches.

As critical as women's groups have been of the population "establishment," they have often become uncomfortably aligned with family planning advocates in the face of organized religious opposition to the availability of contraceptives and abortion. For example, in 1987, Filipino women's groups and professionals from the population community successfully blocked an executive order to ban most modern methods of contraception as well as government policies to encourage lower fertility or set demographic goals; the same year, women's groups campaigned against a fetal protection clause in the new Philippine constitution that was introduced by church and "pro-life" organizations. They were unable to block the clause entirely but won a guarantee of equal protection of the mother. Similarly, in 1986, when Brazilian women's groups successfully fought a constitutional ban on abortion introduced by religious and "right-to-life" organizations, they broke a long-standing alliance with the Catholic Church based on a shared interest in social reforms and opposition to population control policies.[39]

In many ways, mainstream women's groups find themselves in an antagonistic yet somewhat interdependent relationship with the population community—critical of its sometimes top-down, demographic approach but supportive of women's individual freedom to control their own fertility. The dilemma this situation poses is further illustrated by the use of the feminist critique by non-feminist groups to suit their own agendas. In countries like Kenya and the Philippines, conservative, anti-abortion activists have added feminists' criticisms of population control to their rhetorical ammunition.[40]

Environmental Activism

The relatively recent entry of the environmental movement into the population scene has added another dimension to the debate. Environmentalists have long been concerned about the relationship between growing human numbers and environmental degradation. Many private U.S. environmental groups became active on international population issues in the 1960s and early 1970s, but then retreated to a more domestic agenda in the face of anti-population-control attitudes in the developing world and other pressing issues at home.[41] In the 1980s, many environmental groups were also wary of becoming involved in the abortion controversy and thereby jeopardizing the support of their diverse memberships. In recent years, however, there has been a resurgence in environmental attention to population at the grassroots level that has grown increasingly international in scope.

Women's groups have been concerned that a focus on the links between high fertility and environmental stress would imply that women are primarily responsible for yet another global problem and further justify top-down population control policies. In 1991, the World Women's Congress for a Healthy Planet, an international forum of the Women's Environment and Development Organization (WEDO), declared that the "major causes of environmental degradation are industrial and military pollutants, toxic wastes, and economic systems that exploit and misuse nations and people"—not women's fertility.[42] Some feminists doubt that environmental groups have women's interests at heart because many do not have a formal position on abortion rights.[43] At the same time women's groups have a strategic ally in environmentalists who are vocal supporters of universal access to family planning.

At the grassroots-level in developing countries, environmentalists are less inclined to focus on population issues. Some environmentalists do not want to distract attention from issues of overconsumption and resource distribution.[44] Similarly, grassroots development organizations in the developing world also seem to concentrate their energies more on the links between the environment and poverty than those between the environment and population.[45]

The commonalities and differences among these various interest groups were played out at UNCED in 1992. To the frustration of population and environmental activists, women's groups and the Vatican—backed by Argentina and the Philippines—succeeded in diluting Agenda 21 language on population. Most of the conference politicking took place at the concurrent NGO Global Forum. Women's groups reiterated the principles of the World Women's Congress and articulated many of the same concerns about socioeconomic equity as the G-77; at the same time, some feminists argued that women's groups were instrumental in getting stronger family planning language reinserted into the final document after some developing countries sought to delete it.[46]

As different as their interests are, these groups are increasingly identifying and acting on their common concerns.[47] Feminists sympathetic to the goals of population programs emphasize the potential compatibility of demographic and individual interests when family planning programs are responsive to women's needs, although they note that programs that ignore women's interests are not likely to succeed and may even create a widespread backlash against family planning efforts in general.[48] Similarly, environmental groups are advocating the empowerment of women both as a desirable goal in itself and as a means to environmental ends.[49] At the same time, they are devoting more attention to the issue of consumption in the industrialized world, not only because it is a legitimate environmental problem, but because it is a crucial first step toward achieving much needed credibility in developing countries.[50]

These constituencies will continue to play an important role in helping to shape the international population debate. The Catholic Church and other religious groups have been an important voice against coercive practices, except coercive pregnancy, but their continued opposition to abortion deflects much needed attention from the tragic health consequences of illegal abortion for women. Women's groups have successfully and constructively contributed to the debate by drawing attention to the health needs of women—important for individual welfare *and* necessary to achieve population goals; however, feminist advocates have also rejected contraceptive methods that, with proper medical care and quality services, can be sources of empowerment for poor women. Environmental groups have been vocal advocates for attention to population in recent years and continue to generate much needed public support for population activities, particularly in the United States; but the focus on global consequences that is so central in attracting widespread attention is not the best guide for policy design. As other chapters in this volume illustrate, the case for active population policies is strongest at the level of individual welfare (see Overview and Chapter 7).

SOME REGIONAL AND COUNTRY COMPARISONS

The broad overview provided here of the chronological progression of official thinking on population and of the views of the many interest groups (that with varying degrees of success influence population policies and programs) is useful for understanding the historical and current population debate. However, it masks important differences in population and family planning programs at the regional and country levels. For instance, while contraceptive use in developing countries as a whole has increased from only 9 percent of all married women of reproductive age in the 1960s to an estimated 50 percent today, marked differences remain by region and country. In some Asian countries and in many Latin American countries, 60 percent or more of women of reproductive age use contraceptives. In contrast, some African and South Asian countries have contraceptive prevalence rates of 15 percent or less.[51]

What follows are brief descriptions of the population programs and policies of four countries—Brazil, Kenya, India, and China—and their larger regional contexts, that illustrate the diversity (and similarities) across the developing world. Each country represents not only the largest, or one of the largest, national populations in each region, but also various mixes of the issues discussed above. For example, India's experience has followed to some extent the chronological sequence described earlier. Kenya launched a family planning program in the late 1960s but lack of a strong policy until recently weakened its early impact. Brazil has no formal government policy either for or against population but has allowed private-sector initiatives in family planning to flourish. China has followed its own path, beginning with anti-population-control and anti-capitalist rhetoric but shifting dramatically to an aggressive "one-couple, one-child" national policy.

Latin America: Focus on Brazil

According to the latest (1988) population inquiry conducted by the United Nations, 17 out of 33 governments in Latin America had national policies to reduce population growth rates.[52] Most governments have concerns similar to those that prevail in Africa, particularly the impact of a young age structure on social welfare and the future demand for employment. Several nongovernmental organizations have played a pivotal role in bringing down fertility rates and raising "population consciousness" in the region. Caribbean and Central American governments have been almost unanimous in their concern about population growth. In Mexico, for example, the government has been increasingly active in population efforts since the early 1970s, setting targets for growth rates and dominating the provision of family planning services. As of 1988, six out of ten contraceptive users in Mexico relied on government services.[53] In South America, however, only Ecuador and Peru have interventionist population policies. This does not mean that population growth has gone unchecked in other parts of the region; in Brazil, fertility rates have declined substantially without direct government involvement due in good part to the active involvement of NGOs in family planning.

The Brazilian government has maintained a non-interventionist policy toward population that neither supports nor opposes the provision of family planning services. However, through a variety of means, it has indirectly created an environment conducive to fertility decline. With the tacit agreement of the government, the private sector, both commercial and voluntary, has played a dominant role in population activities and has been very successful in increasing contraceptive prevalence. In many ways, the government's approach has been somewhat schizophrenic—declaring on the one hand that the freedom to plan one's family is a human right while resisting pressures to provide the appropriate means for families to exercise that right. It has been suggested that the combined success of private sector efforts along with continued opposition from the Catholic Church has removed the impetus for the government to become actively involved.[54]

Brazil was an outspoken proponent of the NIEO position at the 1974 U.N. conference in Bucharest. As recently as 1992, the government reiterated the need for social and economic development to bring about demographic change.[55] The Brazilian country statement prepared for Bucharest included language that could be construed as a demographic policy declaration (see Box 1), but no national population policy followed. Instead, family planning services have been provided through pharmacies, private physicians, and international NGOs such as BEMFAM, the Brazilian affiliate of IPPF.

A negative consequence of the government's laissez-faire approach has been the limited choice of birth control methods. According to Demographic Health Survey (DHS) data, a high proportion of married women using some method of fertility control are sterilized (despite the fact that it is legally regulated) and 25 percent use oral contraceptives.[56] Abortion is illegal, but unofficially tolerated; in 1990, approximately 400,000 women were hospitalized for complications from an estimated 1.4 to 2.4 million clandestine abortions.[57] Women's groups have advocated that the Brazilian government promote a policy focused on women's health needs. In 1983, a short-lived program known as the Integrated Women's Health Program (PIASM) was developed by Brazilian feminists at the invitation of the military government. The aim of the plan was to provide extensive reproductive health care services and family planning through the public health care system. But this initiative, which was implemented through the state and local health secretariat, had very limited impact.[58]

Even without a modern and effective health system providing a range of contraceptives under safe conditions, there has been a marked fall in fertility rates. Between 1970 and 1989 Brazil's total fertility rate dropped from 4.9 children per woman to 3.3 and the population growth rate declined from 2.5 percent to 2.0.[59] Brazil's contraceptive prevalence rate of 66 percent in 1986 is comparable to the average of the developed world.[60] The decline in fertility is largely attributable to efforts by the Brazilian family planning movement to provide services and educate the public through mass media campaigns. However, other "modernizing" factors such as education and urbanization, which facilitate greater access to information and the adoption of different life styles, have also affected demographic trends. Similarly, growing consumer expectations without commensurate increases in income have made limiting family size more desirable.[61]

Africa: Focus on Kenya

As reported in the 1988 Population Inquiry, 30 out of 52 countries in Africa considered their population growth rates too high and expressed concern about the demands of growing numbers on both natural and government resources.[62] Due to traditional pro-natalist attitudes and optimism about the effect of population growth, most countries of Sub-Saharan Africa were slow to adopt population policies. Even where national programs exist, the demand for family planning remains relatively low. A number of governments have established publicly funded family planning programs, while some also support private organizations. Many countries, such as Egypt, Niger, and Rwanda have integrated family planning with maternal and child health services. Kenya has had a fairly longstanding population program but has persistent high fertility and a high rate of population growth, although it is now beginning to decline. Other countries in Africa with incipient fertility decline include Botswana, Zimbabwe, and part of Nigeria.[63]

In 1969, the Government of Kenya adopted an official population program, becoming one of only three African countries to do so prior to the 1974 U.N. conference.[64] Kenya's country statement at Bucharest criticized its own family planning effort and committed to strengthening the program by establishing targets (see Box 1). In 1979, Kenya had the highest rate of population growth in the African region (3.9 percent) and the highest number of children per woman (a total fertility rate [TFR] of 8.1).[65]

In 1984, at the U.N. conference in Mexico City, Kenya reported progress toward implementing the recommendations of the 1974 World Plan of Action. The government recognized that rapid population growth was a constraint on meeting basic education, health, housing, food, and employment needs. It identified a number of strategies to improve its family planning program but did not see family planning as the solution for all population issues. Nevertheless, the DHS data show a dramatic fall in fertility rates after 1984; in 1989, the TFR for women aged 15 to 44 was down to 6.5 from 8.3 in 1977–78 and by 1993 it had dropped to 5.4.[66] Contraceptive prevalence among married women was 33 percent in 1993.[67] However, according to DHS data from 1989, 36 percent of women desire to limit or space births but do not use contraceptives.[68] The majority of women use traditional methods, followed by sterilization and pills. Abortion has remained illegal.

Kenya's family planning program is considered to have had limited early success because the idea was largely foreign and lacked the support of the country's political and social leadership. Lower fertility rates in the 1980s can be attributed to a combination of socioeconomic factors, including improvements in the education of women, declines in infant mortality, and rising costs of children, all of which increased the desire for smaller families. Also important was the greater political attention to population concerns with the election of President Moi in 1978. Moi's personal commitment to the issue conveyed a sense of urgency that affected both individual behavior and bureaucratic priorities. With the establishment of the National Commission on Population and Development (NCPD) in 1982, the importance of family planning took hold.[69] Another important factor has been the widespread involvement of the commercial and NGO sectors in population activities funded mainly by bilateral, multilateral, and private donors.

Asia: Focus on India and China

Countries in the Asia and Pacific region had interventionist population policies long before African and Latin American governments started confronting the population issue. The largest countries in the region (Bangladesh, China, India, Indonesia, and Pakistan) all have specific population policies and family planning programs aimed at reducing fertility. The Governments of Bangladesh and Pakistan have maintained a sense of urgency about population issues, stressing the social and economic costs of growing numbers. Bangladesh has set goals for contraceptive prevalence and, like other Asian countries, incorporated economic incentives and disincentives into its family planning program. Pakistan, however, has not matched official statements with full government support for and action toward family planning or for associated social sector development (such as education, health services, etc.). Its 3.1 percent annual population growth rate is one of the highest in the world and its proportion of girls in school one of the lowest. Indonesia's strategies include greater community participation in the management and implementation of family planning services. India and China both have implemented population control programs based primarily on the promotion of family planning, although they are quite different from one another. Generally, population growth rates have declined in East and Southeast Asia but have remained high in most South Asian countries, where the problem is compounded by low levels of development and limited access to family planning.

INDIA. In 1951, when the Government of India decided to include population in its economic planning, it became the first developing country to recognize officially the obstacles to development posed by rapid population growth and to adopt a national population policy. From that time on, India has administered a nationwide family planning program with varied results in different states. Consequently, it was a surprise when India led the ranks of developing countries that eschewed population policies at the 1974 U.N. conference (see Box 1). However, India continued to pursue a demographically oriented population policy based on ambitious contraceptive acceptance targets. By the 1984 U.N. conference in Mexico City, the Indian Health Minister gave an optimistic impression of the achievements of the Indian family planning program.

However, the success of India's family planning efforts is tempered by the concerns that have surrounded the program since the widespread sterilization campaigns of the 1970s, which went through a highly coercive phase during the period of emergency rule in 1976.

Although such action was never officially sanctioned, men were routinely rounded up and brought forcibly to vasectomy camps. Violent opposition to these campaigns ultimately contributed to the defeat of Indira Gandhi's government in 1977. The program was subsequently theoretically broadened; in practice, however, it continued to emphasize targeted family planning throughout the 1980s, with a greater focus on *female* sterilization instead of vasectomies.[70] In 1989–1990, women accounted for 92 percent of all sterilizations.[71] Today, the limited choice of contraceptive methods and the poor quality of services have resulted in a high level of unmet need for family planning; in 1988, it was estimated that 18 percent of couples desired to limit their families but were not using any method of birth control.[72]

Furthermore, although abortion has been legal since 1971 and is supposedly available at government facilities free of charge, long waits and a common unofficial stipulation that a woman must agree to sterilization in order to have an abortion cause many women to resort to unsafe "back alley" procedures.[73] The present Government of India has demonstrated an interest in improving the family planning program, but it is too early to judge the impact of its efforts.

Today, India's annual population growth rate is down to 2.1 percent, and the downward trend is expected to continue.[74] The average number of children per woman has dropped to below four, and the contraceptive prevalence rate has increased to nearly 44 percent. However, there is concern about the slow progress in lowering fertility in the four large northern states (Bihar, Madhya Pradesh, Rajasthan, and Uttar Pradesh), which contain over 40 percent of the national population and accounted for 43 percent of India's population growth from 1981 to 1991. In this region, the low average ratio of 923 females per 1000 males implies a disturbingly strong gender bias against girls[75]; other indicators of women's status, such as literacy and age at marriage, are also well below the national average. Not surprisingly, fertility rates are high in these four states, while contraceptive prevalence is very low.[76]

The large voluntary sector in India has played a pioneering role in the provision of quality family planning services, mainly through the Family Planning Association of India (FPAI), which is among the largest voluntary organizations in the country. A founding affiliate of the International Planned Parenthood Federation, FPAI has 41 branches and its leaders are often included in government committees and delegations. However, other voluntary groups uncomfortable with the government's demographically driven policy reject such collaboration and seek to broaden the scope of the government's efforts. For example, environmental and women's groups are pressing for more emphasis on women's health and poverty issues such as income and employment. Many observers suggest that the women's movement was responsible for preventing Norplant from being licensed in India. But overall, the extent of NGO involvement in the national population program has been limited, and there is little discernible evidence of significant policy influence by NGOs on the massive government endeavor. The government considered (and later dropped) the idea of establishing a population commission to coordinate and facilitate the input of NGOs.[77] Their limited influence is further diminished by the fact that there is very little networking among NGOs in related sectors.[78]

CHINA. Alarmed by the implications of a steeply declining death rate in the 1950s, the People's Republic of China set aside Marxist doctrine that overpopulation is a capitalist problem and recognized the need for family planning services. Over the next several years, it passed laws that legalized abortion and sterilization and liberalized the import and sale of contraceptives. By the early 1970s, China had begun a vigorous program of "birth planning" with annual targets established at the national and provincial levels.[79]

At the Bucharest population conference in 1974, the head of the delegation from the People's Republic of China denounced the proponents of the "population explosion," criticized the two superpowers, and staunchly defended China's policy of "planned population growth" (see Box 1). The speech obscured the fact that China had already embarked on a determined path of population control through delayed marriages and fewer births.

Although China reduced its fertility rate by half between 1970 and 1979, the government was concerned that, given the population age structure, even replacement level fertility would generate unsustainable population growth in the future. In 1979, it adopted a draconian "one couple, one child" policy, which contained an array of economic rewards and penalties to encourage compliance. Many allegations have been made subsequently of coercive practices, such as forced abortion, sterilization, and IUD insertion (although these were never official policy) by overzealous family planning workers primarily in rural areas. Due to a cultural bias against girls, the one-child policy also unintentionally resulted in cases of infanticide or abandonment of female children.

At the 1984 population conference in Mexico City, China openly declared its advocacy of the one-child family norm, acknowledged the importance of controlling rapid population growth to help economic development, and proclaimed its self-reliance while giving a friendly nod to "international cooperation."

China has achieved a rapid and remarkable fertility decline. Between the late 1960s and 1979, the total fertility rate dropped from 6 to 2.7. The decline continued during the 1980s, and today, 72 percent of couples in their childbearing years use effective modern contraception. In recent years, reports of abuses under the "one couple, one child" policy have been less common; while the government is continuing the policy, it has acknowledged the need for more socioeconomic measures to encourage the small family norm, such as improving the status of women.[80] With the exception of the semi-autonomous China Family Planning Association, China's population program remains entirely a government effort without any commercial or NGO involvement.

CONCLUSIONS

Since the 1950s and 1960s, developing countries have approached the population debate with a blend of pragmatism and political sensitivity. In the face of donor-driven pressure on population issues and perceived threats to their national sovereignty, developing-country governments have managed to overcome their differences and gain leverage (through ad-hoc or permanent coalitions such as the Group of 77) against developed-country positions on "population control." At the same time, developing countries have addressed domestic population issues within their own economic and political constraints, regardless of international political considerations. Today, most are committed to acting on population based on their self-identified national interests. Developing countries are calling on the international donor community to match this commitment with adequate resources not only for high quality family planning services but also for the related socioeconomic measures now widely recognized as central to lowering fertility. This sentiment was captured in the G-77 statement to the third meeting of the Preparatory Committee of the ICPD:

> . . . it is a fact beyond any doubt that developing countries have become aware of the demographic challenge facing them and will continue to strive to make the necessary efforts and sacrifices in order to implement population policies in keeping with their needs and requirements. And this is their primary responsibility. Sustained and more coordinated support by the international community is vital in this area.[81]

Over time, developed and developing countries have moved toward a consensus on the importance of population factors in development and on a number of specific population issues. Evidence of this shift is most discernable in the widespread agreements emerging on population and sustainable development from the many preparatory meetings leading up to the 1994 International Conference on Population and Development. Some degree of convergence is also apparent among members of various women's, population, and environmental NGOs who have worked together to advance their common interests and to challenge the efforts of religious groups to limit women's access to family planning and abortion. Women's advocates in particular have had a remarkable influence in the Cairo process and, along with allies on developing- and developed-country delegations, have succeeded in focusing unprecedented attention on the needs of women and individuals in the population debate.

The challenge ahead is to translate this emerging substantive consensus on objectives into action. Developing countries must make the necessary investments in health and social sectors, with a particular emphasis on the health and status of women. Donors, in turn, should not miss the opportunity presented by this remarkable degree of convergence on population issues, and move quickly to commit the necessary financial resources for population and reproductive health programs broadly defined.

Notes

[1] United Nations, "Population Policies and Programmes," *Proceedings of the United Nations Expert Group Meeting on Population Programmes,* Cairo, Egypt, April 1992.

[2] The list of dangers included, among other things, nationalism and political instability (which would jeopardize U.S. access to markets and natural resources), war, civil strife, disease, and the spread of communism. Peter J. Donaldson, *Nature Against Us: The United States and the World Population Crisis 1965-1980* (Chapel Hill, NC: The University of North Carolina Press, 1990).

[3] Paul R. Ehrlich, *The Population Bomb* (New York: Ballantine, 1968).

[4] Jason L. Finkle and Barbara B. Crane, "The Politics of Bucharest: Population, Development, and the New International Economic Order," *Population and Development Review*, Vol. 1, No. 1 (September 1975).

[5] Ibid.

[6] Finkle and Crane, "The Politics of Bucharest," op. cit.; and Frederick S. Jaffe, "Bucharest: The Tests Are Yet to Come," *Family Planning Perspectives*, Vol. 6, No. 4 (Fall 1974).

[7] Finkle and Crane, "The Politics of Bucharest," op. cit.

[8] Quoted in Finkle and Crane, 1975 from "Statement by HEW Secretary Weinberger issued to the press, August 30," reprinted in The Department of State Bulletin 71, No. 1840 (30 September 1974).

[9] Finkle and Crane, "The Politics of Bucharest," op. cit.

[10] Michael Cardu and Bob Pack, "Bread Not Loops: The Politics of the World Population Conference," *Science for the People*, Vol. 7, No. 1, 1975.

[11] Quoted in Betsy Hartmann, *Reproductive Rights and Wrongs: The Global Politics of Population Control and Contraceptive Choice* (New York: Harper & Row, 1987); and John Ensor Harr and Peter J. Johnson, *The Rockefeller Conscience: An American Family in Public and in Private* (New York: Charles Scribner's Sons, 1992).

[12] Quoted in Paul Demeny, "Bucharest, Mexico City, and Beyond," *Population Notes* (New York: The Population Council, September 1984).

[13] Michael Teitelbaum, "The Population Threat," *Foreign Affairs* Vol. 71, No. 5 (Winter 1992-93).

[14] Ian Pool, "From Bucharest to Mexico: The Politics of International Population Conferences," *New Zealand Population Review*, April 1975.

[15] United Nations, op. cit.

[16] Jason L. Finkle and Barbara B. Crane, "Ideology and Politics at Mexico City: The United States at the 1984 International Conference on Population," *Population and Development Review*, Vol. 11, No. 1 (March 1984).

[17] Ibid.

[18] This analysis was informed by the "revisionist" economic theories of the New Right. See Teitelbaum, op. cit.

[19] Finkle and Crane, "Ideology and Politics at Mexico City," op. cit.

[20] Ibid.

[21] International Planned Parenthood Federation, "Mexico '84: Conference Report," *People*, Vol. 11, No. 4, 1984.

[22] United Nations, "Report of the International Conference on Population, 1984" (New York: United Nations, 1984).

[23] Findings of the Sixth Population Inquiry, in United Nations Fund for Population Activities (UNFPA), "Population Growth and Economic Development" *Report on the Consultative Meeting Convened by the United Nations Population Fund*, New York, 28-29 September 1992.

[24] Susan A. Cohen, "The Road from Rio to Cairo: Toward a Common Agenda," *International Family Planning Perspectives,* Vol. 19, No. 2 (Washington, DC: The Alan Guttmacher Institute, June 1993).

[25] Martha Madison Campbell, "Schools of Thought: Negotiation Analysis Applied to Interest Groups Active in International Population Policy Formulation," discussion paper for Population Association of America Annual Meeting, Cincinnati, Ohio, 1–3 April 1993.

[26] Ibid.; and Population Crisis Committee (now Population Action International or PAI), "The Nearly Forgotten Factor: Population at the UN Conference on Environment and Development," An Issues Guide for Reporters Covering UNCED and the Global Environment (Washington, DC: PAI, 1992).

[27] Tenth Conference of Heads of State or Government of Non-Aligned Countries, "Draft Decision on Population" Jakarta, Indonesia, 1-6 September 1992.

[28] Pamela Chasek and Langston James Goree VI, "An Interim Report on the International Conference on Population and Development (ICPD), *Earth Negotiations Bulletin*, Vol. 6, No. 13 (Winnipeg: International Institute for Sustainable Development, November 1993).

[29] Statement by The Honorable Timothy E. Wirth, United States Representative to the Second Preparatory Committee for the International Conference on Population and Development, at the Preparatory Meeting, New York, 11 May 1993.

[30] Statement by Dr. Nafis Sadik, Secretary-General of the International Conference on Population and Development on "Item 5: Proposed Conceptual Framework of the Draft Recommendations of the Conference," Second Preparatory Committee, New York, 14 May 1993.

[31] Sally Ethelson, "PrepCom3 Draws to a Close. Next Stop Cairo"; and Daniel J. Shepard, "Weary PrepCom Delegates Prepare for Home," in *The Earth Times*, 22 April 1994.

[32] This discussion refers to religious organizations, particularly the Catholic Church, which oppose population programs based primarily on a rejection of contraceptives and abortion. It is important to note that other denominations support efforts to stabilize population growth, including the use of non-traditional methods of birth control.

33 Barbara Crane, "International Population Institutions: Adaptation to a Changing World Order," in Peter M. Haas, Robert O. Keohane and Marc A. Levy (eds.), *Institutions for the Earth: Sources of Effective International Environmental Protection*, (Cambridge, MA: Massachusetts Institute of Technology, 1993).

34 Feminist ideas on a range of issues have been widely embraced by women all over the world. However, it is important to not gloss over significant differences between Western ideas of women's liberation and those of other countries. At the 1984 Mexico City conference, feminists from the United States and other parts of the West were surprised to find their ideology rejected as imperialist and divisive by many women from developing countries who, in the context of indiscriminatory poverty and deprivation, felt a sense of common struggle with men and were more compelled by nationalist goals than the pursuit of emancipation from male providers. See Jennifer Seymour Whitaker, "Women of the World: Report from Mexico City," *Foreign Affairs*, Vol. 54, No. 1 (October 1975), pp. 173-181.

35 "Women in development" (WID) efforts have successfully drawn attention to the vital roles women play in development as agricultural producers and economic agents. Some are extending this logic to argue that the focus in women and the environment should be less on women's fertility and more on their crucial roles in environmental management. See Margaret Lycette, "Women, Population and the Environment: A Misplaced Focus" (Washington, DC: International Center for Research on Women, December 1993).

36 "Coercive" implies a range of activities—from the use of economic incentives that question the extent to which participation is truly "voluntary" (see Betsy Hartmann, "And the Poor Get Sterilized," *The Nation*, New York, 30 June 1984) to the application of methods without consent.

37 Reliance on sterilization and surgical or hormonal methods is not the optimal long-term solution to shortcomings in reproductive health services. However, in resource poor areas like Nepal where medical facilities are few and far between and rates of maternal and infant mortality are high, sterilization may unfortunately be the most immediate and reliable route to survival. Meaningful "choice" therefore requires access to a full range of contraceptive methods.

38 Betsy Hartmann argues that poor women are often not given sufficient information to legitimately "consent" and that, under conditions of poverty and limited health care, women may inadvertently compromise their safety to get any kind of desperately needed medical attention. See Hartmann, op. cit.

39 Ruth Dixon-Mueller, *Population Policy and Women's Rights: Transforming Reproductive Choice* (Westport, CT: Praeger, 1993).

40 Hartmann, op. cit; and Dixon-Mueller, op. cit.

41 Chantal Worzola, "Conservation Through Contraception: The Environmental Lobby for International Population Assistance," *Journal of Public and International Affairs*, No. 2 (Princeton, NJ: Princeton University, 1992); and PAI, op. cit.

42 "Women's Action Agenda 21," World Women's Congress Report (New York: Women's Environment and Development Organization, 1992).

43 Cohen, op. cit.

44 PAI, op. cit.

45 Julie Fisher, *The Road From Rio: Sustainable Development and the Nongovernmental Movement in the Third World* (Westport, CT: Praeger, 1993).

46 Cohen, op. cit.; and PAI, op. cit.

47 For a useful analysis of the competing and complimentary interests of the various groups concerned with population issues, see Campbell, op. cit.

48 Jodi Jacobson blames India's forced sterilization campaign in the 1970s for a distrust of family planning programs that remains today (cited in Cohen, op. cit.).

49 PAI, op. cit.

50 Cohen, op. cit.

51 UNFPA, op. cit.

52 Much of this discussion of regional trends and the findings of the 1988 Population Inquiry is based on UNFPA, ibid.

[53] Thomas W. Merrick, "The Evolution and Impact of Policies on Fertility and Family Planning: Brazil, Colombia, and Mexico," in *Population Policy: Contemporary Issues*, Godfrey Roberts (ed.), (Westport, CT: Praeger, 1990).

[54] Dixon-Mueller, op. cit.

[55] Statement by the Brazilian delegation at the 39th meeting of the UNDP Governing Council in 1992, noted in UNFPA, op. cit.

[56] Demographic Health Survey data in Thomas Merrick, "The World Bank and Population: Case Studies of Fertility Decline in Brazil, Columbia, and Mexico," Operations Evaluation Department (Washington, DC: World Bank, December 1990). Evidence from other countries suggests that the greater the variety of contraceptives on offer, the higher the rate of use. See Overseas Development Administration, *The ODA Population Guide* (London: ODA, 1993).

[57] *The New York Times*, 21 July 1991, and quoted in Dixon-Mueller, op cit.

[58] Dixon-Mueller, op. cit.

[59] Operations Evaluation Department, "Brazil, Columbia, Mexico: Demographic Trends, Development, and the Role of Government," *Population and the World Bank* (Washington, DC: World Bank, 1992).

[60] Merrick, "The World Bank and Population," op. cit.

[61] Ibid.

[62] UNFPA, op. cit.

[63] John C. Caldwell, I.O. Orubuloye, and Pat Caldwell, "Fertility Decline in Africa: a New Type of Transition?" *Population and Development Review*, Vol. 18, No. 2 (New York: The Population Council, June 1992).

[64] The other two were Ghana and Mauritius. Ibid.

[65] Richard Anker and James C. Knowles, *Fertility Determinants in Developing Countries: A Case Study of Kenya* (Geneva: International Labour Organisation, 1982).

[66] DHS and Family Planning Services (FPS) data in Population Information Program, "Population Reports: The Reproductive Revolution; The New Survey Findings," Series No. 11 (Baltimore, MD: John Hopkins School of Hygiene and Public Health, 1992); and Institute for Resources Development, "Kenya Demographic and Health Survey, 1993" Preliminary Report (Columbia, MD: Macro International, Inc., September 1993).

[67] Institute for Resources Development, op. cit.

[68] Demographic Health Survey data in Stephen Sinding, "The Demographic Transition in Kenya," "The Demographic Transition in Kenya: A Portent for Africa?" *Asia-Pacific Journal of Public Health*, Vol. 5, No. 2 (1991).

[69] Ibid.

[70] Shanti R. Conly and Sharon L. Camp, "India's Family Planning Challenge: From Rhetoric to Action," *Country Study Series No. 2* (Washington, DC: Population Action International, 1992).

[71] T.K. Sundari Ravindran, "Women and the Politics of Population and Development in India," *Reproductive Health Matters*, No. 1, May 1993. Sterilization may avert unintended pregnancies, but its impact on fertility rates overall is questionable—most women who seek sterilization in India are older and already have the desired number of children.

[72] Operations Research Group, "Family Planning Practices in India, Third All-India Survey" (New Delhi, 1991) in Ravindran, op. cit.

[73] Ibid.

[74] J.S. Bajaj, "Population Stabilization: A Continuing Evolution of Perspectives and Policies," in Vasant Gowariker (ed.), *The Inevitable Billion Plus: Exploration of Interconnectivities and Action Possibilities* (Delhi, India: Vichar Dhara Publications, 1993).

[75] The national average in 1985 was 933. See "Health Statistics of India, 1985" in *The Lesser Child: The Girl in India*, Government of India.

[76] Usha Vohra, "The Indian Family Planning Programme—Impact and Prospects," in Gowariker, op. cit.

[77] World Bank, "Strengthening the Role of the Non-Governmental Organizations in the Health and Family Welfare Program in India," *Volume I: Summary of Major Findings and Recommendations* (Washington, DC: World Bank, June 1990).

[78] Ravi and Kaval Gulhati and Associates, "Strengthening Indian Voluntary Action in Three Inter-Related Sectors: Health-Family Planning, the Environment, and

Women's Development" (New Delhi: Centre for Policy Research, forthcoming Spring 1994).

[79] Shanti R. Conly and Sharon L. Camp, "China's Family Planning Program: Challenging the Myths," *Country Study Series No. 1* (Washington, DC: Population Action International, 1992).

[80] Ibid.

[81] Statement by Ambassador Ramtane Lamamra, Permanent Representative of Algeria to the United Nations and Chairman of the Group of 77, to the Third Session of the Preparatory Committee of the International Conference on Population and Development, New York, 4 April 1994.

Chapter Two

Population Dynamics in Developing Countries

Thomas W. Merrick

Developing countries are currently undergoing a massive surge in population—a result of death rates declining earlier and faster than birth rates. Total population in these countries grew by 2.4 billion between 1950 and 1990. Their population growth rates have started to diminish after rising to an average peak level of over 2.5 percent per year around 1970, but the demographic momentum created by youthful age structures will generate further increases of nearly a billion people during each of the next two decades. Several additional billions could be added before population growth levels off later in the next century. Much of this increase is projected to occur in cities. Substantial numbers will move across international borders. It is too early to tell how and when population growth will end; in the meantime, it will have enormous implications for developing-country economic and social development prospects, relationships with developed countries, and preservation of the global environment. This chapter reviews current demographic trends and explores the potential of public policies and programs to create alternative demographic scenarios.

Today's developed countries experienced similar surges in population during the two centuries before 1950.[1] However, those expansions took centuries rather than decades and involved much smaller absolute increases in population than have occurred since 1950 in the developing countries. For example, the total increase in population in today's more developed regions from 1750 to 1950 was a third less than the absolute increase that is projected to occur in developing countries during the current decade. Over those two centuries, population in more developed countries more than quadrupled, from 191 to 832 million. During the same time period, population nearly tripled in developing regions, from 567 to 1,684 million (Table 1). International migration from more to less developed regions contributed to this growth, as did mortality reductions that occurred in developing regions before 1950 (which increased the growth potential for populations that were already large in 1900).

Over 85 percent of the 2.8 billion increase in global population between 1950 and 1990 occurred in developing countries.[2] The largest *absolute* increases in population in the developing world occurred in Asia, because of the large population base this region already had in 1950 (Table 2). China and India, the world's two most populated countries, accounted for almost 40 percent of global population growth over the last four decades. At the same time, Africa and Latin America had the largest *percentage* increases in population. The populations of Mexico and Nigeria nearly tripled, compared to the just more than doubling that occurred in China. Moreover, the surge in population is far from being finished. Despite declines in growth rates, large absolute increases will continue for at least two more decades. By 2025, global population is projected to increase by nearly 3 billion to 8.1 billion with virtually all the increase occurring in developing countries.

DEMOGRAPHIC TRANSITIONS

Underlying the surges in population in both developed and developing countries is a process demographers refer to as the *demo-*

TABLE 1. POPULATION TRENDS, DEVELOPED AND DEVELOPING COUNTRIES (millions)

	Year				
	1750	1900	1950	1990	2025
World	760	1,630	2,516	5,265	8,126
Developing Countries	567	1,070	1,684	4,050	6,762
Developed Countries	191	560	832	1,215	1,364

Sources: Data for 1750–1950 from Thomas W. Merrick and Population Reference Bureau Staff, "World Population in Transition," *Population Bulletin*, Vol. 41, No. 2, December 1989; estimates for 1990 and projections for 2025 from Eduard Bos et al., *World Population Projections, 1992–93 Edition* (Washington, DC: World Bank, 1992).

TABLE 2. GLOBAL POPULATION, 1950–2025, KEY REGIONS AND SELECTED COUNTRIES (millions and percent)

	Population (millions)			Percentage Share of Total		
	1950	1990	2025	1950	1990	2025
World	2,516	5,265	8,126	100.0	100.0	100.0
Developing Countries	1,684	4,050	6,762	66.9	76.9	83.2
Developed Countries	832	1,215	1,364	33.1	23.1	16.8
Africa	222	628	1,431	8.8	11.9	17.6
Ethiopia	20	48	140	0.8	0.9	1.7
Nigeria	33	96	217	1.3	1.8	2.7
South Africa	14	38	69	0.6	0.7	0.8
North America	168	281	362	6.7	5.3	4.5
Latin America and Caribbean	166	435	686	6.6	8.3	8.4
Brazil	53	149	224	2.1	2.8	2.8
Mexico	27	82	136	1.1	1.6	1.7
Asia	1,377	3,104	4,758	54.7	59.0	58.5
China (excluding Taiwan)	547	1,134	1,471	21.7	21.5	18.1
India	348	850	1,370	14.2	16.1	16.9
Indonesia	80	178	265	3.2	3.4	3.3
Europe	398	501	514	15.8	9.5	6.3
Former Soviet Union	174	289	338	6.9	5.5	4.2
Oceania	13	27	38	0.5	0.5	0.5

Sources: For 1950 data, see United Nations, *World Population Prospects: The 1992 Revision* (New York: United Nations, 1993); for 1990 data, see Eduard Bos et al., *World Population Projections: 1994–95 Edition* (Washington, DC: World Bank, forthcoming 1994).

graphic transition. Prior to a demographic transition, high death rates offset the high birth rates characteristic of pre-industrial societies. In the two centuries prior to 1950, there were periodic fluctuations in population growth in various regions, but global population grew very slowly. In Europe, this changed around the time of the industrial revolution. Improved living conditions, followed by advances in public health and medical technology, brought slow but steady declines in mortality. Initially birth rates remained steady or even increased as a result of improvements in living conditions, but eventually the social, economic, and cultural changes associated with the industrial revolution brought declines in fertility. This lag between the onset of mortality decline and the commencement of fertility decline accelerates population growth—which is a major characteristic of the transition process. The transition started earlier in some areas (Northwestern Europe) and later in others (Southern and Eastern Europe). It also took place in countries settled by Europeans through immigration.

Similar transitions began with the acceleration of mortality declines in developing countries just after World War II, again varying by region and country. It differed from Europe's transition in a number of ways, particularly in the speed with which the changes occurred and the magnitude of the accompanying surges in population growth. These differences result from different fertility and mortality patterns prevailing in both developing and developed countries during the early stages of their transitions. Sweden and Mexico provide examples of such contrasts (Figure 1). In Sweden, because of an earlier transition to later and less universal marriage patterns, the crude birth rate had already declined to well below 40 per thousand at the beginning of the nineteenth century when the death rate started to decline. The rate of population growth in Sweden averaged about 10 per thousand (1 percent per year) during its transition; during the later stages (from the 1870s through the early 1900s), emigration served as an escape valve for population pressures. In the 1870s, Sweden's crude birth rate started to decline, and by the 1950s, both birth and death rates were approaching the low levels that characterize today's developed regions.

In Mexico, as in several other Latin American countries, the death rate started declining as early as 1920, but the birth rate remained high until the 1970s. Moreover, because of earlier and more universal marriage patterns, the birth rate was well above 40 per thousand. Mortality decline accelerated after 1945 with the introduction of more effective measures to control infectious diseases. Mexico's population growth rate climbed to more than 30 per thousand (3 percent per year) during the 1960s and 1970s, before it began to decline during the mid-1970s. Emigration did not function as an escape valve for Mexico until the 1980s (because the young adults who accounted for the surge in Mexican emigration were born during the 1950s and 1960s).

At the global level, mortality was universally high before 1800 because of the high prevalence of infectious diseases and fluctuated with periodic bouts of plagues, famines, and wars. The average life expectancy at birth (a better measure of mortality patterns than the crude death rate, which reflects differences in age structure as well as mortality) was only 25 years in Europe in the mid-eighteenth century. This was a reflection of high mortality at all ages but particularly among infants and young children. Only about half of the children born survived beyond age five, with as many as half of the deaths occurring during the first year of life.

The declines in mortality that initiated European demographic transitions resulted from societal changes as well as from advances in public health and medicine. Improvements in agricultural technology

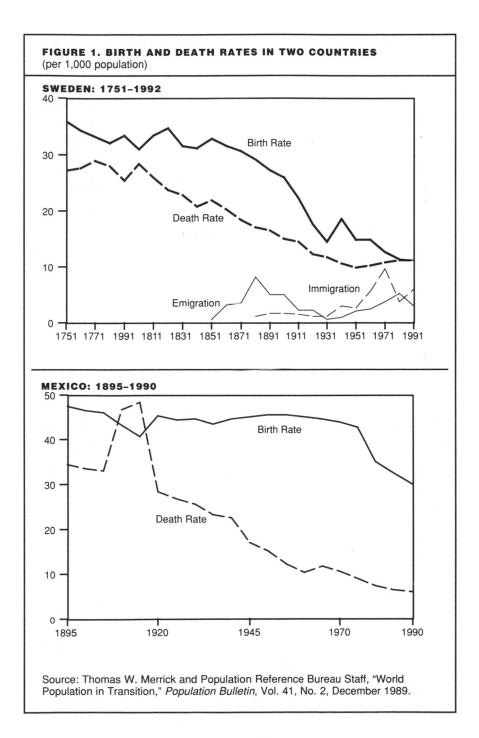

FIGURE 1. BIRTH AND DEATH RATES IN TWO COUNTRIES
(per 1,000 population)

SWEDEN: 1751–1992

Birth Rate

Death Rate

Immigration

Emigration

1751 1771 1991 1811 1831 1851 1871 1891 1911 1931 1951 1971 1991

MEXICO: 1895–1990

Birth Rate

Death Rate

1895 1920 1945 1970 1990

Source: Thomas W. Merrick and Population Reference Bureau Staff, "World Population in Transition," *Population Bulletin*, Vol. 41, No. 2, December 1989.

and transport helped reduce the frequency of famines, and a combination of improved living conditions and public health practice helped reduce epidemics of infectious diseases. Still, mortality decline was gradual. Life expectancy in Europe did not reach 50 years until 1900. Only in this century has the spread of immunizations and the introduction of antibiotics to prevent and cure infections made it possible to push life expectancy above 60 years.

Most of the decline in mortality in developing countries came after 1950, except in Latin America and other areas with European settlements or colonial enclaves where some program was made earlier. (Among some indigenous communities, however, the arrival of Europeans and their diseases increased mortality at first). As Table 3 shows, average life expectancy at birth was only 41 years for developing countries in 1950. By 1990, average life expectancy had risen to 62 years, accomplishing in 40 years what had taken a century or longer in

TABLE 3. MORTALITY TRENDS, MAJOR REGIONS AND SELECTED COUNTRIES (per 1,000 live births)

	Life Expectancy at Birth		Infant Mortality	
	1950–54	1990–94	1950–54	1990–94
World	46.5	64.7	155	62
Developing Countries	40.7	62.4	180	69
Developed Countries	66.0	74.6	56	12
Africa	37.7	53.0	185	95
Ethiopia	33.0	47.0	190	122
Nigeria	36.5	52.5	207	96
South Africa	45.0	62.9	96	53
North America	69.0	76.1	29	8
Latin America and Caribbean	51.4	68.0	125	47
Brazil	51.0	66.2	135	57
Mexico	50.8	70.3	114	35
Asia	41.0	64.8	181	62
China (excluding Taiwan)	40.8	70.9	195	27
India	38.7	60.4	190	88
Indonesia	37.5	62.7	160	65
Europe	65.7	75.2	63	10
Former Soviet Union	64.1	70.4	73	20
Oceania	61.1	72.6	68	22

Sources: For 1950 data, see United Nations, *World Population Prospects: The 1992 Revision* (New York: United Nations, 1993); for 1990 data, see Eduard Bos et al., *World Population Projections: 1994–95 Edition* (Washington, DC: World Bank, forthcoming 1994).

TABLE 4. FERTILITY TRENDS, MAJOR REGIONS AND SELECTED COUNTRIES (births per woman)

	Total Fertility Rates				
	1950s	1960s	1970s	1980s	Current[a]
World	5.0	5.0	4.5	3.6	3.3
Developing Countries	6.2	6.1	5.4	4.2	3.6
Developed Countries	2.8	2.7	2.2	1.9	1.9
Africa	6.7	6.8	6.6	6.4	5.8
Ethiopia	6.7	6.7	6.8	6.5	7.5
Nigeria	6.8	6.9	6.9	6.9	6.4
South Africa	6.5	6.5	5.5	4.8	4.1
North America	3.5	3.3	2.0	1.8	2.1
Latin America and Caribbean	5.9	6.0	5.0	3.9	3.1
Brazil	6.2	6.2	4.7	3.8	2.8
Mexico	6.8	6.8	6.4	4.3	3.2
Asia	5.9	5.7	5.1	3.8	3.2
China (excluding Taiwan)	6.2	5.9	4.8	2.5	2.4
India	6.0	5.8	5.4	4.7	3.9
Indonesia	5.5	5.4	5.1	4.1	2.9
Europe	2.6	2.6	2.2	1.8	1.7
Former Soviet Union	2.8	2.5	2.4	2.4	2.3
Oceania	3.8	3.9	3.2	2.6	2.4

[a]Estimate for 1990–1994.

Sources: For 1950 data, see United Nations, *World Population Prospects: The 1992 Revision* (New York: United Nations, 1993); for 1990 data see Eduard Bos et al., *World Population Projections: 1994–95 Edition* (Washington, DC: World Bank, forthcoming 1994).

developed countries. The rapidity of post-1950 increases in life expectancy is related to the introduction of modern health interventions in low-income settings. The impact has often been dramatic, as illustrated by the reductions in infant and child mortality resulting from immunization programs and other interventions. Infant mortality in developing countries was reduced by nearly two-thirds—with Asia, Latin America, and the Caribbean leading and Africa lagging behind in these declines.

Rapid mortality decline is the first reason for the surge in population growth rates in developing countries after 1950. The second is that fertility rates remained high until at least the mid-1970s. In some cases, fertility actually increased during the 1950s and 1960s.[3] As Table 4 shows, the total fertility rate (TFR) was below 3 births per woman in developed regions during the 1950s and 1960s, but over 6 in developing regions, where they remained until the 1970s. Since then, fertility declines in Asia and Latin America have brought the developing-country average down, although fertility transitions remain problematic in Africa.

In some cases, declines have been quite dramatic—in China, for example, the TFR fell from around 6 in the 1960s to 2.4 by the early 1990s. Substantial declines have also occurred in India, Indonesia, and several other Asian countries, and in Brazil, Mexico, and a number of other Latin American countries. Many of these countries are now more than halfway through the transition to fertility levels that are close to the replacement level of around 2, which is common in developed regions. Several developing countries, such as South Korea, Taiwan, and Thailand, have already reached this level.

The average TFR for Africa is still close to 6. Even in countries such as Kenya and Zimbabwe, where transitions began during the 1980s, TFRs still average 5 or higher—an improvement from previously observed levels of 7 and over but still a long way from completion of the transition to low fertility.

FERTILITY DETERMINANTS

Fertility declines now occurring in developing countries can be attributed to both the increased availability of family planning services and to broader social and economic changes.

Availability of Family Planning Services

Concern about the negative impact of rapid population growth on efforts to raise living standards in those countries as well as about the adverse effect of high fertility on the health and welfare of women and children has motivated development assistance agencies and developing-country governments to subsidize family planning. This coincided with the introduction of modern methods of fertility regulation that came into popular use in developed countries during the 1960s, including the birth control pill and the intrauterine device (IUD), as well as improved surgical sterilization methods. Publicly supported family planning is now dispensed through both public and private service providers. In Latin America, nongovernmental organizations, along with private physicians and commercial outlets, play a lead role in providing services, while governments either finance services or, in some cases (Mexico), provide them directly in public health clinics. In Asia, the majority of users obtain services from public health posts, hospitals, etc. This is also true for the few countries in Africa where contraceptive use began to expand during the 1980s.

As a result of these developments, fertility regulation has increased dramatically in developing countries. In 1960, around 40 million women in developing countries—about 10 percent of the estimated 400 million married women of reproductive age—were using some form of fertility control, including traditional methods. By 1990, the proportion of users had increased to an estimated 51 percent— around 365 million women. Contraceptive use has expanded most in East and Southeast Asia and in Latin America. There are also signs of progress in South Asia, the Middle East, and North Africa. Even in Sub-Saharan Africa, where the average prevalence remains low, some countries such as Kenya and Zimbabwe have growing proportions of women regulating fertility.

The increase in the number of contraceptive users is even more impressive than the increase in rates. However, the numbers also hold some sobering challenges. During the thirty-year period from 1960 to 1990, the number of married, reproductive-age women using contraceptives increased by nearly 325 million. Because the total number of women of reproductive age increased by 300 million during this time, the number not using contraceptives showed little change, leaving 350 million women without the means to regulate their fertility. Furthermore, a large proportion of the increase in contraceptive use occurred in China, which accounts for 40 percent of current users in the developing world. Excluding China, the proportion of users drops to 41 percent for all methods and 34 percent for modern methods.[4]

As already noted, birth rates were generally higher in developing countries at the initial stages of fertility transitions than in Western European countries at similar stages because of earlier and more universal marriage. Other factors have also influenced both the initial levels of fertility rates and the pace of fertility declines. Traditionally, prolonged breastfeeding, which extends post-partum amenorrhea and provides a natural contraceptive effect, as well as practices such as post-partum abstinence and separation of recent mothers from their spouses, have helped to keep fertility rates lower in many parts of Asia and Africa than the physiological maximum. Although the onset of fertility declines has coincided with the introduction of modern fertility control methods in these regions, the initial impact of increased use of contraceptives on fertility has been dampened by offsetting declines in these traditional fertility-limiting practices.[5] The same social and economic changes—urbanization, increased female education, and labor force participation—that motivate increased use of contraceptives also contribute to declines in breastfeeding and post-partum abstinence.

Because they play a mediating role between broader social and cultural variables and fertility, these variables (marriage, post-partum amenorrhea, and abstinence, along with the availability of contraception and abortion) are referred to as *intermediate variables* or *proximate determinants* of fertility.[6] For example, higher educational attainment is related to later age at marriage and smaller desired family size (which affects the demand for contraception), and is probably a factor in the more effective use of contraceptive methods. Most research on fertility now examines the effects of socioeconomic and cultural changes on fertility in terms of their impact on one or more of these proximate determinants. According to available research, among the proximate determinants, increased availability of high-quality, user-oriented family planning services has played the key role in speeding up fertility declines in developing countries.

The Role of Socioeconomic Change

Countries with the most rapid fertility declines have also experienced profound social and economic changes. These include rapid urbanization, expansion of nonagricultural activities, improved child survival, increased educational attainment and narrowing of the gender gap in education, and other improvements in the status of women. These changes affect fertility through their influence on the proximate determinants of fertility just mentioned and work through a variety of channels. Formal and informal education including mass media and information campaigns by family planning organizations have contributed to changes in attitudes about ideal family size and other reproductive mores. The complexity of these changes and the difficulties in measuring them accurately have sometimes made it difficult to disentangle the effects on fertility of increased availability of contraceptives and of the forces that motivate increased use. Cross-national studies using composite indices of program effectiveness and socioeconomic setting have shown that fertility declines fastest in countries with high scores on both scales.[7] At the same time, the experience of countries such as Bangladesh show that increased family planning and fertility decline is possible even in low-income settings provided that services address the needs of individual users and take advantage of synergies inherent in the local social and cultural context.[8]

The factors that motivate couples to begin contraceptive use are a topic of continuing debate and remain a key question for population policy. On one side of the debate are those who argue that merely expanding the availability of contraceptive supplies through family planning programs encourages couples to use them, and that fertility decline will result. Others, however, place greater emphasis on demand factors, arguing that for contraceptive use to become widespread, people's perceptions of desirable family size and the value of children must change. This debate about the relative importance of "supply" and "demand" factors in motivating couples to practice family planning has continued since the 1974 U.N. World Population Conference in Bucharest, where many advocated that fertility would decline faster if spending were shifted from family planning programs to changing the underlying social structure that generates demand for large families.

Demand theory has both economic and sociological facets. The economic theory of fertility decline has emphasized structural aspects, such as contributions of children to family economic activity, the role of women in the labor market, and the role of children to provide old-age insurance. The sociological approach has emphasized the importance of culture and social institutions, such as religion and the family. Both approaches view fertility behavior as a matter of personal choice, with couples balancing the social and economic costs and benefits of fertility. Demand proponents see a limited role for family planning programs.

In contrast, supply-side proponents hold that family size is often larger than is desired by couples because they lack access to contraceptive methods and information on how to use them effectively. Proponents of the supply theory attribute a significant proportion of fertility decline to effective service delivery by well-managed family planning programs.

Experience has shown that the supply-demand dichotomy is inadequate for addressing linkages between adoption of family planning and socioeconomic setting. Neither theory by itself adequately accounts for fertility decline: in low-income settings such as Bangladesh, contraceptive prevalence has risen, and fertility subsequently declined. In other countries, the availability of family planning services is only weakly correlated with contraceptive prevalence. The debate should not be a matter of an "either-or." In many settings, latent demand for family planning exists, but high-quality family planning services that are compatible with the social, economic, and cultural circumstances of the society are needed to increase contraceptive use. Socioeconomic characteristics such as educational attainment clearly play an important function in making contraception acceptable and desirable. Supply and demand aspects play important, mutually reinforcing roles.[9]

The relationship between education and fertility offers some powerful synergies. For a variety of reasons including increased opportunities for alternatives to childbearing and inculcation of new attitudes about family life, increased educational attainment, particularly for girls, plays an important role in the motivation to use family planning. At the same time, lower fertility makes it easier to provide educational opportunities and keep girls in school. Countries such as Indonesia and Kenya that made early investments in primary education *and* expanded access to family planning are now benefiting in terms of fertility decline and other health and welfare benefits associated with increases in both contraceptive use and educational attainment.

DEMOGRAPHIC MOMENTUM

The acceleration of fertility declines in developing countries is an encouraging sign that efforts to expand family planning services and motivate couples to have smaller families are paying off in terms of slower population growth rates than would otherwise have occurred. According to an analysis by John Bongaarts, population in developing countries will be about 400 million lower at the end of this century because of these declines.[10] Moreover, future increases in population will be less because the population base is expanding less rapidly. According to Bongaarts, by the time the population stabilizes at the end of the next century there will be 4.6 billion fewer people than would have occurred in the absence of family planning programs.

This encouraging news needs to be tempered by recognition that individuals born when birth rates were still high are now entering their reproductive ages. As Figure 2 illustrates, the average total fertility rate for developing countries has declined by about 40 percent since the 1960s, from more than six to approximately four. However, because the number of women in reproductive ages has doubled, the number of births has continued to rise. Demographers refer to this effect as *population momentum*. Because of momentum, the absolute *numbers* of population increase remain high even after fertility *rates* have declined. During the next two decades, global population will increase by close to 100 million people annually, with most of that increase occurring in developing countries.

Population momentum is a result of the youthful age structure of developing-country populations. Because of high fertility, 35 percent of the population in developing countries is under age 15, compared with 21 percent in developed countries. In high-fertility countries of Sub-Saharan Africa, the proportion of the population under age 15 is nearly 50 percent. In addition to its effect on total population size,

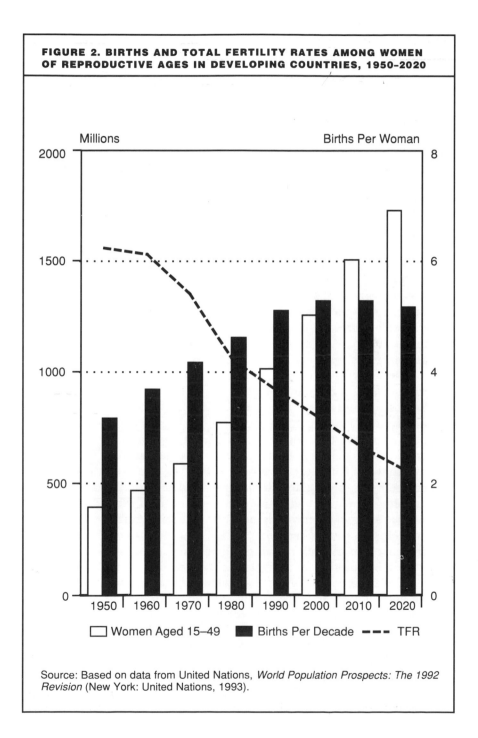

FIGURE 2. BIRTHS AND TOTAL FERTILITY RATES AMONG WOMEN OF REPRODUCTIVE AGES IN DEVELOPING COUNTRIES, 1950–2020

Millions

Births Per Woman

☐ Women Aged 15–49   ■ Births Per Decade   ▬ ▬ ▬ TFR

Source: Based on data from United Nations, *World Population Prospects: The 1992 Revision* (New York: United Nations, 1993).

population momentum impacts on public services such as health and education. For example, demographic momentum required family planning programs *to run faster in order to stand still* during the 1980s. This phenomenon will continue during the 1990s. Fertility declines in developing countries are so recent that the increase in the number of women continues to outrace the decline in the fertility rate. Momentum will be even more pronounced during the next two decades.

Another 170 million married women will be added to the number of potential contraceptive users during the 1990s and 180 million during the following decade. Simply to maintain current levels of contraceptive prevalence (i.e., 51 percent), services will have to be expanded to accommodate 87 million more women during this decade. To continue the pace of fertility declines assumed in standard World Bank population projections would require an increase in prevalence to 58 percent by 2000, implying an expansion of services to at least 62 million women who are not now users.[11] This means that during the 1990s services will need to be expanded to reach an additional 150 million women—about half as many as were reached during the previous three decades. In large countries such as India, this implies an enormous effort to expand services at the same time that program managers struggle to improve the quality of existing services.

The growth of young adult populations (the 15-to-29-year-old group) affects a variety of development objectives: employment creation, housing, and other types of social infrastructure whose demands are sensitive to the growth of population in the household-forming age groups. From 1970 to 1990, the young adult population in developing countries grew by half a billion. Even after accounting for fertility declines that have already occurred, the size of this group is projected to increase by another 350 million between 1990 and 2010. Countries such as Mexico, which had TFRs of more than 6 in the 1960s, experienced a doubling of their young adult populations during the last two decades. Mexico's rapid fertility decline since 1975 will help to slow that increase substantially during the next two decades, resulting in a 25 percent increase compared to the earlier doubling. In countries where fertility remains high, the growth of the young adult population will be substantial. In Nigeria, for example, the young adult group doubled from 1970 to 1990 and is projected to double again by 2010.

Because of demographic momentum, the full effect of fertility declines on the size and age structure of developing-country populations will take several decades to occur. Some effects, however, are more immediate. The benefits of fertility decline appear earliest in sectors that serve children: education and child health. For example, with lower fertility, countries that have struggled for decades to build schools and train teachers to keep up with a rapidly increasing school-age population can apply their educational resources to improvements in quality and equity of access to education. The experience of countries such as Thailand demonstrates that these benefits accrue at both community and family levels because parents with fewer children are more able to provide for books, uniforms, and other needs related to their children's schooling.

Although it takes longer to manifest itself, population aging is another effect of rapid fertility and mortality declines. The global population aged 65 and over in 1990 is estimated to be 295 million. Although the percentages of those 65 and over are highest in the developed world, developing countries are aging as well. Large developing countries such as China and India have large numbers of elderly even though they comprise only around 5 percent of total population; older age groups are growing at twice the rate of population at all ages. The dependency and health needs of the elderly population mean these trends will have significant consequences for social expenditures.

Developing countries still have time before their populations reach levels now observed in European countries; 14 percent of the population was in the age group 65 and over in 1990, and 22 percent is projected to be in that group in 2025. Nevertheless, the aging of the large cohorts now reaching young adulthood could pose serious problems unless adequate investments in health and social infrastructure are made during the working lifetimes of those generations. Human resource investments at younger ages is an important factor in the capacity to support aging populations later on. Developing countries experiencing rapid demographic transitions will have less time than European countries to prepare themselves for population aging.

FUTURE POPULATION PROSPECTS

The largest and most important impact of high fertility rates combined with demographic momentum is the large increase in absolute population size that is projected to occur in developing regions over the next three decades. According to the World Bank, global population is expected to increase by nearly 3 billion people by the year 2025, when total population would reach 8.1 billion (see Table 2). In absolute terms, that increase is larger than the increase from 1950 to 1990, with 95 percent of the growth expected to occur in developing countries. The largest absolute increase—1.7 billion—is expected to occur in Asia, where India is projected to add nearly half a billion people and China could add over 330 million. The percentage increase is lower than it was from 1950 to 1990, but the absolute increase is larger despite lower population growth rates because of the very large populations that these countries currently have. In Africa, where the transition to lower fertility is just getting under way, both absolute and percentage increases are projected to be very large.

The projections in Table 2 are based on country-by-country assessments of recent trends in fertility and mortality applied to age-specific population estimates for each country. The accuracy of these and other projections discussed in this chapter depends on the quality of the baseline data and on the assumptions used to calibrate the projections. The effects of small differences in either of these factors become greater as the time scale of the projection increases. Thus demographers will talk with some confidence about projections that span a decade, but view long-run projections mainly as exercises to demonstrate how future combinations of fertility, mortality, and migration rates could affect future population size and age composition.[12]

Recent projections are particularly sensitive to shifts in fertility rates. For example, earlier projections for a number of Latin American countries failed to anticipate the rapid declines in fertility that occurred there, and current projections for that region are lower than those of a decade ago. In other cases such as Pakistan, fertility has declined less than previously anticipated, so that current projections are higher than in the past. The U.N. Population Division has also prepared alternative projections incorporating both slower and more rapid fertility decline than in Table 2. For the developing countries, total population in 2025 is projected to be a half billion lower in the "low" variant and higher by an equal amount in the "high" variant.[13]

Until the spread of the human immunodeficiency virus (HIV) that causes AIDS, population projections generally assumed that there would be too little variation in mortality trends to warrant separate assumptions for that variable. With the growing HIV/AIDS pandemic, analysts have attempted to assess the potential demographic impact of AIDS. They have reached widely varying conclusions, particularly for African countries with high HIV prevalence. Some have argued that HIV/AIDS will lead to an absolute reduction in population in that region. Others argue that HIV prevalence is likely to plateau at levels that make population decline on a regional or even national scale unlikely, though they do accept the possibility that such decline could occur in the high-prevalence regions of several countries and in a small number of major cities. Even without actual population decline, the impact of HIV/AIDS is likely to be serious. This impact is complicated by the fact that a high proportion of infected adults will survive long enough to have children, many of whom will themselves be infected, but not long enough to raise those children to young adulthood; these AIDS orphans will create enormous burdens for relatives and other survivors.

The most recent U.N. population projections have attempted to account for potential AIDS mortality. In 15 high-prevalence countries, the aggregated population in the year 2005 is projected to be 310 million without including AIDS mortality; after accounting for AIDS mortality, it is 298 million, a difference of 12 million. For Uganda, the 2005 projection is 29.2 million without AIDS and 27.8 million with it.[14]

ALTERNATIVE LONG-TERM PROJECTIONS

Population projections beyond the next couple of decades require even more speculative assumptions about the future course of fertility and mortality rates. The main value of such projections is that they demonstrate the powerful long-term effects of demographic momentum on the total size of the population in different regions as well as the effect of relatively small differences in the speed with which developing countries finish their demographic transitions. Recently revised long-term population projections by the World Bank are based on country-by-country assessments of when the demographic transition will be completed. They show what the stable or nearly-stable size of population would be under such conditions. Table 5 summarizes the results of these projections for developing countries as a whole and for the two largest developing countries, China and India. The projections assume that fertility rates in most developing countries will be at or near replacement level by approximately 2030, with that level occur-

TABLE 5. LONG-RANGE POPULATION PROJECTIONS	(billions)		
	Year		
	2025	2075	2150
Developing Countries	6.8	9.1	10.0
China	1.5	1.6	1.7
India	1.4	1.8	1.9

Source: Eduard Bos et al., *World Population Projections, 1994–95 Edition* (Washington, DC: World Bank, forthcoming, 1994).

TABLE 6. POPULATION IN 2150 WITH VARIOUS TFRs (billions)			
	Middle Variant[a]	Mid-Low Variant[b]	Low Variant[c]
All Developing Countries	10.0	5.7	5.1
China	1.4[d]	0.7	0.5
India	1.9	0.9	0.7

[a]Middle variant assumes replacement level fertility rate.
[b]Mid-low assumes TFR goes below replacement around 2040 but returns to replacement later.
[c]Low assumes TFR goes below replacement and stays there.
[d]The asumptions underlying these projections differ from the World Bank projections in Table 5. The World Bank assumes that China will stay at replacement-level fertility over the next century, while the United Nations assumes that it will fall below replacement. On average, the country-by-country differences in assumptions cancel each other out in the developing-country total.

Source: Carl Haub, *The UN Long-Range Population Projections: What They Tell Us* (Washington, DC: Population Reference Bureau, Inc., 1992).

ring somewhat earlier for East Asia and Latin America and later for South Asia, the Middle East, and Africa. Because of momentum, the population of developing countries is projected to continue growing beyond the projected level of 6.8 billion in 2025 to a stable total of 10 billion by the end of the next century. China, with a projected 1.5 billion in 2025, continues to grow to 1.7 billion by 2150, and India, with 1.4 billion in 2025, reaches 1.8 billion in 2075. Even though it starts with a smaller base, India is projected to overtake China's ultimate size because of the added momentum associated with its later transition to replacement fertility.

These projections assume that when countries complete their transitions to low fertility, their TFRs will be near the so-called "replacement" level of 2.1 births per woman. This rate is called replacement-level fertility because the parent generation would be equal in size to their children's generation after taking account of deaths likely to occur between birth and the reproductive ages. Recent experience in several Western European countries has been that decline in TFRs does not stop at 2.1. Some countries (Italy, Spain, Germany) now have TFRs below 1.5; others (Sweden) have gone below replacement but later returned to near-replacement levels.

The United Nations recently prepared a set of population projections to demonstrate the possible impact of transitions to below-replacement fertility in developing countries.[15] Table 6 summarizes some results from these projections; they demonstrate that fertility decline beyond the replacement level could have a powerful effect on the ultimate size of a country's population. For developing countries as a whole, projected population size in either the "mid-low" or "low" variant is about half that of the "middle" variant. In China, the projected "mid-low" total of 694 million in 2150 is considerably lower than its current population of nearly 1.2 billion, and in India the long-term total is a little less than its population today. It is important to recognize that these lower alternative long-term totals come *after* an intermediate stage during which total population gets larger because of the effect of *current* demographic momentum. Thus in the "mid-low" variant, China's population size reaches a peak level of 1.3 billion during the first decade of the next century before it levels off and declines. In India, the peak occurs at a level of about 1.3 billion in the 2040s.

How likely is it that one of these scenarios might occur in place of the standard "medium" projections? On-going work by John Bongaarts explores policy and program changes that could reduce total population below the standard projection of 10.2 billion people by 2075.[16] He examines three avenues through which this could be done.

The first is to eliminate existing unwanted fertility by immediately expanding high-quality family planning services to couples who have indicated a desire to delay or limit births but are not currently doing so. The impact of this on the population of developing countries is estimated to be 1.9 billion, bringing total developing-country population at the end of the twenty-first century down from 10.2 to 8.3 billion.

A second avenue would be to motivate couples to have smaller families through increased education for girls and other social and economic changes that are known to be closely associated with fertility reduction. This could trim another billion from the projected total and would bring the projected total population to 7.3 billion. That is still 2.8 billion more people than the current population (4.5 billion in 1995) in developing countries. This is again the result of demographic momentum—the growth that will occur even if fertility is reduced quickly to replacement level. It is tempting to take momentum as an inevitable demographic reality. However, exercises such as the United Nations "mid-low" and "low" long-term projections demonstrate that momentum need not be considered inevitable.

Bongaarts' third avenue to reduce population below the standard projection is to emphasize the impact that the *timing* of childbearing has on momentum. Delay of the onset of childbearing and longer intervals between births could cut momentum even if women continue to have two births during their childbearing years.[17] Bongaarts calculates that a five-year delay in the mean age of childbearing would offset 1.2 billion of the expected 2.8 billion increase associated with momentum.

How realistic is the notion that momentum could be reduced through public policy measures? Experience with family planning and reproductive health programs demonstrates that couples will use high-quality services when they are provided and that use of these services contributes to the health and well-being of mothers and children as well as lowers fertility. Social research on reproductive behavior has also shown that the desire for smaller families, which motivates couples to use such services, is related to increased education, particularly for girls, and that education can also raise the median age at marriage and median age of childbearing. Thus, a comprehensive strategy to expand family planning/reproductive health services, to expand educational opportunities, and to bridge the gender-gap in education, in combination with other efforts to improve the status of women, could further accelerate the transition to low fertility in developing countries and could push fertility down to levels that significantly reduce the long-term effect of demographic momentum.

The *timing* of these interventions is critical to the strategy. For developing countries to get ahead of the wave of demographic momentum, significant investments to expand family planning, educational opportunities, and other key social services have to be made now. This is a formidable challenge, because the number of people to be served will increase by such large proportions during the next two decades. The challenge is to design and implement strategic approaches that take account of the needs of particular countries and the time needed for different interventions to take effect. Otherwise social development efforts may continue on a demographic treadmill, *running faster in order to stand still*, and face rising costs over the long run because of the need to continue expanding to keep pace with the numbers associated with momentum.

Something similar to the rapid-accumulation strategy once advocated as a way to generate industrial take-offs may be needed in the social sectors. Such a strategy would maximize the synergistic linkages between direct and indirect measures to slow population growth and achieve other benefits associated with social sector investments. In the short run, lower fertility slows the growth of the school-age population and facilitates efforts to expand access and quality in education. Educational investments, in turn, help to motivate smaller family norms and bring about the delayed childbearing needed to dampen the effect of momentum. The combination produces earlier population stabilization and speeds human resource development. This is, in fact, similar to what occurred in several East Asian countries that simultaneously achieved rapid transitions to low fertility and rapid accumulation of human capital.[18]

GEOGRAPHIC REDISTRIBUTION OF POPULATIONS

An important dimension of rapid population growth in developing countries is the resulting change in geographic distribution of population. Only 17 percent of the population of developing countries was considered "urban" in 1950.[19] However, urban areas accounted for a little more than half the increase in developing-country population between 1950 and 1990; urban areas are projected to account for an increasing share of total population increase between 1990 and 2025 (see Table 7).

In this respect, the developing countries are following a pattern already established in developed areas, where rural-to-urban migration has more than offset higher rates of natural population increase in rural areas. The urban share of developing-country population is about 34 percent today and is expected to increase to around 57 percent by the year 2025. By then, the urban share in developed countries is projected to pass 80 percent.

There are important regional differences in the extent of urbanization. Latin America is much more urbanized (over 70 percent urban in 1990) than Asia or Africa (both about 32 percent urban in 1990). Still, much of the *projected* growth of population is expected to occur in urban areas.

TABLE 7. URBAN POPULATION, 1950–2025 (millions)

	1950	1990	2025
Developing Countries			
Total Population	1,684	4,084	7,070
Urban Population	285	1,401	4,011
Urban Percent	17	34	57
Developed Countries			
Total Population	832	1,215	1,404
Urban Population	452	880	1,177
Urban Percent	54	73	84

Source: United Nations, *World Urbanization Prospects: The 1992 Revision* (New York: United Nations, 1993).

TABLE 8. POPULATIONS OF THE 20 LARGEST DEVELOPING-COUNTRY CITIES, 1970–2010 (millions)

City	1970	1990	2010
São Paulo	8.1	18.1	25.0
Mexico City	9.1	15.1	18.0
Shanghai	11.2	13.4	21.7
Bombay	5.8	12.2	24.4
Buenos Aires	8.4	11.4	13.7
Seoul	5.3	11.0	13.8
Rio de Janeiro	7.0	10.9	13.3
Beijing	8.1	10.9	18.0
Calcutta	6.9	10.7	15.7
Jakarta	3.9	9.2	17.2
Tianjin	5.2	9.2	15.7
Manila	3.5	8.9	16.1
Cairo	5.3	8.6	13.4
Delhi	3.5	8.2	15.6
Karachi	3.1	7.9	17.0
Lagos	2.0	7.7	21.1
Bangkok	3.1	7.1	12.7
Teheran	3.3	6.7	11.9
Dhaka	1.5	6.6	17.6
Istanbul	2.8	6.5	11.8

Source: United Nations, *World Urbanization Prospects: The 1992 Revision* (New York: United Nations, 1993).

Urban growth in developing countries has been concentrated in the largest cities. During recent decades, large metropolitan areas in the developing countries have experienced enormous population increases. Of today's 20 largest metropolitan areas in developing countries (Table 8), only one (Shanghai) had a population of more than 10 million two decades ago. By 1990, nine of them surpassed 10 million, and by 2010 all are expected to have populations of 10 million or more; thirteen are projected to have populations in excess of 15 million. Recent census data suggest that population growth in the largest cities may be slowing, in part because of problems arising from managing and providing services on such a large scale.

Large urban population concentrations present major challenges for the development and maintenance of infrastructure and services—education, health, water and sanitation, public transportation—and particularly, for employment generation. In their efforts to become competitive in international markets, many developing countries have opted for manufacturing technologies that save rather than use labor, exacerbating their already great difficulties in creating enough good jobs. A further concern about the rapid growth of large cities is their impact on the environment and natural resources—soils, water tables, forests—both directly in the form of air and water pollution and indirectly through policies to stimulate food production and agricultural exports needed to sustain large urban populations.

Internal Population Movements

The rapid growth of large cities results both from rural-to-urban migration and urban-to-urban migration. Developing countries have experienced significant movements from towns and small cities to larger cities.

A variety of forces contribute to increased internal population movement in developing countries. Natural increase has remained higher in rural areas, thereby increasing population pressures. Unequal distribution of land and agricultural production resources has forced many off the land, and attempts to increase production using more advanced agricultural technologies have cut the labor-absorptive capacity of the agricultural sector. In some areas, for example the African Sahel, poor management of soil, water, and forest resources has further reduced the labor-absorptive capacity of rural areas. In situations of political instability, rural violence provides an added stimulus. On the "pull" side of the migration equation, potential migrants also perceive that there are greater job opportunities for themselves and educational opportunities for their children in urban areas. Improved transportation and communication have also fostered geographic mobility in developing countries.

International Migration

The same forces that create internal population movements also stimulate increasingly large flows of migrants across international borders. Historically, international migration provided an escape valve during the period when European countries were experiencing the population pressures associated with their demographic transitions. International migration has become similarly important in developing countries over the last two decades (see Chapter 8). Based on census reports, migration experts estimate that more than 80 million people were living outside their countries of birth or citizenship during the 1980s.[20] The number has probably increased since then; a 1992 World Bank report put the figure at 100 million. These numbers include individuals who have moved for a variety of reasons—legal migrants and their dependents seeking jobs and a better life, undocumented and clandestine workers, as well as political refugees fleeing violence and persecution. Accounting for migration flows is complicated by the presence of undocumented movers, by the variety of types of movements, and by changes in international borders in recent years. For example, the numbers do not include the millions of ethnic Russians and other groups who now find themselves living outside of their "home" republic as a result of the breakup of the former Soviet Union.

Most of the recent attention toward international migration has focused on movements from developing countries to developed countries: from Mexico and Central America to the United States, from North Africa to Europe, etc. In fact, the largest share of international movers remain in the developing regions. Africa has by far the largest number of migrants, accounting for an estimated 35 million out of the global total of 80 million reported for the 1980s. Many African migrants are refugees from political violence (Burundi, Mozambique, Somalia). But there are also significant movements of economic migrants (to South Africa and in West Africa). In Asia and the Middle East, the estimates of migrants run at about 15 million, including many laborers in Persian Gulf states whose lives were disrupted by the 1991 Gulf War. Many Asian migrants are refugees from political upheavals, including millions of Afghans and Palestinians. In Latin America and the Caribbean, both economic and political conditions have been factors in the movement of approximately 6 million people *within* the region, in addition to the estimated 13 to 15 million who have moved from the region to the United States and Canada.

International population movements often have greater economic, social, and political than purely demographic significance for both sending and receiving countries. Although the volume of movement represents only a small proportion of total population increase in developing countries and thus has a much smaller dampening effect on their population pressures compared to Europe during the nineteenth century, the movement of even a small proportion of the annual total population increase that developing countries now experience translates into millions of people. The likelihood of these increases continuing for at least a couple of decades as a result of demographic momentum and the continuation or possible worsening of differences in economic opportunities between the sending and receiving countries suggests that the pressures stimulating flows are not likely to abate soon. Rising ethnic and racial tensions, other problems of assimilation of migrants in terms of language and culture, and recognition of the costs of providing social services for migrant workers and their dependents are creating a hostile climate that could make migration less attractive to potential movers. The stakes are quite high. The migration process tends to be selective of better-trained, more ambitious workers, so that many potential employers oppose migration restrictions. Networks among migrants, once established, tend to encourage further movements. Official remittances from migrant workers, estimated to be in excess of $70 billion in 1990, exceed official development assistance, estimated at $54 billion for 1990. Net official remittance flows to developing countries, which are far less than the total including unofficial flows, amounted to $37 billion, roughly 70 percent of ODA to developing countries.

CONCLUSIONS

Many developing countries are now experiencing demographic transitions from high to low fertility and mortality rates. Some are well advanced in that process (China and several other East Asian countries, as well as Brazil, Mexico, and other Latin American countries). Others (most of Sub-Saharan Africa and several Middle Eastern countries) are still at early stages. Many countries (including such large South Asian countries as India and Bangladesh) are in the middle stages. The large population bases and high fertility rates with which developing countries began their transitions, combined with the more abrupt declines in mortality that started the process, have caused the population growth in developing countries to be larger and more rapid than that experienced by the now developed countries during their transitions.

These forces translate into the enormous demographic momentum now being experienced by developing countries. Even with declining population growth rates, many countries are projected to have large absolute increases in population over the next several decades. How much of that increase will actually occur depends on the speed with which the transition to lower fertility is accomplished. Earlier completion of the transition would have both immediate and long-term effects on the ultimate size and composition of population. An immediate effect would be slower growth in younger age groups whose reproductive behavior shapes momentum. For example, slower increase in school-age populations would make it easier to expand primary schooling opportunities and bridge the gender gap in education; this would contribute to smaller family norms and later initiation of childbearing, both of which could sharply slow the momentum process. Later child-bearing and increased spacing between children would also have health benefits for mothers and children.

The demographic future of developing countries depends heavily on the social investment strategies of developing countries during the next two decades, which represent a window of opportunity to influence demographic momentum. A concerted effort to expand investments in family planning, education, and health could accelerate the transition to low fertility in developing countries even more rapidly than currently assumed in the most plausible population projections. There are substantial obstacles to such strategies, including the enormous number of people being added to the user pool for such services as a result of current momentum. A major effort to expand such services is needed to get ahead of the wave of momentum.

The alternative is continuing the treadmill process—*running faster to stand still*—that has been the experience of so many countries over the last two decades. For a variety of reasons, this is not a sustainable approach in poor countries. Sooner or later, significant increases in population will reduce capacity to deal with resulting problems. Whether to avoid potential breakdowns in the capacity to govern and provide services or to reap the high potential returns on social investments in terms of both demographic outcomes and better living standards for large numbers of people in developing countries, the expansion of family planning and related social services is a much more attractive alternative.

Notes

The author would like to thank Ed Bos, Randy Bulatao, Susan Cochrane, Jane Nassim, Sharon Stanton Russell, My Vu, and Chantal Worzala for help and comments. Robert Cassen, Mohammed Nizamuddin, and Tim Dyson also provided valuable comments and suggestions during the review process.

[1] For more information on pre-1950 trends, see Thomas W. Merrick and Population Reference Bureau Staff, "World Population in Transition," *Population Bulletin*, Vol. 41, No. 2 (December 1989) reissue.

[2] Eduard Bos et al., *World Population Projections 1992-93 Edition* (Washington, DC: World Bank, 1992).

[3] For discussion on this point, see Tim Dyson and Mike Murphy, "The Onset of Fertility Transition," *Population and Development Review*, Vol. 11, No. 3, September 1985, pp. 399-440. In the case of Africa, these authors attribute the rise in fertility to a reduction in the practice of post-partum abstinence and of subfecundity associated with venereal disease. "Fertility" in demographic parlance is a measure of the number of births; demographers refer to the capacity to conceive as "fecundity."

[4] For more detailed discussion of these trends, see Thomas W. Merrick, "Demographic Momentum," *Integration*, No. 33 (August 1992), pp. 57-64.

[5] Dyson and Murphy, op. cit.

[6] John Bongaarts, "A Framework for Analyzing the Proximate Determinants of Fertility," *Population and Development Review*, Vol. 4, No. 3 (March 1978), pp. 105-132.

[7] W. Parker Mauldin and John A. Ross, "Family Planning Programs: Efforts and Results, 1982-89," *Studies in Family Planning*, Vol. 22, No. 6 (November/December 1991), pp. 350-367.

[8] For a review of experience in Bangladesh, see John Cleland and James A. Phillips, *The Determinants of Reproductive Change in Bangladesh*, World Bank Regional and Sector Studies, 1993 (Washington, DC: World Bank, forthcoming).

[9] Thomas W. Merrick, "Social Policy and Fertility Transitions," *HRO Working Papers*, No. 3 (Washington, DC: World Bank, 1993).

[10] John Bongaarts, W. Parker Mauldin, and James F. Phillips, "The Demographic Impact of Family Planning Programs," *Studies in Family Planning*, Vol. 21, No. 6 (November/December 1990), pp. 299-310.

[11] World Bank, *Effective Family Planning Programs* (Washington, DC: World Bank, 1993), Table 1; see also W. Parker Mauldin and John A. Ross, "Contraceptive Use and Commodity Costs in Developing Countries, 1990-2000," *International Family Planning Perspectives*, Vol. 18, No. 1 (March 1992), pp. 4-9.

[12] Ronald D. Lee, "Long-Run Global Population Forecasts: A Critical Appraisal," *Population and Development Review*, Vol. 16, Supplement (1990), pp. 44-71; also, Nathan Keyfitz, "The Limits of Population Forecasting," *Population and Development Review*, Vol. 7, No. 4 (December 1981), pp. 579-593.

[13] United Nations, *World Population Prospects: The 1992 Revision* (New York: United Nations, 1993).

[14] United Nations, "Demographic Impact of AIDS in 15 African Countries," in *World Population Prospects*, op. cit., Chapter 3, pp. 53-80. It is important to note that these assessments assume that the AIDS epidemic will continue to follow its unabated course until the year 2005, with the peak impact occurring about 12 years after its onset. Much of this remains speculative, and other assumptions about the time-path of the epidemic could yield different longer-term outcomes.

[15] For a review of the United Nations' longer-term projections, see Carl Haub, *The U.N. Long-Range Population Projections: What They Tell Us* (Washington, DC: Population Reference Bureau, Inc., 1992).

[16] John Bongaarts, "Population Policy Options in the Developing World," *Science*, Vol. 263, No. 11 (11 February 1994), pp. 771-776.

[17] When this occurs, current or period total fertility rates could fall below the replacement level even though individual couples will continue to have about two children each during their reproductive lifetimes (so that the cohort total fertility rate will be two). What changes is the pace at which younger and older couples have those two children.

[18] World Bank, *The East Asian Miracle: Economic Growth and Public Policy* (Oxford: Oxford University Press, 1993), pp. 191-195.

[19] Information in this section is based on United Nations, *World Urbanization Prospects: The 1992 Revision* (New York: United Nations, 1993).

[20] Michael S. Teitelbaum and Sharon S. Russell, *Population Pressure and Migration Movements*, address to The International Parliamentary Workshop on Selected Issues of the ICPD Debate, New York, 1993; Philip L. Martin, "The Migration Issue," *Migration World*, Vol. 20, No. 5 (1992), pp. 11-15; and United Nations Population Fund (UNFPA), "Population, Migration, and Development in the 1990s," *The State of World Population* (New York: UNFPA, 1993).

Chapter Three

Population and Development in Historical Perspective

Allen C. Kelley and William Paul McGreevey

Since 1950, volumes have been written on the consequences of population growth, resulting in an active and somewhat contentious period in the long population debate between those who assess population growth to be significantly adverse to the pace of economic prosperity and those who see the impacts to be relatively modest, or even positive.[1] A striking feature of this scholarly outpouring has been a tendency to eschew the insights and perspectives of history, and instead to advance theories and to interpret evidence within the purview of myopia and tunnel vision: with a short-run time frame and with a focus on limited (mainly macroeconomic) consequences. On the one hand, such a short-sighted and narrow orientation is ironic since the population debate spans two centuries; on the other, this ahistorical orientation in part accounts for the inability of the debating protagonists to reach accord since the rules of the game are not well defined.

This essay attempts a modest reconciliation of the debate by considering two historical themes. First, it examines the history of population ideas in the postwar period and interprets "revisionism"—a "non-alarmist" assessment of population consequences that is dominant among economists in the field. Second, it reviews how modern economic growth since the industrial revolution overcame the constraints posed by rapid population growth, just as it overcame the many other limits that kept most of humankind at very low levels of living for its first two hundred thousand years as a species. But prior to that process of change, a process still only barely under way in most low-income countries, progress could be stalled by many barriers, rapid population growth being one among them. These two doses of historical perspective will not cure the fundamental causes of contention, which lie mainly in the empirical uncertainties surrounding the consequences of demographic change. They can, however, soften the discord by pointing more clearly to important methodological sources of controversy, thereby placing the debate on a firmer footing.

REVISIONISM: A HISTORY OF IDEAS IN THE POPULATION DEBATE

Concern about the adverse consequences of rapid population growth was awakened among population analysts by the original, alarmist treatise on the subject by the Reverend Thomas Malthus, published nearly two centuries ago.[2] This "traditionalist" pessimism has been challenged from time to time by population optimists, most recently with the spread of "revisionism," a view that countered Malthusian pessimism with agnosticism about the linkages between population growth and economic growth.

The key to understanding the "new" assessments is not to focus on the direction of the impact of rapid population growth. (Indeed, most revisionists conclude that many, if not most, developing countries would benefit from slower population growth.) Rather, the key is the adoption of a methodological perspective that highlights the intermediate to longer run, taking into account both direct and indirect impacts, and feedbacks within economic, political, and social systems. This is in contrast to the "traditionalist" perspective, which emphasizes short-run adverse effects deriving from the apparently fixed nature of resources (i.e., diminishing returns), and downplays the capacity of economic systems to adjust through the dynamics of human capital accumulation and technological change.

Revisionism is not distinguished by predicting a net positive impact of population growth. Instead it asserts that: 1) there are medium-term offsetting impacts to counter adverse short-run costs of rapid population growth, 2) these impacts are induced directly and indirectly by population growth, and 3) countervailing forces lessen the often highlighted adverse/direct effects that derive mainly from diminishing returns to land, environment, minerals, forests, and other scarce resources.

Attempting to understand the reasons for the rise of revisionism—today the dominant perspective of U.S. economic demographers—

and how it can (or should be) reconciled with the more traditionalist, population-alarmist perspective, provides a useful historical filter for reviewing and evaluating impacts of population growth on economic development. Such a review may also be useful in predicting the nature of the population debate in the 1990s.

Not a New Idea

It may come as a surprise that revisionist thinking is not all that new, since it is associated by many with events in the 1980s. Indeed, the term "revisionism" may be a misnomer since it is arguably the dominant perspective of U.S. economists working in the population field over the postwar period. This interpretation is documented in a paper presented at the Nobel Jubilee Symposium in Economics in Stockholm, Sweden,[3] which examined in considerable detail the writings of the economists who contributed to two United Nations and two National Academy of Sciences reports on the consequences of population growth.[4] Space precludes reproducing here even a fraction of that evidence, but the conclusions of these four reports merit summary.

The 1953 U.N. report was both seminal and distinctly non-alarmist. The chapters on economics antedated by three decades the key propositions currently associated with revisionism. Specifically, the report discounted the proclivity of population specialists to focus on the "fixity" of resources and strongly urged the adoption of a longer-run perspective, where, to use the report's characterization, "constants" are treated as "variables."[5] This represents the central analytical underpinning of modern economic thinking about demographic change. The report also noted that not all population consequences are negative. Indeed, of the twenty-one direct impacts listed, some were positive (scale, organization), some were negative (diminishing returns), and some were neutral (technology and social progress). While the U.N. report, like most modern assessments, speculated that the net impact of rapid population growth in developing countries was likely to be negative, this conclusion was guarded, especially since international trade and migration could qualify the results and the impacts on saving and investment were, at least theoretically, quite uncertain.[6]

The 1973 U.N. report was somewhat more pessimistic, highlighting several shorter-run impacts of population growth. This is true of the chapters on food, where traditionalist methodology focusing on direct impacts was employed, and, to a lesser degree, the discussion of the impacts on saving and investment. The most significant new finding, however, was the striking conclusion that a net negative impact of population growth on growth in per capita output was not obvious in the data. Given the strong prior assumptions of demographers and policymakers that the negative impacts of population growth on development were quantitatively large, the inability to easily "confirm" this hypothesis through simple, albeit inconclusive, correlations kept the population debate alive and encouraged the continuing elevation of revisionism during the next two decades.

In contrast, the 1971 National Academy of Sciences (NAS) report appeared, at first glance, to be quite "traditionalist," indeed alarmist. The crisply written executive summary lists, in just a few pages, more than twenty adverse impacts of population growth, downplays positive linkages, and ventures a bold quantitative assessment that a 25 percent reduction in birth rates could raise per capita income growth rates by one-third. The pessimism in this summary is both baffling and misleading, since most of the major scholarly papers underlying the report, especially (but not exclusively) those written by economists, provide a different interpretation. While the 1971 NAS report is often cited as the major scholarly justification for the alarmist concern about population growth, this assessment is, in fact, unwarranted, since it is largely based on the executive summary which, lamentably, is unfaithful to the evidence and argumentation of important scholarly contributions to the study. Why this was done remains a puzzle. Surprisingly, the executive summary was never vetted with most of the participants in the NAS study; moreover, the summary is unauthored. On the basis of an exhaustive inquiry into this matter, we conclude that the executive summary was most likely written by an NAS staff assistant, with influential input from the U.S. Agency for International Development, the financial sponsor of the project.[7] At any rate, the 1971 NAS report should not be characterized as traditionalist/alarmist; indeed, in terms of the scholarly writings of the contributing economists, it is not all that different from the 1973 U.N. report.

The 1986 NAS report is the most revisionist of the major studies in the postwar period. It was written almost entirely by economists, and the executive summary represented true collaboration by the scholars who compiled the working papers. The report emphasizes individual and institutional responses to initial impacts of population change—among them, conservation in response to scarcity, substitution of abundant for scarce factors of production, and innovation and adoption of technologies to exploit profitable opportunities. These responses are considered to be pervasive, and they are judged to be quantitatively important. The report also reviews a large number of empirical studies that tend to reinterpret many traditional concerns about rapid population growth. Four of these concerns are of particular note.

First, according to the 1986 NAS report, the concern that population growth will result in resource exhaustion is considered to be misplaced. The relationship between population growth and global resource use is not as strong as some population alarmists had asserted. This conclusion is based on studies of 1) the determinants of resource supply and demand (related most strongly to per capita income); 2) the relative impact of price-induced versus serendipitous technological change on resource discovery, efficiency of use, and lower costs of extraction; 3) the responsiveness of conservation in the face of resource scarcity; and 4) an assessment of the efficacy of markets and political processes in allocating exhaustible resources over time.

Second, the concern that rapid population growth would notably constrain saving and investment is not supported by the data. While some capital-shallowing occurs, no strong impact on economic growth is found. The conclusion regarding saving is based on the inability to obtain reasonably robust empirical results demonstrating the impact of population growth and age structure on saving, deriving mainly (but not exclusively) from international cross section data. The conclusion regarding investment is based on a combination of empirical assessments and simulation models.

Third, the concern that population growth will significantly shift resources from productive physical capital formation into allegedly "less-productive" areas such as education is not supported by the data. Education enrollments, which have expanded significantly even in the face of population pressures, have been financed not so much by diverting resources from other investment areas, but rather by per pupil expenditure reductions and by efficiency gains. While this allocation plausibly reduces the quality of education, the quantitative importance of this impact is judged to be uncertain.

In contrast, a fourth concern about the adverse effects of population growth on renewable resource degradation, where property rights are difficult to assign or maintain (e.g., rain forests), is considered to be warranted. It is important to recognize that this conclusion, which supports population pessimism, is itself revisionist in orientation since it explicitly highlights the role (i.e., the lack) of feedbacks.

While, like most revisionist writings, the 1986 NAS study judged the net impact of rapid population growth in developing countries to be negative, the conclusion was carefully qualified. It merits quotation since it represents in tone the predominant assessment of most U.S. economic demographers over the postwar period: "On balance, we reach the qualitative conclusion that slower population growth would be beneficial to economic development of developing countries."[8] This statement, arduously negotiated to obtain unanimous support by the NAS working group, exemplifies several attributes of modern economic thought on population: 1) population growth has both positive and negative impacts (thus, "on balance"); 2) the actual size of the net impact—even whether it is strong or weak—cannot be determined based on existing evidence (thus, "qualitative"); 3) only the direction of the impact from high current growth rates can be discerned (thus, "slower," not "slow"); and 4) the net impact varies from country to country—in most cases it will be negative, in some it will be positive, and in others it will be neutral (thus "developing countries").

The major summary reports in the postwar period on the consequences of population growth have been quite tempered in their assessments, especially those parts contributed by the economists. It appears that the perception of the "emergence" of revisionism in the 1980s is due to three factors: 1) the increasing influence of economists vis-à-vis others in the population debates; 2) the work of Julian Simon, whose influential book, *The Ultimate Resource*, posed a threat to the population-programming/family-planning establishment and stimulated the compiling of several survey articles (including the NAS report) that systematically exposed the results of two decades of empirical research;[9] and 3) the political environment of the period. While the political environment has since changed, it is the least important factor accounting for revisionism since the revisionist perspective persisted and may have dominated thinking over most of the postwar period, at least among prominent U.S. economic demographers.

The Future of Revisionism

Will revisionism continue to dominate the 1990s and beyond? Can the history of the debate provide clues to its future? Several countervailing factors are at play.

First, and most important, revisionism may well gain strength as the result of the rise of economic liberalism in the 1980s, the increasing prevalence of structural adjustment programs in the developing world during this period, and the collapse of socialism and centralized economic management and the emergence of market economies in the former Soviet bloc countries in the 1990s. Markets are the major institutional mechanism attenuating the short-run adverse impacts of population growth. Put differently, many, if not most, resource pressures are reconciled in and through markets.[10] For example, scarcities (caused by, say, rapid population growth rates) are signaled by high prices, which automatically, flexibly, and often rapidly, expand supply and constrain demand. In contrast, where markets are distorted or controlled, mainly by governments, adverse short-run population impacts will continue, and may in some cases be amplified. The rise of relatively unfettered markets may be the most important single factor that will dampen any negative impacts of rapid population growth in the coming decade and beyond.

Second, numerous efforts in the last decade to liberalize and broaden international relations also help promote revisionism. The economic adjustment processes required to accommodate one factor growing relatively rapidly, such as population/labor, are greatly facilitated in an environment of relatively free movement of capital, labor, as well as goods, which can, to an extent, substitute for factor flows. It is difficult to predict the pace and distribution of such liberalizing forces as private-sector development, expansion of trade, and more effective and democratic governance, but in direction they are well advanced in many areas, Africa being the most important exception.

Third, the diffusion and adoption of technology into production will mute the impact of rapid population growth and act as a powerful feedback in the system. Theoretically, this impact can be illustrated by contrasting an environment where production combinations between, say, capital and labor are limited, and in the extreme "fixed." An increase in the growth of one factor can cause unemployment or under-employment, unless something stimulates the growth of a complementary factor. Much of the revisionist literature illustrates the automatic (feedback) forces that cause the complementary factor to grow. To the extent, however, that production options are not "fixed," but "flexible," through the availability of alternative technologies, there is less need for rapid population growth to be accommodated through the growth of complementary inputs.

The population debate is now on sound footing. The shift in thinking is based not on new and convincing empirical evidence but rather on the adoption of a methodological perspective. Instinctive and genuine concerns about rapid population growth will continue to inspire some to focus on direct, short-run impacts, but this strategy will fail to convince professional economists.

The strength and nature of "feedbacks" that may attenuate or reverse initial negative effects of population growth represent the remaining area of contention in the population debate. Alarmists fail to anticipate such feedbacks, or they downplay them a priori, some-times by trying to change the "rules of scientific engagement" and dialogue. For example, Nathan Keyfitz, a distinguished and brilliant demographer, comments on "feedbacks" as follows:

> The range . . . is limited only by the imagination of the writer, and the scope for cleverness is wide . . . . I submit that the direct effect is primary, and that the burden of proof is on the one who has introduced some intermediate effect that would upset it.[11]

Sound science should require only an even-handed analysis that takes feedbacks into account. Revisionism has brought such even-handedness to the population debate. This contribution will be enduring.

A major insight of revisionism—that the adverse consequences of population growth are greatest where feedbacks are blocked by market failure—helps set the agenda of the population debate. Pessimists may focus on the negatives where feedbacks are weak (as with renewable resource use in situations where information is absent). Optimists may offer counter examples. But if this dialogue and research is explicitly cast to assess the empirical strength of feedbacks in response to rapid population growth, it will represent healthy dialogue, whatever the outcome.

POPULATION AND DEVELOPMENT BEFORE THE INDUSTRIAL REVOLUTION

Having set Malthusianism aside, economists have been seeking empirically based conclusions about economic-demographic relationships. This search has led to a reexamination of the same periods in Europe's past that inspired Malthus' pessimism in *An Essay on the Principle of Population* published in 1798. Starting three decades ago, with greater objectivity, superior data, and better econometrics, economic and demographic historians asked once again whether, in the long run, rapid population growth impedes development. Their finding: Malthus failed initially to anticipate the power to increase consumption and production that arose from capital accumulation and technological innovation, especially in agriculture. As a result, he overestimated the negative impact of population growth. But in looking backward on his country's past, he was right in important respects. Specifically, the poor agrarian society of England and Wales before 1800, with undeveloped markets and an unequal distribution of income between the landless poor and the rentier class, often was strained and became worse off by measures such as wage rates and the income share going to laborers. In periods when population grew more rapidly, landowners prospered at the expense of landless workers.

The historical evidence, described briefly below, prompts the question: How relevant is history to describing the impacts of population growth in today's poorest countries, and for the poorest groups in those countries? Insofar as conditions among the poor today replicate those of the past, the historical findings may be relevant. Moreover, population growth rates, which have often exceeded three percent per annum since 1950, are far more rapid than any observed over long periods in European history. Since post-1950 cross-section data fail to show a consistent negative impact of rapid population growth on per capita income, a challenge to economic-demographic analysis is to set the boundaries in time and space that divide the Malthusian from modern settings (i.e., to define those situations in which population growth can be absorbed by a feedback process that permits sustained economic growth).

Why Historical Data Matter for Today's Experience

What is the evidence that rapid population growth impedes economic development? Taking all countries and sub-periods into account, it appears that, based on evidence from cross-country studies prior to and including the 1970s, there is no association between population growth and economic growth. Recent studies suggest a negative population impact may have emerged during the 1980s; however, the quantitative size of this impact, its robustness, and its causes, are yet to be established. Moreover, such cross-country evidence must be interpreted with great caution, and augmented by historical and other information, to obtain a clearer picture of economic-demographic relationships.

The experience of economic growth since 1945, particularly in the period before the 1973 oil crisis, is unique in human history. Income grew faster, and on a more sustained basis, than in any previous period for which data are available. Per capita product grew in the developed countries of the Organisation for Economic Co-operation and Development (OECD) at a cumulative average annual rate of about three percent, during the period 1950 to 1991; sustained growth rates over any four-decade period since 1800 never exceeded 1.4 percent per annum and were certainly lower in all previous epochs and for all world regions.[12] The spreading effects of new technologies, and the stimulus to growth in poor countries generated by demand in developed countries, could easily have obfuscated, in statistical cross-section studies or in most available time-series data, any measurable ill effects of population growth in Africa, Asia, and Latin America.

More formally, the impacts of population growth may vary with the rate of per capita output growth. For example, one might hypothesize that high rates of economic growth provide more resources for accumulation. This, in turn, provides both time and resources for countering the short-run negative impacts of population growth through diminishing returns. This possible scenario, if true, was positively reinforced in the 1960s and 1970s by capital inflows, and negatively impacted in the 1980s by a virtual curtailment of capital imports. Other hypotheses could be cited to explain the relative ease of "accommodating" rapid population growth in an environment of rapid economic growth. However, only by applying a longer-term perspective of centuries, not merely decades, of interaction between demography and development is it possible to clarify how the two interact. A look at the past is potentially instructive about the present and future because so much of the world remains in abject poverty, has few prospects of immediate improvements, and must anticipate a long upward march out of poverty before economic systems can function as they do in the developed world.

Economies Before the Industrial Age

The low-income countries today, and the high-income countries before 1800 when they also were poor, can be thought of as distorted, poorly functioning market systems out of equilibrium and hence unable to achieve efficient resource allocation. Weak institutions and poorly functioning governments were common in both times and places. The industrial revolution brought markets together, took advantage of economies of scale, and made possible the divisions of labor and gains from trade that raised European incomes from 1800 onward. But before those changes occurred, prices were often wrong— markets did not always bring supply and demand into balance and inefficiencies and misallocations were normal conditions in economic life. These features had desperately negative implications for the well-being of most people, but especially for the poorest. Most people worked and traded within a local market often marked by monopoly, inefficiency, and poor capacity to respond either to tragedy or to opportunity. Before the eighteenth century, for example, there was virtually no change in the share of world population living in cities, a sign of overall, long-term stagnation.[13]

ENGLAND FROM 1200 TO 1750. For Malthus, the operative challenge was the geometrical growth of population pressing against a slower, arithmetical expansion of food supply. "Population, when unchecked, increases in a geometrical ratio. Subsistence [food production] only in an arithmetical ratio. A slight acquaintance with numbers will shew the immensity of the first power in comparison of the second."[14] (In the face of missing evidence, Malthus abandoned this formulation between the 1798 and 1803 editions of his essay.) In the longest period for which there are data to subject to empirical analysis, i.e., in England over the centuries from 1200 to 1750, population change was possibly the dominant cause of long-run changes in wages, rents, industrial prices, and income distribution. The economy absorbed population growth at about 0.4 percent per annum with little effect on these key variables. However, significant deviations of population growth above this trend line appeared to elicit notable consequences. Ronald D. Lee estimates that a 10 percent increase in population depressed wages by 22 percent; raised rents by 19 percent; lowered industrial prices relative to agricultural prices by 17 percent; raised the ratio of industrial to agricultural production by 13 percent; and lowered labor's share of national income by 14 percent.[15] In more recent work, Lee finds a somewhat less elastic response of wages to population growth over those centuries, with a percentage decline in wages equal to the percentage increase in population growth rate above the trend line. The effect of population growth on wages and income distribution between labor, land, and capital has been shown to be quite robust to various modeling approaches.

The distributional consequences of rapid population growth may have been as important, or more important, than the aggregate impacts on economic growth. This finding accords with David Weir's analysis of Great Britain and France over three centuries, from 1500 to 1800, in which he concludes that, "Population growth's strongly negative consequences for real wages were balanced by equally strong positive consequences for rents."[16]

Population growth above a fairly slow rate, far slower than the two percent per annum that is often referred to as rapid population growth, favored landlords over workers and lowered labor's share of total income. In England, as well as on the continent, periods of rapid population growth and price increase were also periods in which real wages sank and the relative price of foodstuffs rose. Population growth had strong and predictable effects, beneficial for some social classes and damaging for others.[17]

MEIJI JAPAN. This finding for Europe appeared in similar form in Japan as well. A study combining the tools of formal computer general equilibrium modeling with data from Meiji Japan posed the following question: What would have happened to Meiji economic history had population growth tripled from 0.9 to 2.7 percent per annum to approximate the demographic pressures in developing countries today?[18] The results were surprising. The impact of rapid population growth on Meiji Japan would have been quite small: the levels of output per capita, urbanization, and industrialization would have been only 7.7, 4.4, and 3.8 percent lower, respectively. The reasons for this are similar to what happened in Europe. In the short run, capital-shallowing occurred and average labor productivity declined, but over a quarter century there were offsetting feedbacks on savings, the capital-output ratio, and the productivity of capital. These feedbacks would have muted initial diminishing returns to a more numerous labor force and higher dependency rate. The simulation exercise showed that the overall consequences of rapid population growth can be found not only in the aggregate numbers, but also in the distribution of the impacts between the owners of labor and capital.

THE EXPERIENCE OF THE REST OF EUROPE. David Weir recently extended the analysis of the British case to the United Kingdom, Netherlands, France, Germany, Italy, and Spain, showing a negative response of wages to population growth over six fifty-year periods, between 1500 and 1800. Weir concluded that "population growth in early modern Europe not only had negative consequences for real wages, but also consequences greater in magnitude than would be produced by simple changes in the land/labour ratio."[19] But this is a qualified finding. He identified a sharp distinction between the "successful" areas, the United Kingdom and the Netherlands, and the other four: "Any positive population growth in most of Europe had negative consequences, while in the United Kingdom and the Netherlands, economic growth allowed for modest growth without declines in real wages." This result caused him to hypothesize that these two economies' capacity to absorb population growth, without real-wage declines, improved in the sixteenth century, and especially after 1750, just prior to the onset of modern economic growth. "There appears to have been a transition to the 'modern' pattern of very little cross-sectional correlation of population growth and economic growth in the second half of the eighteenth century."[20]

LESSONS FOR TODAY'S DEVELOPING COUNTRIES

What lessons applicable to the developing countries today might be gleaned from the historical experience of the now developed countries? This historical assessment suggests that two factors are central to population- and economic-growth linkages. First, rapid population growth appears to be best accommodated in situations where 1) institutions (e.g., markets and government policies) are well developed and can attenuate short-run adverse population-growth impacts, and 2) strong forces encourage productivity growth in agriculture, resulting in a shift of the share of the total labor force from lower-productivity agriculture to higher-productivity nonagricultural pursuits. Second, market and other institutional development and agricultural productivity increases have gone hand-in-hand.

The Growth of Markets

Historically, strengthened markets and other institutions helped foster effective adjustment to population growth. Improved markets helped counteract the adverse effects of diminishing returns by eliciting adjustments in resource use, capital accumulation, and agricultural innovation. The capacity to adjust, and the pace of economic development, differed markedly from period to period and from country to country, as it does today. Government policies—important in developing countries today—were probably less important than market responses in early European history, unless, of course, one considers private institutional development and the relative absence of adverse government policies a hallmark of the European success. This process of institutional and market change was slow, uneven, and incomplete even in the parts of Europe that led the industrial revolution. The transition to sustained development was achieved in substantial part by building more efficient markets and reducing the many kinds of market failure that hindered growth-promoting allocations of resources—the same forces that conditioned the size and direction of the impacts of rapid population growth. Although industry and manufacturing led the way in that transition, a constant problem was how to overcome the resistance to change in the traditional agrarian societies from which the new bourgeoisie had sprung.

The Growth of Agricultural Labor Productivity

As markets and institutions were developing, yet another force—an agricultural productivity revolution—accounted for much of the observed success of the industrial revolution and, importantly, the success in coping with rapid population growth. Before the industrial revolution, the vast majority of all countries' and regions' workers were farmers. Elites excepted, up to 80 percent of consumption was in the form of food. Farm productivity was too low to free many workers for non-farm occupations.

Concurrent with the beginning of the industrial revolution, an exceptional and often-ignored historical trend emerged in England and subsequently in several other European countries and areas of European settlement—a substantial and sustained growth in farm productivity. Farm-worker productivity in industrializing European countries rose at about two thirds of the rate of improvement in manufacturing, permitting a rapid shift of labor out of agriculture to more productive manufacturing. Without this development, the pace of nonagricultural output growth would have been much slower.[21]

Might the industrial revolution have been stymied altogether if farm-labor productivity had not improved? The answer to that question goes to the heart of the contemporary issue of whether rural population growth, with its implications for potentially *declining* labor productivity, may pose a difficult barrier to low-income countries striving to make the transition from poverty to sustained economic development.

As late as 1880, the countries we now call developed had over half of their labor force working in agriculture—a share that subsequently fell dramatically. In Japan, for example, the proportion of labor working in agriculture fell from 75 percent to 51 percent between 1880 and 1900, at the same time that productivity in farming was growing at the unprecedented rate of two percent per annum. A double transformation was taking place: the shift of labor out of farming, and technical progress permitting higher productivity among agricultural workers who remained.[22]

In most industrializing countries, women's participation in the nonagricultural labor force grew rapidly as well, adding to the growing cost of children, the resultant decline in fertility, and the demographic transition to low fertility and mortality. Without these labor-force changes, the costs of childbearing may not have grown, fertility may not have fallen as rapidly, and persistent poverty may have resulted.

Labor Force Shifts in Recent Decades

Today's low-income countries have had no experience of rapid labor-force change similar to that experienced in the industrialized countries, either historically or recently. Indeed, even in the period since 1960, the industrial countries have been transforming their economies and societies at a faster rate than have low- and middle-income countries (see Table 1). For the low-income economies, excluding China, total fertility rates declined by 30 percent in the 1960–1990 period, and the share of labor force in agriculture declined by an equivalent percentage. Among the industrial and upper-middle-income countries, total fertility rates declined 39 percent, and the share of labor force in agriculture declined by more than 60 percent. The low-income and lower-middle-income countries changed far less on these socioeconomic indicators. By these measures, the rate of transformation, even in the past three decades, has been considerably faster in the

TABLE 1. DECLINES IN FERTILITY AND SHARE OF LABOR FORCE IN AGRICULTURE, SELECTED COUNTRY GROUPS, 1960–1990 (percent)

	Change in Total Fertility Rates, 1960–1990 (percent)	Change in Share of Labor Force in Agriculture, 1960–1990 (percent)
Low-Income Countries[a]	−6	−15
China	−27	−9
Lower-Middle-Income Countries	−29	−30
Upper-Middle-Income Countries	−39	−61
Industrial Countries	−39	−69

[a]Excludes China

Sources: For fertility data, World Bank, Internal World Bank Data System, Washington, DC. For labor force data, United Nations, PC/METS: Macroeconomic Data System, New York, 1991.

developed than in the low-income and lower-middle-income countries. Low agricultural productivity growth in many developing countries is a major part of the explanation.

Low-income countries, in relative terms and with some important exceptions, are not transforming their economies nearly fast enough to avoid falling further behind the industrial countries. The reasons for the growing gap in incomes may be the interrelated factors of the inability to cope with high fertility and the lack of innovation in agriculture. These, in turn, are related to inappropriate government policies, poorly developed markets, and indeed the impacts of governments on markets.

Consequences of Rural Inertia

Rural inertia, characterized by little or no productivity growth, increasing population density, and limited capacity to change, remains common, especially in Africa and South Asia, where raising farm-worker productivity depends on exogenous sources of technical change. What accounts for this inertia? One explanation is that although there may be more technologies available today than historically, few of them are economically viable for skills-poor, capital-poor rural workers where government policies favor urban areas. The capacity to "accommodate" rapid population growth requires "flexible" technological response to rapidly changing labor-to-land and labor-to-capital ratios. Few low- and lower-middle income countries have absorbed the lessons of earlier experience, with the result that too many countries have experienced stagnation in the post-World War II period, especially in agriculture.

Raising labor productivity in agriculture will be difficult in African and South Asian countries that face continuing large increases in the absolute size of their agricultural work forces. Kenya, for example, could experience as much as a ninefold increase in the size of its agricultural work force by the year 2050.[23] In contrast, Japan's agricultural work force was already falling in absolute numbers by 1900; Korea's began to fall in 1955; and Brazil's in 1970. Despite mechanization, Egypt's agricultural labor force grew by nearly half between 1960 and 1980, as high fertility and stagnant labor productivity perpetuated rural poverty.[24]

Some newly industrializing countries provide a refreshing contrast. In the past two decades, several countries in East and Southeast Asia have experienced rapid growth in farm productivity. In South Korea, for example, farm-worker productivity grew at sustained rates of 6 percent per annum for more than two decades. In most such cases, governments have promoted agricultural development, and markets have provided prices that reward farmers using new technologies.

Less successful countries are, almost by definition perhaps, largely unsuccessful at transforming their rural economies: they shift labor out of agriculture only slowly, and they may even experience a decline in per worker product, as did India in the years 1960 through 1981 before market reforms were introduced.

While some rural societies have succeeded in escaping from poverty,[25] more than a billion people living in rural poverty today are unable to raise their productivity, and may remain unable to do so because of their inability to absorb greater numbers.[26] Raising farmworker productivity in an environment of a farm labor force growing at more than two percent per annum may be an insurmountable task, especially over long periods of time. To date, however, there has been insufficient analysis of population and labor force interactions in cases of extreme and growing scarcity to pass judgment on these issues.

In many countries, poorly developed markets and ill-advised government policies have led to stagnation and lack of technical progress in agriculture. On the one hand, farmer-managed innovations that raise worker productivity by mechanization are unlikely until labor scarcity and rising wages make them attractive to the farm manager. And, the more rapid the growth rate of population, the more delayed the onset of labor scarcity in the agricultural sector, and thus the more delayed the farmer-based innovations that would raise labor productivity.[27] On the other hand, Green Revolution innovations that are labor intensive are unlikely to be adopted without government support in the form of infrastructure and market prices for inputs and outputs that are conducive to favorable farmer responses.

It may be even more important today than in the past to speed the pace of technical change in agriculture. Innovation occurs mainly where output can grow into expanding export markets, and where governments provide an enabling environment conducive to farmer innovation and adoption of new crop varieties, complementary inputs, and farm management systems. Otherwise, the capacity to accommodate rapid population growth will be undermined, and the panacea of technology can be distressingly elusive.

RECENT SUCCESSES (AND FAILURES) IN TRANSITION

There is no inevitable Malthusian barrier to economic progress. Some of the world's most populous, high-fertility countries have experienced high rates of growth in per capita income in recent decades, and these countries may someday have the same standard of living as today's developed countries. China, India, Pakistan, Indonesia, Thailand, Turkey, and Korea, all with populations above 50 million, have achieved rates of economic growth above 2.3 percent per capita per annum between 1980 and 1991, a rate equal to the average of the developed countries during the same period.[28] But many low-income countries fell even further behind, and many middle-income countries in Latin America went through a lost decade of per capita GNP decline in the 1980s. Overall, the number of people living in poverty grew about 2 percent per annum in the late 1980s and early 1990s, the same rate as population.[29] Despite some big-country successes, it remains reasonable to question whether a transition to sustained development has been made in many of the smaller countries, especially in Sub-Saharan Africa.

The macroeconomic linkages between rapid population growth and economic development are complex and contingent on the development of markets, institutions, and facilitating government policies—all of which can dramatically affect how well societies adjust to population growth. Concerns about population no longer need to be justified on the basis of an uninformed application of the law of diminishing returns. The ground for discussion has shifted to concern about poverty, the well-being of particular segments of the population, and especially women's reproductive health and choice. This focus on individual well-being represents a return to the traditional concerns of

Malthus, who emphasized the distributional consequences of rapid population growth. In the contemporary setting, market failure, associated with rural isolation and low productivity, can lead to more births and higher fertility than would be socially optimal as parents use children as a means of old-age security or cheap labor.

Numerous "traps" abound. Fertility differentials in rural areas can exacerbate income inequalities. The poor continue to give birth more often and, with declining infant mortality, have more surviving children than higher-income groups. Gaps between rich and poor widen as the poor are unable to make investments in human capital. Escaping these traps will require institutional settings characterized by developing and integrated markets and facilitating government policies.

If the population debate continues to focus on the short run, or to constrain attention to just one or two factors, it will continue to result in unbalanced and unproductive assessments. The broadened themes found in this volume—the modus operandi both of revisionism and of the historical debates—will assist to rectify this deficiency.

Malthus gave up Malthusianism in the 1803 revised edition of his essay on population with the introduction of positive checks—the observation that people can and do decide to limit their fertility well short of the point of starvation. But he did not give up the suspicion that more people might yield more misery, perhaps because the arithmetic-geometric metaphor was so beguiling. The contradictions in the mind of Malthus still confront many analysts and policymakers in the population field, those whose feelings, impressions, and personal certainties about the negative effects of rapid population growth are not supported by a careful sifting of the facts. The revisionists shift of attention away from rapid population growth to such factors as market failure and errant government policies highlights many economists' view that these other factors may be more important and more amenable to change in the effort to speed the process of economic development than would be the effort to slow population growth. Nonetheless, there are significant pockets of poverty, particularly among nearly one billion low-productivity rural workers, a not inconsiderable fifth of world population, where high fertility and population growth continue to interact with bad policies to yield an environment of low prospects for economic change. In such environments, efforts to slow population growth, difficult though they may be, may have no less a chance of leading escape from poverty than would other policies. Alarmists and revisionist might find grounds for agreement that, in such circumstances, slower population growth and market-friendly government policies could both contribute to the development objective.

Notes

[1] This literature is summarized in Nancy Birdsall, "Economic Approaches to Population Growth and Development," in Hollis B. Chenery and T. N. Srinivasan (eds.), *Handbook of Development Economics* (Amsterdam: Elsevier Science Publications, 1988), pp. 477-542; Robert H. Cassen, "Population and Development: A Survey," *World Development*, Vol. 4, No. 10 and 11 (1976), pp. 785-830; Robert H. Cassen, "Economic Implications of Demographic Change," *Transactions of the Royal Society of Tropical Medicine and Hygiene*, Vol. 87 (1993), pp. SI13-18; Allen C. Kelley, "Economic Consequences of Population Change in the Third World," *Journal of Economic Literature*, Vol. 36 (1988), pp. 1685-1728; National Research Council, *Population Growth and Economic Development: Policy Questions* (Washington, DC: National Academy Press, 1986); Geoffrey McNicoll, "Consequences of Rapid Population Growth: An Overview and Assessment," *Population and Development Review*, Vol. 10, No. 2 (1984), pp. 177-240; T. N. Srinivasan, "Population Growth and Economic Development," *Journal of Policy Modeling*, Vol. 10, No. 1 (1988), pp. 7-28; and World Bank, *World Development Report 1984* (New York: Oxford University Press, 1984).

[2] Thomas R. Malthus, *First Essay on Population* (London, 1798).

[3] Allen C. Kelley, "Revisionism Revisited: An Essay on the Population Debate in Historical Perspective," in Rolf Ohlsson (ed.), *Population, Development and Welfare: The Nobel Jubilee Symposium in Economics* (Berlin: Springer-Verlag, forthcoming).

[4] United Nations, *The Determinants and Consequences of Population Trends*, Department of Social Affairs, Population Division, Population Studies No. 17 (New York: United Nations, 1953); United Nations, *The Determinants and Consequences of Population Trends*, Department of Social Affairs, Population Studies No. 50, Vols. 1 and 2 (New York: United Nations, 1973); National Academy of Sciences, *Rapid Population Growth: Consequences and Policy Implications*, Vols. 1 and 2 (Baltimore, MD: Johns Hopkins Press for the National Academy of Sciences, 1971); and National Research Council, *Population Growth and Economic Development: Policy Questions* (Washington, DC: National Academy Press, 1986).

[5] U.N. 1953, ibid., p. 181.

[6] U.N. 1953, ibid., pp. 137 and 237.

[7] The author interviewed the living participants in the study, including staff at the NAS, and consulted hundreds of pages of memoranda, letters, and various drafts of key papers, including the executive summary. The research benefited significantly from the assistance of Professor George Stolnitz. For a summary, see footnote 19 in Allen C. Kelley, op. cit.

[8] National Research Council, op. cit., p. 90.

[9] Julian Simon, *The Ultimate Resource* (Princeton, NJ: Princeton University Press, 1981).

[10] Of course, markets are largely ineffective in the cases of public goods and externalities; in such cases, governmental allocations and regulation provide one (but not the only) mechanism for modifying resource allocations.

[11] Nathan Keyfitz, "Population and Development Within the Ecosphere: One View of the Literature," *Population Index*, Vol. 57, No. 1 (1991), p. 3.

[12] William McGreevey, "Economic Aspects of Historical Demographic Change," World Bank Staff Working Paper 685 (Washington, DC: World Bank, 1985), pp. 79-81.

[13] Paul Bairoch, *Cities and Economic Development from the Dawn of History to the Present*, Christopher Braider (trans.), (Chicago: University of Chicago Press, 1991), pp. 494-495.

[14] T.R. Malthus, op. cit., p. 14.

[15] Ronald Demos Lee, "A Historical Perspective on Economic Aspects of the Population Explosion: The Case of Preindustrial England," in Richard A. Easterlin (ed.), *Population and Economic Change in Developing Countries* (Chicago: University of Chicago Press, 1980), pp. 517-557 and 563-566. See also World Bank, *World Development Report 1984* (New York: Oxford University Press, 1984), p. 57. This work summarizes the evidence.

[16] David Weir, "A Historical Perspective on the Economic Consequences of Rapid Population Growth," *Consequences of Rapid Population Growth in Developing Countries* (New York: Taylor and Francis, 1991), p. 61.

[17] H.J. Habakkuk and M.M. Postan, *The Cambridge Economic History of Europe, Vol. 6, The Industrial Revolutions and After: Incomes, Population and Technological Change*, 2 parts (Cambridge: Cambridge University Press, 1965), pp. 1-59.

[18] Allen C. Kelley and J.G. Williamson, "General Equilibrium Analysis of Agricultural Development: The Case of Meiji Japan," in Lloyd Reynolds (ed.), *Agricultural Development and Theory*, (New Haven: Yale University Press, 1974).

[19] Weir, op. cit., p. 55.

[20] Ibid., pp. 57-58.

[21] Simon Kuznets, *Modern Economic Growth: Rate, Structure and Spread* (New-Haven: Yale University Press, 1966).

[22] William McGreevey, "Economic Aspects of Historical Demographic Change," World Bank Staff Working Paper 685 (Washington, DC: World Bank, 1985), p. 31, summarizes evidence from several sources.

[23] World Bank, *World Development Report 1984* (New York: Oxford University Press, 1984).

[24] Ismail Sirageldin, "The Population Dynamic Basis for Sustainable Egyptian Agricultural Development," The Johns Hopkins University, Department of Economics, 1992, mimeo.

[25] Ester Boserup, *The Conditions of Agricultural Growth: The Economics of Agrarian Change Under Population Pressure* (Chicago: Aldine, 1965); and Ester Boserup, *Population and Technological Change: A Study of Long-term Trends* (Chicago: The University of Chicago Press, 1981).

[26] Partha Dasgupta, "An Enquiry into Well-Being and Destitution," *The Population Problem*, Ch. 12 (Oxford: Clarendon Press, 1993).

[27] Teresa Ho reports evidence of labor-productivity decline even at very low intensities of use in Sub-Saharan African agriculture. "Increased farming intensity apparently leads to reduced labor productivity in the absence of a change in technique; The loss in productivity can be reversed by a shift from the hoe to the plow or tractor." Teresa Ho, "Population Growth and Agricultural Productivity in Sub-Saharan Africa," in Ted Davis (ed.), *Proceedings of the Fifth Agriculture Sector Symposium*, (Washington, DC: World Bank, 1985), p. 103. But these innovations have to be induced by labor scarcity.

[28] World Bank, *World Development Report 1993* (New York: Oxford University Press, 1993), Table 1.

[29] S.G. Datt Chen and M. Ravaillion, "Is Poverty Increasing in the Developing World?" WPS1146 (Washington, DC: World Bank, 1993).

Chapter Four

Population Growth and Poverty

Dennis A. Ahlburg

Rapid population growth is said to be a major cause of poverty. However, it is often not clear whether population growth is thought to increase the *number* of people in poverty, the *percentage* of the population in poverty, or the *severity* of poverty. Others describe economic factors as being primarily responsible for poverty, with population growth being an *important additional factor* affecting poverty.[1]

This chapter presents estimates of the number of people in poverty (including changes over time), identifies factors related to poverty, and evaluates the role of population growth in determining poverty. It demonstrates that, at the household level, additional children reduce the educational attainment and health of other children in the household but not to a significant extent. Econometric studies across countries have found net negative effects on such poverty-related variables as income, education, and health, but little evidence of a direct effect on poverty itself. While it is not clear whether population growth *causes* poverty in the long run or not, it is clear that high fertility leading to a rapidly growing population will increase the *number* of people living in poverty in the short run, and at least in some cases make escape from poverty more difficult.

POVERTY: DEFINITIONS, NUMBERS, AND TRENDS

Poverty exists when one or more persons fall short of a level of consumption of goods and services deemed to constitute a reasonable minimum, either in some absolute sense or by the standards of a specific society.[2] But poverty is not just a question of inadequate income. Poverty may exist where people have inadequate education, health, and freedom to "develop [and use] their full potential and to have a reasonable chance of leading productive and creative lives in accord with their needs and interests."[3] This expanded definition offers a host of new measurement problems but emphasizes that traditional measures of well-being and poverty are inadequate. In addition to their focus on income, traditional measures fail to take account of the satisfaction derived from children, thereby underestimating well-being or overestimating poverty.

How Many People Are Poor?

More than one billion people, a third of the population of the developing world, live below a poverty line of $370 per person per year, using purchasing power parity (ppp) dollars.[4] Of the 1.116 billion people in poverty, 630 million are in extreme poverty, defined as annual consumption below $275 (Table 1). For developing countries as a whole, 18 percent of the population is extremely poor; for Sub-Saharan Africa and South Asia, the percentages are 30 and 29 percent, respectively. Table 1 also shows an estimate of the poverty gap—the additional income (measured as a share of aggregate consumption) that would be required to lift all individuals above the poverty level. In 1985, a 3 percent increase in the total consumption of the developing world would have been sufficient to lift all individuals out of absolute poverty as measured; a 1 percent increase would have lifted the extremely poor of the developing world out of poverty.[5] Those regions with the highest incidence of poverty tend to have lower life expectancy, higher infant mortality, and a lower primary school enrollment rate, although the association is not perfect.

Poverty in the developing world is not evenly spread. Almost half the population in Sub-Saharan Africa and South Asia is poor, compared to around 20 percent in East Asia and ten percent in Eastern Europe. The incidence of poverty differs both within regions and within countries. In South Asia in the mid-1980s, 51 percent of the population was in poverty. In India, the figure was 43 percent, and in Pakistan and Sri Lanka the figures were 23 and 27 percent, respectively.[6] The ratio of rural to urban poverty rates for thirteen developing countries in the 1980s varied from 1.3 to 1 for Guatemala, Mexico, and Malaysia to 3.7 for Indonesia, 4.6 for Ivory Coast, and 6.0 for Kenya.[7] Rural areas also fare relatively poorly on other measures of well-being. Infant mortality rates in rural areas are often 30 to 100

TABLE 1. ESTIMATES OF WORLD POVERTY BY REGION, 1985

Region	Number of Poor (Including Extremely Poor)[a]		Poverty[b] Gap	Number of Extremely Poor		Poverty[b] Gap	Social Indicators		
	(millions)	(percent)		(millions)	(percent)		Under Age 5 Mortality[c] (per thousand)	Life Expectancy (years)	Net Primary Enrollment Rate (percent)
Sub-Saharan Africa	180	47	11	120	30	4	196	50	56
East Asia	280	20	1	120	9	0.4	96	67	96
China	210	20	3	80	8	1	58	69	93
South Asia	520	51	10	300	29	3	172	56	74
India	420	55	12	250	33	4	199	57	81
Eastern Europe	6	8	0.5	3	4	0.2	23	71	90
Middle East and North Africa	60	31	2	40	21	1	148	61	75
Latin America and the Caribbean	70	19	1	50	12	1	75	66	92
All Developing Countries	1,116	33	3	633	18	1	121	62	83

[a]The poverty line in 1985 purchasing power parity dollars (PPP) was $370 per capita per year for the poor and $275 per capita per year for the extremely poor.
[b]The poverty gap is defined as the aggregate income shortfall of the poor as a percentage of aggregate consumption.
[c]Under age 5 mortality rates are for 1980–85, except for China and South Asia, where the period is 1975–80.

Source: World Development Report 1990, Poverty (New York: Oxford University Press, 1990), Table 2.1, p. 29.

percent higher than in urban areas, and access to safe water is generally half to two-thirds the urban level.[8]

Has Poverty Increased or Decreased?

Table 2 shows changes in poverty from the 1960s or 1970s to the mid-1980s for selected countries. All countries for which data were available show declines in the *percentage* of the population in poverty; except for India, Morocco, and Sri Lanka, the countries experienced declines in the *number* of people in poverty, despite growing popula-

TABLE 2. CHANGES IN POVERTY 1960–1986, SELECTED COUNTRIES

	Length of Period (years)	Percentage of Population Below Poverty Line		Number of Poor (millions)		Average Income Shortfall (percent)	
		First Year	Last Year	First Year	Last Year	First Year	Last Year
Brazil (1960–80)[a,b]	20	50	21	36.1	25.4	46	41
Colombia (1971–88)[a]	17	41	25	8.9	7.5	41	38
Costa Rica (1971–86)[a]	15	45	24	0.8	0.6	40	44
India (1972–83)	11	54	43	311.4	315.0	31	28
Indonesia (1970–87)	17	58	17	67.9	30.0	37	17
Malaysia (1973–87)[a]	14	37	15	4.1	2.2	40	24
Morocco (1970–84)	14	43	34	6.6	7.4	46	36
Pakistan (1962–84)[a,b]	22	54	23	26.5	21.3	39	26
Singapore (1972–82)	10	31	10	0.7	0.2	37	33
Sri Lanka (1963–82)[a]	19	37	27	3.9	4.1	35	29
Thailand (1962–86)[a,b]	24	59	26	16.7	13.6	..	35

Note: This table uses country-specific poverty lines. Official or commonly used poverty lines have been used when available. In other cases, the poverty line has been set at 30 percent of mean income or expenditure. The range of poverty lines, expressed in terms of expenditure per household member and in PPP dollars, is approximately $300–$700 a year in 1985 except for Costa Rica ($960), Malaysia ($1,420), and Singapore ($860). Unless otherwise indicated, the table is based on expenditure per household member. The average income shortfall is the mean distance of consumption or income of the poor below the poverty line, as a proportion of the poverty line.

[a]Measures for this entry use income rather than expenditure.
[b]Measures for this entry are by household rather than by household member.

Source: World Bank *World Development Report, Poverty* (New York: Oxford University Press, 1990), Table 3.2. p. 41.

tions. The average income shortfall (the mean distance of income or consumption of the poor below the poverty income, as a percentage of the poverty line) also declined. There are no reliable data for Sub-Saharan African countries, but World Bank calculations indicate that, between 1965 and 1985, the number of individuals in poverty in Sub-Saharan Africa increased by at least 55 million.[9]

By 1990, it appears that the economic difficulties experienced in the 1980s eroded earlier gains made in the alleviation of poverty. The percentage of people consuming less than $370 per year was constant at 33 percent in both 1985 and 1990, and the number in poverty grew during this time by about 2 percent per year, the average increase in population. There was some variation by region. Poverty fell in East and South Asia but increased in Latin America, the Middle East and North Africa, and Sub-Saharan Africa. Sub-Saharan Africa now has the greatest poverty gap, and, with forecasts of low economic growth, prospects for improvement are grim.[10]

Developments in other measures of well-being slowed down in the 1980s as well. While significant improvements in health status and educational attainment were made in the 1970s, only modest gains were made in the 1980s.

Once Poor, Always Poor?

Do people move into and out of poverty in developing countries, or is poverty a permanent affliction of a particular segment of society? If poverty is chronic, policies that attempt to make the poor more productive (land reform, education, and credit) are appropriate. If poverty is more transitory, then income stabilization schemes such as public relief work schemes, like those used in famine relief in South Asia, and credit programs are appropriate.[11]

The longitudinal data on individuals[12] needed to address these questions are rare. One study in India of 211 agricultural households over the period 1975 to 1983 found that, although there is a substantial core of persistent chronic poverty, a relatively large group moves into and out of poverty. On average 50 percent of households were poor; the highest poverty rate in any single year was 64 percent, and the lowest 41 percent. On average, in a particular year, 84 percent of the poor had been poor the previous year. Only 12 percent of households were never in poverty, 19 percent were poor in every year, and 44 percent were poor in six or more of the nine years studied.[13] These kind of data could also help in identifying the factors responsible for individuals and families moving into and out of poverty.

WHY ARE THE POOR POOR?

Poverty is associated with low wages, lack of human capital such as education and health, and lack of income earning assets such as land; with income inequality and lack of economic growth; with large family size; and with gender, race, and ethnicity.

Lack of Income, Human Capital, and Assets

The major source of income for the poor is labor earnings, primarily from unskilled labor. For most countries in Sub-Saharan Africa, Latin America, and Southeast Asia, poverty is closely associated with the head of household being self-employed in farming. The pattern is more varied in South Asia.[14] Among the urban poor, income comes primarily from informal sector work resulting in low and highly variable income.

The children of the poor complete less school than children of higher income families. This is partly because they are less able to afford school fees and partly because overall educational expenditures by governments tend to favor the non-poor.[15] In addition, the quality of schooling provided to the poor is lower than that provided to children from wealthier families; the poor are more likely to attend under-funded rural schools and are less likely to attend high quality private schools.[16] Quality differences are particularly important since children of poorer households benefit more than children from richer households from increases in the availability and quality of education.[17]

The poor also receive less health care, both privately purchased and publicly provided, and consequently have a higher level of morbidity and mortality. Morbidity lowers earnings capabilities and higher mortality increases the probability of the loss of the principal income earner in the family. The poor die younger and have more disability. For example, in the late 1980s in Porto Alegre, Brazil, adult death rates in poor areas were 75 percent higher than in rich areas.[18]

There are important linkages between health and education. Parent's education and children's health are positively associated. Among children, poor health and nutrition reduces enrollment, particularly for girls, and academic achievement. Among children in a poverty-stricken area of northeast Brazil, inadequately nourished children lagged 20 percent behind the average gain in achievement scores over a two-year period. These effects lower future productivity at both the individual and national level.[19]

The poor are also less likely than the non-poor to have other income-generating assets, especially land. In South Asia, Southern

Africa, and much of Latin America, poverty is associated with land-lessness.[20] Where the poor have access to land, it is either of poor quality, farmed under tenancy arrangements, owned communally, or is common property and has a lower return than privately owned land. In some regions of the world, landlessness is increasing, putting the poor at greater risk because of an increased reliance on wage employment for subsistence.

Rural households are fairly adept at dealing with seasonal fluctuations in income due to the crop cycle. Some income smoothing comes from increased hours of work; some from employment of men in the cash economy; some from the employment of women on the family farm and in cottage industries, services, and small-scale commerce; some from selling assets; and some from limited borrowing from money lenders or through credit from shopkeepers. Further smoothing comes from the migration of household members and the marrying out of daughters. Households with more volatile income from crops marry-out daughters to men from different rainfall or climate zones in order to more efficiently reduce the variability in consumption.[21] Access to such sources for smoothing consumption reduces the correlation between poverty and current family earnings. Very poor families are probably less likely to have assets to sell to avoid poverty in times of crop failure, as well as less likely to have access to income insurance through migration and marriage; they are thus more reliant on current labor earnings.

The Role of Economic Growth and Income Inequality

Economic growth is considered to be the main avenue by which the incomes of the poor and near-poor rise and thus is an important means by which poverty will be reduced. Evidence from about a dozen countries suggests that income growth from the 1960s to the 1980s reduced the incidence of poverty in the developing countries and that the economic difficulties of the 1980s increased it somewhat.[22] Poverty reductions were largest in those countries that grew fastest (greater than 3 percent per year) and lowest in those that grew the slowest (less than 1 percent per year). An analysis of changes in poverty data for the 1980s for 16 countries found that a 1 percent growth in mean consumption was associated with a 2 percent reduction in poverty, although this varied considerably among countries depending upon the level of poverty.[23]

Further reductions in poverty can come about through a reduction in income inequality, even if there is no increase in mean income. Income growth and inequality are not necessarily independent. The

World Bank found that in countries such as Colombia, where growth raised average income and reduced income inequality, poverty fell by more than that explained by the increase in average income alone.[24] Another study found that changes in relative inequalities and the initial level of poverty accounted for most of the progress in reducing poverty not accounted for by growth in mean consumption.[25]

The Role of Family Size

Large family size is positively correlated with being poor, so it has been concluded by some that large family size is a cause of poverty.[26] Large family size can lead to poverty by decreasing the ability of women to work for pay, by decreasing the human capital (education and health) of children, and by reducing the family's ability to save and invest to protect itself from unexpected decreases in income.[27] Studies in developed countries generally find evidence of a negative impact of family size on child well-being (educational attainment, intellectual ability, and health), but the empirical findings for developing countries are varied.[28]

Identifying an effect of family size is complicated by the fact that the existence and strength of the relationship may be affected by the country's level of economic development; the position of the family in its life cycle; the living arrangements of the household's children, not just their number; whether the family receives income from nonresident family members; the spacing of children and whether births are premature; and government contributions to education and health.[29] Particularly troublesome is the fact that the number of children in a family and family expenditures on the education and health of children may be jointly determined; that is, family size may be both a cause and consequence of poverty. If this joint determination is ignored, the estimate of the effect of family size on poverty will be inaccurate. In addition, lower fertility and slower population growth may not translate into better education and health and lower levels of poverty. As one author notes, "an exogenously induced decline in fertility may also mean a reduction in the amount devoted to children, leaving the amount available to each child unaltered."[30]

Many of these problems are overcome in a set of methodologically sophisticated studies examining the relationship between family size and investment in human capital. Studies in Malaysia, India, and Indonesia found that an unanticipated extra birth due to twins reduced the schooling of siblings by 17 percent if the extra birth occurs at first pregnancy, and by 34 percent if it occurs at the third or fourth pregnancy. These studies also indicate that the postponement of births, wider birth intervals, and fewer births increase the weight of children at birth, an important determinant of infant mortality and of the development of surviving children. These biological effects are small. For example, doubling birth intervals would increase birthweight by about 3 to 6 percent, and postponing a birth for a year increases birthweight by 1.4 to 3.2 percent.[31]

The impact of poverty on children is important, in part, because of the transmission of poverty from one generation to the next. On the whole, it seems that a large number of children in a family has negative effects on the education and health of children, but these seem to be quantitatively small; moreover, some studies show a positive impact, and some show no impact. (See Chapter 6 in this volume for more on conditions that affect the effect of family size).

Gender, Race, Age, and Ethnicity

While females are over-represented in poor households in developed countries, this does not appear to be the case in most developing countries.[32] However, women are disadvantaged relative to men on most other measures of well-being. Because their wages are lower, they must work longer than men to achieve a comparable standard of living, female infant mortality rates are higher in some countries, and males are favored in access to education.

Although it is difficult to prove, it is likely that inequality *within* a household is greater in larger households; direct empirical tests of this hypothesized relationship, however, are rare.[33] Larger households place an additional burden on women and, probably, on female children. Such intra-household dynamics are significant for the design of poverty-alleviation policy. For example, additional income in the hands of a woman will raise the share of the household budget spent on education and health by about four times more than if the additional income went to a man.[34]

Even though women may not be over-represented in poverty, they do have a lower probability of escaping from poverty. They must spend more of their time on household chores; overt discrimination prevents them from fully exploiting opportunities in the labor market; and employment opportunities for women are more seasonally sensitive than those for men.[35] Because women generally have a weaker claim on the resources of the household, they depend more than men on children for economic security and social status. Such effects are stronger in Africa than in Asia. Poverty alleviation schemes, therefore, need to address the economic and social dependence of women on children.

Race and ethnicity are also related to poverty. In Latin America, as in many developed countries, indigenous peoples are disproportionately poor. Children and the sick are heavily over-represented among the poor, while the elderly are currently under-represented. This, however, is changing in Asia and Latin America as populations age.[36]

THE EFFECT OF POPULATION GROWTH ON POVERTY

If population growth affects poverty, it probably does so by affecting one of the correlates of poverty discussed above. That is, population growth may affect poverty by influencing economic growth, the distribution of income, and the value of earnings and other assets; by affecting the provision of education and health services; or through the size and structure of families.

Population Growth and Economic Development

Does population growth decrease economic development, at least as measured by income per capita? A 1987 National Academy of Sciences study concluded that while there are both negative and positive impacts of population growth, on balance slower population growth would be beneficial to economic development.[37] This study examined the relationship between population growth and economic development by regression analysis of data on 75 developing countries. Two measures of economic development were examined: per capita GNP in 1989 and annual growth in per capita GNP between 1980 and 1989. Population growth was broken into recent and past growth, with recent growth defined as annual growth between 1980 and 1989, and past growth defined as annual growth between 1965 and 1980. This distinction was made because the short- and long-run effects of population growth may differ and population effects may take time to occur. Earlier analyses of the relationship between population growth and economic development generally failed to distinguish between recent and past population growth. The study found that higher recent population growth (i.e., 1980 to 1989) was associated with lower per capita GNP in 1989 and slower annual growth in per capita GNP, while past population growth was positively related to these measures of economic development.[38] These findings are similar to others for the early 1980s.[39]

The negative effects may occur because population growth decreases saving and investment and shifts government expenditure away from capital and infrastructure into education and health, which take longer to pay off. The longer-run positive effects may occur because of a growing labor force, or because of induced efficiencies in production that accompany larger markets and improved government organization, public services, and infrastructure from increased population density.[40] One study concluded that "countries with more sharply declining rates of population growth tend to have a higher rate of per capita income growth, both because they are able to enjoy higher rates of labor force per capita and because of increases in GDP per worker."[41]

To assess well-being—not just per capita income (which is only one measure of well-being)—the United Nations Development Programme's human development index (HDI) was regressed on population growth. The HDI (1990 version) is a scale combining a country's scores on (logarithm of) per capita GDP, life expectancy, and literacy and thus captures the dimensions of the broader definition of poverty discussed above.[42] The regressions suggest that recent population growth is associated with poorer performance in delivering income, health, and education, while past population growth is positively associated with the index.[43] As with the economic development regressions, the negative short-run effect is larger than the positive long-run effect, indicating that the net effect of population growth on human development is negative.[44]

These results must be handled with some caution. Economic growth and human development are as likely to affect, as to be affected by, population change. The lags with which these variables affect each other are unknown and may be mis-specified in the above analysis, and the correlations between population and economic growth may reflect special historical circumstances (omitted variables), not causality. If there is no causal relationship between population growth and economic development, then policies to reduce population growth will not necessarily affect development or poverty.

Population Growth and the Distribution of Income

What effect does population growth have on the distribution of income? There is widespread belief that population growth worsens the distribution of income. However, a thorough review of the literature on the topic suggests that the evidence for the theoretical impact is ambiguous. The effect of population growth depends on the measure of inequality used and on the source and nature of population change. Population growth that comes from higher fertility among the poor may have a different effect on inequality than fertility increases from all income groups in society or from a decline in mortality.[45] Consequently, hypotheses about the effect of population growth on the relative economic position of the poor cannot be tested using either cross-section or time-series observations on standard measures of inequality. Policy interventions to reduce the rate of population growth that are based solely on the adverse effects of population growth on the distribution of income among the existing population may be unfounded.[46]

Evidence of a negative effect of family size on a child's birthweight, nutrition, education, and future earnings prospects, and increased inequality in subsequent generations could offer a defensible argument that rapid population growth is inconsistent with the welfare of future generations. However, while appealing as a proposition, evidence on the quantitative importance of this hypothesis is not yet established.

Population Growth and Earnings and Other Assets

If population growth from high fertility increases poverty, then it is likely to do so, at least in part, by depressing wages. In the archetypical case, population growth leads, with a lag, to labor force growth; land availability increases slowly or not at all; industrialization absorbs only a small portion of the labor force increase; land per worker declines and landlessness increases; as a result, real wages fall, and poverty increases. However, at least in the period 1960 to 1980, most countries did not fit this pattern. Despite unprecedented population growth, developing countries were generally able to "absorb" the new labor supply at higher productivity and higher income per capita with a shift toward more productive employment.[47] There were exceptions, however, principally in Africa and in Latin America.

The relatively successful absorption of a growing labor force does not mean that wages would not have been higher in the absence of population growth; it does mean, however, that accommodations were made in many countries that kept wages from falling. Examples of these accommodations include: expansion of land and increased intensity of use (in Punjab, India; Pakistan; Thailand; Philippines; and Kenya); land reform (in China and Taiwan); increased rural non-agricultural employment (in Taiwan, China, Punjab, and Pakistan); and increasing urban employment (in Taiwan, Thailand, and Korea).[48] The countries that most successfully absorbed labor and reduced poverty did so by promoting growth that favored the assets of the poor (primarily labor, but also land) and by developing the human capital of the poor.

An important question raised by the past success in accommodating population growth is whether this success will continue. Labor force growth is expected to continue at about 2 percent per year. In the past 30 years, this added 700 million to the labor force in developing countries; in the next 30 years, it will add 1.2 billion.[49] Prospects for successful absorption in Africa are bleak because suitable agricultural innovation has proven illusive, land quality is declining, and export markets for traditional products are weak. Agricultural prospects are also dim in Latin America, where there is little possibility of agricultural expansion, and hope lies in employment growth in urban areas. Prospects are best in Asia, where further innovations in technology and off-farm employment seem possible. However, even in Asia, the intensity of agriculture is already high, further reductions in farm size will probably reduce productivity, and landlessness (particularly in Bangladesh and India) is a serious problem.

Some evidence indicates that population growth has decreased the non-exchange component of income that affects the poor more than other groups. The non-exchange component includes wild fruit and animals; firewood; building and thatching materials; water from tanks, streams, and ponds; free-ranging of poultry; and some limited grazing for livestock. A study of the dry tropical parts of India found that production from common property resources comprised 14 to 23 percent of the income of the poor. From the 1950s to the 1980s, common property resources available to villagers declined 30 to 55 percent, with villages with the largest population growth having the largest declines.[50] This was the result not only of population growth, but also of changes in government policy, technological change, and the fact that community property increased in economic value, thereby creating an incentive to sell it to a business concern. Similar results were found in a study in Bangladesh.[51]

Population Growth and Family Size

If larger numbers of children in a family lower well-being, how are family size, birth spacing, fertility, and population growth related? This is a more difficult question than it seems. The data show that higher fertility and more rapid population growth are not automatically linked either to a large number of siblings who compete for household resources or to close spacing of births. For example, although the total fertility rate (TFR) in Mali is nearly twice that of the Dominican Republic (6.9 and 3.6, respectively), on average a child in Mali has 3.4 living siblings compared to 3.7 for a child in the Dominican Republic.[52] Despite different TFRs, both countries had an annual rate of population growth of 2.4 percent in the 1980s.

Countries with similar TFRs, rates of population growth, and average numbers of siblings have very different percentages of their population in poverty. For example, the populations of Indonesia and Colombia both grew at an annual rate of 2.1 percent in the 1980s, and both had TFRs and average numbers of siblings close to 3.0. Yet 25 percent of Columbia's population lived in poverty compared to 17 percent of Indonesia's population. Thailand, with a TFR and average number of siblings only two-thirds as large as these two countries, had 26 percent of its population living in poverty.[53]

When correlations among average number of siblings, child spacing, fertility, and population growth are calculated for 19 developing countries for which data were available, they are not uniformly positive and statistically significant. However, this reflects heterogeneity in the sample of countries. When the sample is split into three separate groupings—Sub-Saharan African countries, North African and Asian countries, and Latin American and Caribbean countries— the number of siblings is positively and statistically significantly correlated with higher population growth and fertility for all but the Sub-Saharan African countries. Closer spacing of births is not significantly associated with fertility and population growth.[54]

These empirical findings suggest that larger numbers of siblings and closer spacing of births, rather than population growth per se, are associated with negative impacts on well-being and, possibly, with poverty.[55] The macro-level associations are harder to establish. Thus for policy formulation, data on population growth may be a poor proxy for the relevant micro-level variables, number of siblings and birth spacing.

Population Growth and Education and Health

If education and good health are important components of well-being and lack of access to them directly and indirectly contributes to poverty, is there any evidence that population growth has adverse impacts on the supply of education and health services at the macro-level?

A cross-national study of school expenditures and enrollments in the 1960s and 1970s found that countries in which larger proportions of the population are children of school age tend to have lower educational expenditure per child of school age, achieved largely by decreasing teacher salaries, rather than by lowering enrollment rates. In fact, many countries had significant increases in enrollment rates. The negative effects were noted particularly at the secondary level.[56] The study concluded that population "plays an indirect role in diluting public resources allocated to the school system." This role probably varies among countries. In some countries with efficient use of educational resources, slower population growth could increase educational performance. In others, with inefficient resource use, slower population growth may have little effect. This point is supported by a recent study of education in Asia. In countries with efficient educational sectors and sound government policies, reduced population growth has allowed improvements in education. Where such efficiency and sound policy are lacking, the potential improvements in education from lower population growth have been squandered.[57]

Does a decrease in educational expenditure per child lower educational attainment? Unfortunately there is no clear answer to this question. Some studies find educational inputs affect educational outcomes while others do not.[58] All schools and all countries are not equally efficient at producing education. Clearer information is needed on the link between educational inputs and outputs (the efficiency of educational organizations) before conclusions can be drawn about the link between rapid population growth and educational outcomes at the national level.

In the 1980s in a number of developing countries, and particularly in Sub-Saharan Africa, school enrollment rates as well as expenditure per pupil decreased, raising concerns about the formation of human capital. These decreases were largely due to the economic difficulties of the 1980s but were exacerbated by population growth.[59]

At the micro-level, there is evidence that poorer nutrition and higher child mortality is associated with larger family size. At the macro-level, it is very difficult to establish a relationship between population growth and nutrition, but there is some evidence of adverse effects on the provision of health service. In the case of extreme inadequacy of food, that is, famines, it has been argued that policy failure rather than population growth is the underlying cause.[60] In a study of small South Pacific nations, countries with a larger and more rapidly growing population tended to have lower provision of health services (doctors and hospital beds per capita) and also lower educational attainment.[61]

Population Growth and Poverty

What evidence is there at the macro-level of a direct effect of population growth on poverty? Changes in poverty, as measured by changes in the percentage of the population who were poor were regressed on population growth for 22 countries from the 1960s and 1970s to the mid-1980s.[62] Population growth was not statistically significantly related to declines in poverty. This result was found when different measures of poverty were used, when different models were used, and when different time periods were examined. Differentiating between recent and past population growth did not affect the conclusion.

There are, of course, a number of reasons to be skeptical of these aggregate regressions. Changes in poverty are likely to affect the rate of population growth.[63] It is also possible that population growth does affect poverty, but the effect is masked by variables omitted from the regression. Thus, the regression results do not necessarily mean that population growth has no effect on poverty, but, if an effect exists, it is not strong enough at the national level to show through, given the possible methodological problems mentioned. As Allen Kelley and William McGreevey note in Chapter 3 of this volume, these and other aggregate regressions should be taken only as first approximations.

There are few other studies of the effects of population on poverty. Several studies of rural poverty in 13 Indian states from 1959–60 to 1970–71 concluded that population size did not affect poverty independently of per capita agricultural output. A re-analysis of the data, correcting for methodological problems in these studies, concluded that for most states a 10 percent increase in population would increase the percentage of the population in poverty by about 0.01 percent. For some states, the effect was about 1 percent. Population growth may have increased poverty through adverse shifts in the distribution of income due to increased rural unemployment.[64] Thus, negative effects of population growth were found, but they were not very large. Replications of this study for other countries and time periods would be valuable.

CONCLUSION

Poverty is the result of many factors including population growth. However, the importance of population growth's contribution to poverty is far from clear. At the level of the household, it appears that additional children reduce the education and health of other children in the family but estimates of the size of these effects vary considerably: sometimes they are positive, sometimes insignificant, and more often than not negative and fairly small. At the national level, it is even harder to establish the effect of population growth on poverty. Net negative effects have been found on variables related to poverty, such as income, education, and health, but there is little direct evidence of a significant negative effect on poverty itself. Overall, the evidence shows that many countries have been able to reduce poverty while population has been growing, but in many other countries population has contributed to the difficulties of reducing poverty.

In seeking to improve the economic position of the poor, governments should use the most direct policy instruments available, including policies to increase access of the poor to land, credit, public infrastructure, and services, particularly education and health.[65] In regions where there is an insufficient resource base, policies to aid out-migration are also needed. Not only does a strategy of land reform, early concentration on agriculture, the development of nonagricultural rural activities, and infrastructure development support growth, it also fosters more equal income distribution. It appears that East Asian governments have been able to lower poverty by fostering vigorous growth in both agricultural and nonagricultural sectors.

Family planning programs may help reduce poverty, but the effects may be small and take a long time to be felt. Even intergenerational transmission of poverty is better addressed through changes in government policies and expenditures on child health and education than through family planning programs. Indeed, a family planning program that emphasizes health services to the poor is better justified on the grounds that it directly redistributes health resources to the poor than on the grounds that lower fertility may decrease poverty.[66] Still, family planning programs are a useful complement to such direct policies. They are generally easier to implement, relatively inexpensive, and their effects tend to be cumulative, that is effects on health will enhance later education and productivity.

Although it is not clear whether population growth causes poverty in the long run or not, it is clear that high fertility leading to rapidly growing population will increase the number of people in poverty in the short-run, and in at least some cases make escape from poverty more difficult.

Notes

The author has benefited from comments from Allen Kelley, Robert Cassen, Jere Behrman, Ragui Assaad, Tim Dyson, Sandy Korenman, Deborah Levison, Cynthia Lloyd, and Vern Ruttan.

[1] World Bank, *World Development Report 1990* (New York: Oxford University Press, 1990).

[2] For an excellent survey of poverty in developing countries, see Michael Lipton and Martin Ravallion, "Poverty and Policy," World Bank Policy Research Paper WPS 1130 (Washington, DC: World Bank, April 1993).

[3] United Nations Development Programme, *Human Development Report 1990* (New York: Oxford University Press, 1990). This approach owes much to the writings of Amartya Sen who has stressed the role of "capabilities" and "functionings" in the assessment of standard of living enjoyed. Capability is the ability to achieve, that is, the real opportunities an individual has regarding the life they may lead. Functionings are achievements, that is, different aspects of living conditions. See, for example, Amartya Sen, *The Standard of Living* (Cambridge: Cambridge University Press, 1985) and Partha Dasgupta, *An Inquiry into Well-Being and Destitution* (Oxford: Oxford University Press, 1993), p.1.

[4] World Bank, *World Development Report 1990*, op. cit., pp. 26-27. The PPP is much better than official exchange rates for converting currencies and appears to be the best available method of establishing internationally comparable poverty lines. See Shaohua Chen, Gaurav Datt, and Martin Ravallion, "Is Poverty Increasing in the Developing World?" World Bank Policy Working Paper WPS 1146 (Washington, DC: World Bank, June 1993). The importance of converting income figures into purchasing power parity equivalents is illustrated by looking at Russian incomes. Based on April 1993 income figures, the average Russian earned $360 per year, less than the average Indonesian (*The Economist*, "Poverty of Numbers," 10 July 1993). However, it is highly unlikely that living standards are lower and poverty higher in Russia than in Indonesia.

[5] Martin Ravallion, Gaurav Datt, and Dominique van de Walle, "Quantifying Absolute Poverty in the Developing World," *Review of Income and Wealth*, Vol. 37, No. 4 (December 1991), pp. 345-361.

[6] World Bank, *World Development Report 1990*, op. cit., p. 41.

[7] Lipton and Ravallion, op. cit., p. 42.

[8] World Bank, *World Development Report 1990*, op. cit., p. 31.

[9] Ibid., p. 42.

[10] Chen, Datt, and Ravallion, op. cit., p. 13.

[11] See Lipton and Ravallion, op. cit., pp. 56-69, for a discussion of poverty alleviation policies.

[12] Longitudinal data on individuals, or panel data, are data on individuals (or families, households, etc.) observed over time. Variation is observed *across* individuals and *over* time.

[13] Raghav Gaiha and Anil. B. Deolalikar, "Transitory, Permanent and Innate Poverty: Estimates for Semi-Arid Rural South India, 1975-83" (Seattle, WA: University of Washington, 1989), mimeo.

[14] World Bank, *World Development Report 1990*, op. cit., pp. 33-34.

[15] Even though in many countries government allocations to primary education tend to favor the poor, disproportionate shares of the education budget go to secondary and, particularly, tertiary education. For example, in Sub-Saharan Africa only 2 percent of young people go on to higher education, but 22 percent of the region's education budget is spent on tertiary education (World Bank, op. cit., p. 79).

[16] Donald Cox and Emmanuel Jimenez, "The Relative Effectiveness of Private and Public Schools," *Journal of Development Economics*, Vol. 34, Nos. 1-2 (November 1991), pp. 99-121.

[17] Nancy Birdsall, "Public Inputs and Child Schooling in Brazil," *Journal of Development Economics*, Vol. 18, No. 1 (May/June 1985), p. 84.

[18] World Bank, *World Development Report 1993* (New York: Oxford University Press, 1993), p. 21.

[19] Ibid., pp. 19 and 21.

[20] World Bank, *World Development Report 1990*, op. cit., p. 32.

[21] See Mark Rosenzweig and Kenneth Wolpin, "Credit Market Constraints, Consumption Smoothing, and the Accumulation of Production Assets in Low Income Countries: Investments in Bullocks in India," *Journal of Political Economy*, Vol. 101, No. 2 (April 1993), pp. 223-244; and Mark Rosenzweig and Oded Stark, "Consumption Smoothing, Migration, and Marriage: Evidence from Rural India," *Journal of Political Economy*,

Vol. 97, No. 4 (August 1989), pp. 905-926, for a discussion of these consumption smoothing strategies.

[22] World Bank, *World Development Report 1990*, op. cit., p. 47.

[23] Chen, Datt, and Ravallion, op. cit. The short-run effect is probably smaller due to consumption smoothing.

[24] World Bank, *World Development Report 1990*, op. cit., pp. 46-47.

[25] Chen, Datt, and Ravallion, op. cit.

[26] For example, in the Philippines in 1985, 44 to 50 percent of households with one child, but 60 to 78 percent of households with five children, were in poverty. In Russia, in 1992, 40 percent of families with one child were poor, while almost 80 percent of families with three or more children were poor. John Bauer, Dante Canlas, Maria Theresa Fernandez, and Andrew Mason, "Family Size and Family Welfare in the Philippines," paper presented at the Regional Conference on Priority Health and Population Issues, Honolulu, HI, 25-28 February 1992. *The Economist*, op. cit.

[27] For instance, in Thailand, 60 percent of small families (one or two children) had financial savings in 1988. In contrast, 60 percent of large families (four or more children) had no savings at all. See Napaporn Havenon, John Knodel, and Werasit Sittitrai, "The Impact of Family Size on Wealth Accumulation," working paper, Institute of Population Studies, Chulalongkorn University, 1989. However, a study of the Philippines found that larger rural families had greater *lifetime* accumulation of wealth because older children work and contribute to household income (Bauer et al., op. cit.). It seems that the effect of the number of children on wealth is influenced by the age profile of production in a society and the rules governing resource flows from children to parents (and the reverse). For reviews of this literature see Andrew Mason, "National Saving Rates and Population Growth: A New Model and New Evidence," in *Population Growth and Economic Development: Issues and Evidence* (Madison, WI: University of Wisconsin Press, 1987), pp. 523-560; and Allen C. Kelley, "Economic Consequences of Population Change in the Third World," *Journal of Economic Literature*, Vol. 36, No.4 (December 1988), pp. 1685-1728.

[28] These studies are discussed in Lloyd (Chapter 6 in this volume).

[29] See Sonalde Desai, "The Impact of Family Size on Children's Nutritional Status," Research Division Working Paper No. 46 (New York: The Population Council, 1992); Stephen S. Kyereme and Erik Thornbecke, "Factors Affecting Food Poverty in Ghana," *Journal of Development Studies*, Vol. 28, No. 1 (October 1991), pp. 39-52; Cynthia Lloyd and Anastasia Gage-Brandon, "Does Sibsize Matter? The Implications of Family Size for Children's Education in Ghana," Research Division Working Paper No. 45 (New York: The Population Council, 1992); and Jane Miller, James Trussell, Anne Pebley, and Barbara Vaughan, "Birth Spacing and Child Mortality in Bangladesh," *Demography*, Vol. 29, No. 2 (May 1992), pp. 305-318.

[30] Desai, op. cit., p. 8. Joint determination assumes reasonable control over fertility. In a survey of wanted fertility in 48 countries Bongaarts found that 78 percent of births were wanted. The proportion wanted was highest for countries at the beginning of the fertility transition and lowest for countries in midtransition. For example, in Cameroon in 1978, 94 percent of births were reported as wanted while in Peru in the same year, only 61 percent of births were reported as wanted. See also John Bongaarts, "The Measurement of Wanted Fertility," Research Division Working Paper No. 10 (New York: The Population Council, 1990).

[31] Mark Rosenzweig, "Population Growth and Human Capital Investments: Theory and Evidence," *Journal of Political Economy*, Vol. 98, No. 5 (part 2), (October 1990). Note that biological effects should be distinguished from behavioral effects. Rosenzweig concludes that the observed negative correlations between family size and per-child measures of human capital do not appear to have a strong biological component.

[32] Lipton and Ravallion, op. cit., p. 33.

[33] Ibid., p. 20.

[34] Duncan Thomas, "The Distribution of Income and Expenditure Within the Household," *Annales d'Economie et de Statistique*, Vol. 29, No. 1 (January/March 1993), pp. 109-136.

[35] Lipton and Ravallion, op. cit., p. 33.

[36] Ibid., p. 12.

[37] D. Gale Johnson and Ronald D. Lee (eds.), *Population Growth and Economic Development: Issues and Evidence* (Madison, WI: University of Wisconsin Press, 1987).

[38] The negative effects were found to be larger than the positive effects, particularly when the positive effects are discounted since they do not occur until sometime in the future.

[39] David Bloom and Richard Freeman, "Economic Development and the Timing and Components of Population Growth," *Journal of Policy Modelling*, Vol. 10. No. 1 (April 1988), pp. 57-82. For a similar result see Didier Blanchet, "Population Growth and Income Growth During the Demographic Transition: Does a Malthusian Model Help Explain Their Relationship?" *Population* (English Selection), Vol. 2 (1990), pp. 37-52. Bloom and Freeman also show that the impact is sensitive to whether population growth comes from rising fertility or declining mortality.

[40] For a discussion of these effects, see the papers in Johnson and Lee, op. cit., and Julian Simon, *The Ultimate Resource* (Princeton, NJ: Princeton University Press, 1981).

[41] Bloom and Freeman, op. cit., p. 77.

[42] For a skeptical view of the index see Kelley (1991).

[43] The human development index has been revised twice since its inception. The regression results were repeated using 1991 version of the index on a sample of 122 developed and developing countries. The same pattern of results was found.

[44] A problem with these regressions is that mortality changes affect both population growth and the index and the association between the index and population growth could reflect this. Thus, the regressions were rerun using the income and education components as dependent variables. The results were similar to those using the full human development index.

[45] David Lam, "Distribution Issues in the Relationship Between Population Growth and Economic Development," in *Population Growth and Economic Development*, op. cit., pp. 589-630.

[46] Ibid., p. 608. Lam (p. 610) suggests that focusing on relative wage effects maybe more illuminating. In studying the history of inequality in the United States Williamson and Lindert [See J.G. Williamson and P.H. Lindert, *American Inequality: A Macroeconomic History* (NY: Academic Press, 1980), pp. 80-82] found that wage differentials for skilled and unskilled workers moved in the same direction as summary inequality measures. Thus data on wage ratios alone could be used to infer movements in inequality. Population increase decreased relative wages for the unskilled and increased inequality. However, there is insufficient data for developing countries to test whether the Williamson-Lindert finding holds for developing countries. It should be noted that care need be taken in interpreting data on relative wage effects. It is possible for relative wages to decline and increase measured inequality, but the absolute income of the poor to rise.

[47] David Bloom and Richard Freeman, "Population Growth, Labor Supply, and Employment in Developing Countries," in *Population Growth and Economic Development*, op. cit., pp. 105-148; Azizur Khan, "Population Growth and Access to Land: An Asian Perspective," in *Population, Food, and Rural Development* (Oxford: Clarendon Press, 1988), pp. 143-161; and David Turnham, *Employment and Development: A New Review of the Evidence* (Paris: Organisation for Economic Co-operation and Development, 1993).

[48] Bangladesh has been viewed as the country that best fits the archetype, but even here there is conflicting evidence. A recent study using district level data found that districts with higher population density had higher agricultural wages, and, between 1953 and 1981, districts with more rapid population growth experienced a slower decline in real wages over the period. See James K. Boyce, "Population Growth and Real Wages of Agricultural Labourers in Bangladesh," *Journal of Development Studies*, Vol. 25, No. 4 (July 1989), pp. 467-485. It appears that population growth is associated with the emergence and diffusion of more intensive cultivation techniques, which raised land productivity and led to agrarian institutional change that was conducive to labor absorption and rising wages. Specifically, population growth was associated with a decline in the average size of landholdings, an increased use of both family and hired labor, a higher

incidence of sharecropping, and a shorter duration of tenancies. All of these changes were associated with a higher demand for labor and higher wages. It is possible, however, that population density was high because of migration into these districts resulting from the higher wages.

[49] Turnham, op. cit., p. 249.

[50] N.S. Jodha, "Depletion of Common Property Resources in India: Micro-Level Evidence," *Population and Development Review*, Vol. 15, special supplement, 1990, pp. 261-283.

[51] Mohammed Alauddin and Clem Tisdell, "Poverty, Resource Distribution, and Security: The Impact of New Technology in Rural Bangladesh," *Journal of Development Studies*, Vol. 25, No. 4 (July 1989), pp. 550-570.

[52] Cynthia Lloyd and Sonalde Desai, "Children's Living Arrangements in Developing Countries," Research Division Working Paper No. 31 (New York: The Population Council, 1991).

[53] Ibid.

[54] The samples are quite small, so these findings should be viewed with some caution. Ibid.

[55] The sample of countries for which we have data on number of siblings, spacing of births, and poverty is too small to carry out a meaningful statistical test of association.

[56] T. Paul Schultz, "School Expenditures and Enrollments, 1960-1980: The Effects of Incomes, Prices, and Population Growth," in *Population Growth and Economic Development*, op. cit., pp. 413-478.

[57] For a discussion of these studies see Allen Kelley, "The Consequences of Rapid Population Growth on Human Resource Development: The Case of Education" (Durham, NC: Duke University, February 1994), mimeo.

[58] See Cox and Jiminez, op. cit., p. 120.

[59] World Bank, *World Development Report 1990*, op. cit.

[60] See Amartya Sen, *Poverty and Famines: An Essay on Entitlement and Deprivation* (Oxford: Oxford University Press, 1981).

[61] Dennis A. Ahlburg, "Is Population Growth a Deterrent to Development in the South Pacific?" *Journal of the Australian Population Association*, Vol. 5, No. 1 (May 1988), pp. 46-57.

[62] The data were taken from World Bank, *World Development Report 1990*, op. cit., Lyn Squire, "Fighting Poverty," *American Economic Review*, Vol. 83, No. 2 (May 1993), pp. 377-382, uses the data to investigate the effect of economic growth on changes in poverty. Data from Chen et al. on a variety of measures of poverty for the late 1980s were also analyzed. Population growth was not found to be related to changes inpoverty.

[63] See Nancy Birdsall and Charles Griffin, "Fertility and Poverty in Developing Countries," *Journal of Policy Modeling*, Vol. 10, No. 1 (April 1988), pp. 29-55. The argument for poverty affecting family size and population growth runs as follows: infant mortality is higher among poor families, so to ensure that sufficient children survive to look after the parents in old age, fertility is higher in poor families. In addition, poverty may be alleviated by having more workers. When young, children can perform household tasks that release an adult for work outside the home or production in the home for sale to the market. Children may also be directly employed in the market to increase family income. Child labor is often at the expense of school attendance. Thus the short-run necessity of having the child work increases the probability that the family and the child will remain in poverty.

[64] Dominique van de Walle, "Population Growth and Poverty: Another Look at the Indian Time Series Data," *Journal of Development Studies*, Vol. 21, No. 3 (April 1985), pp. 429-439.

[65] See the World Bank, *World Development Report 1990*, op. cit., and Lipton and Ravallion, op. cit., for a discussion of policies to reduce poverty.

[66] This is not to say that family planning could not be justified on these grounds. A child growing up in a smaller family may well be better off. The point is that there are other, stronger, justifications for family planning programs.

Chapter Five

The Population, Environment, and Development Nexus

Theodore Panayotou

Views on the effects of population growth on the environment span the entire range from unequivocally negative, even catastrophic, to unequivocally positive and highly beneficial. According to the neo-Malthusian view, population growth is the root cause of environmental degradation, as it pits growing demands against the planet's finite resources and limited carrying capability. Direct population control is seen as the only effective means for reversing environmental degradation and averting a Malthusian catastrophe of massive famines.[1]

At the other extreme, population growth is viewed as a driving source of increased efficiency, economies of scale, and technological innovation that not only expands the earth's carrying capacity, but also makes possible increases in living standards and environmental improvements.[2] According to this view, there is no environmental justification for population interventions.

In between these diametrically opposing positions there is an entire spectrum of views that ascribe a contributory or proximate role for population growth in environmental degradation.[3] According to these views, poverty, inequality, distortionary policies, and export demand are the ultimate causes of environmental degradation, exacerbating the impact of population on the environment.[4] The implication is that the primary focus of environmental policy should be to deal with these root causes.

Most examinations of the relationship between population and environment are cast at such an aggregate or macro level that they have limited behavioral content and largely ignore human responses to population growth. By implication they overstate, understate, or misstate the impact of population density and growth on natural resources and the environment, and can lead to misguided policy prescriptions.

This chapter analyzes the relationship between population and local ecosystems by focusing on household, community, and national economy responses to population growth. Inevitably, the impact of population on the environment depends on the ability of these social units to respond, i.e., their "response elasticities." The chapter examines the factors that affect the responsiveness or speed of adjustment, including the role of population itself. While formal estimation of response elasticities is beyond the scope of this paper, evidence from all regions of the developing world supports the eclectic view that population growth can be an agent either of sustainable development or of environmental degradation depending on how free households, communities, and societies are to respond.

Accommodating growing numbers of people against a fixed endowment of resources requires a flexible response that will improve the productivity of both resources and people, substitute dwindling resources with more abundant ones, import additional resources, and/or export people to other areas and other occupations. When scarcity is general across resources, sectors, and areas, there is an increasing premium on technological and institutional innovation to induce changes in production and consumption and the development of new substitutes. When the response is muted, constrained, or blocked, population growth has decidedly negative impacts on local ecosystems.

This chapter's focus therefore is on the impact of population growth on local ecosystems. Global impacts are no less significant but they are beyond the scope of this study. The chapter begins with a discussion of how households, communities, and societies respond to population growth under conditions of natural resource depletion and scarcity. It examines the linkage between population growth and environmental degradation, looking particularly at the role of economic growth, poverty, and income distribution. It also presents an overview of the available evidence for the population-environment link with respect to specific environmental problems (deforestation, pollution).

ACCOMMODATING POPULATION GROWTH WITHIN THE HOUSEHOLD

If a pregnancy is a desired one (i.e., part of the household's demand for children), the benefits to the household must exceed the costs. The child is accommodated by dividing the household's resources for food, shelter, and education more finely between a larger number of household members who are obviously poorer in per capita terms with than without the additional member. However, this is only a temporary cash flow problem. Once the child is old enough (usually over 5), he/she will begin to contribute to the household's income sufficiently to defray the cost of his/her upkeep, and will eventually generate a surplus that more than offsets the negative cash flow of his/her earlier years. The child contributes to the family income in one or more of the following ways: gathering fuelwood, fetching water, collecting fodder, tending animals, working on the farm (planting, harvesting, weeding, and irrigating), collecting food and other non-timber products from the forests, fishing from inland streams and reservoirs, helping with landclearing, earning income from off-farm employment, food processing, and looking after younger siblings so that other members of the household can engage in the above activities.

As a result of these multiple contributions, the household could, within a relatively few years from the child's birth, become better off than if it did not have the additional child. For a complete private cost-benefit analysis of an additional birth, one should also include the costs of early child mortality and schooling, the risk of maternal mortality, and the insurance and old-age security benefits to the parents, as well as the direct utility derived from a larger family.

Notice, however, that most contributions by children consist of capturing and appropriating open-access natural resources such as water, fodder, pastures, fish, fuelwood, and other forest products, and clearing open-access[5] land for cultivation. This has two critical implications:

1) Appropriation by capture makes the number of children the decisive instrument in the hands of the household: the household's share of open-access resources depends on the number of hands it employs to convert open-access resources into private property. This is not unlike the case of the common pasture, where the share of each household depends on the number of animals it grazes.

2) While having a large number of children (or animals) exploiting the commons is optimal from the individual household's perspective, it is not optimal socially, and in the long run could become devastating for the resource, the community, and eventually the individual household.[6] The rule of capture puts a premium on the deployment of as many human hands (and animal mouths) as possible, in order to appropriate open-access resources before others do. A household's share is roughly proportional to the number of "transformers" of common resources into private property it employs. Machines can

rarely be afforded and are not always helpful for the tasks at hand, such as gathering fodder and fuelwood; animals can only be helpful if pasture is available, and in any case, they need children to tend them. This leaves children as the primary vehicle of resource capture, with the result that a large number of children is seen as an asset rather than a liability.[7] The consequences are as predictable as they are catastrophic. Natural resources become overexploited and degraded just as pastures become overgrazed and degraded as a result of overstocking. Entry to open-access resources continues until excessive capture costs dissipate all rents (that is, profits attributable to the scarcity of the resource) and damage to the resource base has occurred.

It is tempting to conclude that the large number of children, and hence population size and growth, is the cause of overexploitation and degradation of resources. After all, it is the additional child that puts additional pressure on resources, both directly through his/her engagement in resource extraction, and indirectly through the need to feed, clothe, shelter, and educate an additional person. However, the decision to have an extra child is not independent of the expected benefits. Since a major part of these expected benefits is the capture and appropriation of open-access resources for the household, the larger the unappropriated resources available for capture, the greater the incentive for the household to add more hands to the task. Equilibrium only occurs where excessive effort and environmental degradation dissipate all the rents from the resource in question.

Even if population growth is not influenced by resource availability, there are many ways for a household to accommodate an extra member. These include intensifying agricultural production, seeking non-farm employment, and migrating to other areas.

Agricultural Intensification

The household can seek to intensify agricultural production by investing in land improvement, soil conservation, irrigation, and purchase and use of productivity enhancers such as fertilizers.[8] Given the household's limited cash resources and the increased consumption due to the added person, agricultural intensification is critically dependent on access to credit. Institutional rural credit, however, is extremely scarce due to interest rate ceilings, supposedly aimed at protecting the rural poor from exploitation and usury. The limited rural credit that may be available is rationed against the high-cost small borrower. Furthermore, lack of collateral precludes small farmers from institutional credit. Land, the poor farmer's only mortgageable asset, is often untitled or under short-term tenure and transfer restrictions, ostensibly aimed at protecting poor farmers from land speculators and ultimately from themselves. For instance until recently, 40 percent of agricultural land in Thailand was untitled.[9] Non-institutional credit is usually available, but the rates are as high as 10 percent a month, reflecting the high cost and risk of lending scarce funds to small borrowers without collateral. At these rates, no agricultural investment is profitable. The lack of rural credit in Java, for example, has prevented upland farmers from undertaking investments and adopting technologies with long payback periods such as stump clearance, land leveling, terracing, irrigation, drainage, and tree cropping (Box 1). The worst government policies in Sub-Saharan Africa have kept food and fuelwood prices artificially low, thereby reducing the incentives for intensification of food and wood production.[10]

Non-Farm Employment

When agricultural intensification is not possible, the rural household may attempt to accommodate the additional family member by seeking non-farm employment. While pregnancy and childcare may temporarily reduce the mother's time available for outside employment, the institution of the extended family makes it possible for mothers to work at other times. Older children may also be available for part-time employment. Yet non-farm employment in the rural areas of poor countries is notoriously scarce. In the name of development and industrialization, infrastructure and public services have been concentrated in the capital and a few other urban centers, as have industry and services.[11] Protection and subsidization of capital- and energy-intensive industry, as well as minimum wage laws, severely limit industrial employment. The economy's limited investible funds, extracted mostly through taxation of the rural sector and foreign borrowing, are often wasted on megaprojects that create little employment but benefit the urban elite while rural industry and non-farm employment are neglected for lack of resources. The few rural non-farm jobs available (usually in local government) require a level of education and skills that the household lacks.

The population growth-induced demand for non-farm employment paired with a very limited supply results in further softening of the labor market and a decline in rural wages. Lower non-farm wages and the inability to raise (or even maintain) agricultural productivity amount to a reduction in the alternatives open to labor. Under an open-access regime, reduction in these employment possibilities results in increased encroachment on natural resources until a new open-access equilibrium is established in which the resource base is smaller and

BOX 1. JAVA: A CASE OF MUTED RESPONSE TO POPULATION PRESSURE

Java's population quadrupled during the last 100 years to reach 100 million people today, resulting in one of the world's highest population densities. Millions of landless and near-landless Javanese maintain intense pressure on the uplands, while large numbers of underemployed migrants and homeless city dwellers exert an equally intense pressure on the urban environment. The government has pursued vigorous population policies to reduce fertility and to promote out-migration to the outer islands. However, even under the most successful scenario, population policies cannot reduce the already severe pressures in Java that result in rapid deterioration of watersheds and soil erosion, which ranges between 23 and 38 millimeters per year, more than 10 times the average rate of soil formation. Moreover, considering the poverty and fragility of soils in the outer islands, transmigration may not amount to much more than export of environmental degradation from Java to the outer islands. Indeed, many transmigrants were located on lands that could not sustain annual cultivation with consequent rapid decline in yields and incomes; in response, settlers reverted to shifting cultivation and petty logging already produced by native inhabitants. One set of environmental problems in Java has simply been exchanged for another set of equally severe problems on the outer islands.

A correct diagnosis would have attributed the degradation of the uplands in Java to economic rather than demographic failures. "People cultivate unsuitable lands with low and declining yields for lack of better opportunities, either in rural or urban labor markets."[1] A remarkable economic growth of almost 8 percent during the 1970s and early 1980s was not translated into a proportionate increase in employment. In Java, employment grew at one-third the growth of output and two-thirds the growth of the labor force. While Javanese agriculture has reached its limits in terms of labor absorption, the nonagricultural sector failed to create adequate numbers of new jobs to absorb the new entrants into the labor force because of a policy bias in favor of capital-intensive heavy industries.

The result has been persistent labor surplus both in urban and rural areas, softening of the labor market, and depression of real wages. Predictably, the economic and demographic pressure on the open-access uplands and eroding watersheds intensified. Since the uplands received little development assistance such as irrigation infrastructure, research, and extension, and had limited access to markets, the productivity and profitability of upland agriculture remained low or declined. The scarcity of rural credit prevented upland farmers from investing in land improvement, higher productivity inputs, soil conservation, and such measures as terracing, shelter plantings, and mixed tree cropping systems. Under these circumstances, environmental degradation predictably takes place regardless of population growth.

Recent policy reforms in Indonesia have reduced the policy bias against upland farmers and labor-intensive industry; interest rates have been relaxed, rural credit programs introduced, and the relative price structure changed to favor the use of labor. As a result, Java is now in a better position to absorb its growing labor force despite the phasing out of the large-scale, state-sponsored transmigration program.

....

[1] R. Repetto, "Soil Loss and Population Pressure on Java," *Ambio*, Vol. 15, No. 1 (1986).

more degraded, and the resource-dependent population is larger and more impoverished. One familiar household response is to shorten the fallow cycle—a response that undermines future productivity and sustainability.[12]

Rural to Urban Migration

This need not be the outcome of population growth if yet another avenue remains open. If industries and jobs do not come to the rural area despite low wages, the household may attempt to accommodate the additional child by moving to a large urban center in search of employment. Mobility is severely constrained, however, if the land cannot be sold (except perhaps at a great loss), and if credit cannot be secured to finance the costs of relocation and the acquisition of new skills. Limited education is an additional barrier. Furthermore, governments, labor unions, and urban elites, in an effort to safeguard their benefits from adverse rural-urban terms of trade, higher wages, and exclusive access to public services and infrastructure, create administrative or political barriers to rural-urban migration. Despite these barriers, large numbers of rural inhabitants, pushed out by a depleting resource base and declining incomes, and pulled by the prospect of high-wage employment and public services, find their way to the large urban centers. At the same time, the strong urban bias of economic and investment policies in most developing countries, notably in Sub-Saharan Africa, causes a "land flight." Some succeed, many fail. Formal employment is scarce and well protected; housing is only available to those who can afford it.

Many migrants, lacking both capital and skills, find accommodation in squatter settlements and employment in the informal sector, both of which are subject to the same rule of capture—a rule that favors larger families. Whether as vendors, street hawkers, scavengers, or beggars, there is an advantage to having a larger number of children, as long as ownership is established mainly by capture. Public property, open spaces, unused private property, urban infrastructure, and the general urban environment become the new open-access resources to be captured and appropriated for household use. Crowded urban slums, squatter settlements, unsanitary conditions, uncollected solid waste, anaerobic rivers, congestion, and overburdened infrastructure are the urban equivalents—the urban manifestations—of deforestation, soil erosion, overfishing, overgrazing, degraded watersheds, and other rural environmental problems left behind. The congestion and pollution of cities such as Manila, Bangkok, and Mexico City are a mirror image of the degradation of the rural resource base.[13]

Open-access resources are fewer and the rule of capture weaker in urban settings than in rural areas; this may be one reason why fertility rates are commonly lower.[14]

Again, it is tempting to blame population growth for rural-to-urban migration and for the degradation of the urban environment, but this is largely a symptom of severely constrained responses to the interlocking forces of poverty and environmental degradation in the face of massive institutional and policy failures that are biased against agriculture and in favor of urban areas.[15] Of course, whatever the degree of responsiveness, the more rapidly population grows, the larger the rural-to-urban migration and consequent urban environmental degradation, especially when urban responsiveness is also constrained.

COMMUNITY RESPONSES TO POPULATION GROWTH

Communities have traditionally recognized the problem of overexploitation of open-access resources, and have sought to establish communal management systems that exclude outsiders, and regulate the use by insiders. They try to prevent the loss of profitability and the destruction of resources caused by excessive harvesting. These systems, based on social functions, peer group pressures, taboos, and customs, implicitly or explicitly assign community members rights of access and responsibilities 1) to protect communal resources from encroachment by outsiders, and 2) to regulate individual use of the resource in the interest of the community welfare. Examples include forests in Papua New Guinea, fisheries in Sri Lanka and the Côte d'Ivoire, and land in Kenya, Ghana, and Rwanda.[16]

Traditional Resource Management Systems

Increased population pressure from within the community is accommodated by expanding communal resources (claiming a larger area of surrounding lands and forests for the community) and/or tightening the rules of harvesting and introducing more active management. Sharing systems are introduced to insure members against growing risks of crop failures due to cultivation of increasingly marginal lands or shorter fallows, and to ensure a more equitable distribution of resources in the face of growing scarcity.[17]

Another possible response to growing population pressures on community resources is a community decision to terminate open-access grazing rights and to practice stall-feeding of livestock. Because it is a community decision, no fencing is necessary, thus significantly containing the transaction costs of the enclosure of the commons. The community may further improve the pastures by calling on its members to contribute labor to planting forage grasses. This is practiced, for example, among communities on the overgrazed hills around Phera Tal Lake in Nepal.

When fuelwood resources become depleted, communities may establish village woodlots and when local watersheds are threatened, communities may introduce management and rehabilitation of local watersheds. In India, for example, villages have successfully created forest-related employment opportunities and protected the forests from encroachment (Box 2). In northern Thailand, villages have protected their water resources for rice irrigation through the establishment of protected forest areas in local watersheds and systems of management known as *muang fai*.[18] In Katheka, Kenya, community self-help groups (mostly women) have undertaken self-funded projects such as terracing land, digging cut-off drains, installing check dams, and planting trees to control soil erosion, improve water catchment, and increase food production (Box 3).[19]

The Disintegration of Traditional Systems

Traditional resource management systems began to disintegrate in modern times as a result of commercialization, introduction of new technologies, and assertion of state ownership over forests, water, and other natural resources in disregard of traditional customary rights and communal management systems. Without official sanctioning of these rights, communities have been unable to defend their resources against external forces such as encroachment from commercial interests or from other communities. Under these circumstances, communal ownership degenerates into open-access, and additional children again become an asset rather than a liability to the household and the community, though detrimental in broader social terms.

Population growth can be accommodated by a rural community, even in the absence of a land frontier, if there are alternative employment opportunities either in the proximity of the community or in the urban centers. The response to population growth has often been limited by barriers to mobility (including the lack of education) and subsidization of capital intensity in industry and services. The role of rapid population growth itself in the disintegration of traditional management systems cannot be ruled out a priori. Aside from rising transaction costs (i.e., the costs of collective decisionmaking, monitoring, and enforcement) with growing community population, encroachment

BOX 2. THE ARABARI EXPERIMENT IN INDIA: COMMUNAL RESOURCES MANAGEMENT

India's Arabari experiment began in West Bengal in 1970 as a response to rapid deforestation in that region. The objective of the experiment was to discover how to stop villagers from encroaching on the forest for illegal firewood. Interviews with 1,300 people in eleven villages revealed that villagers were earning much of their income from the illegal cutting and selling of firewood.

The experiment offered the villagers forest-related employment opportunities from which they could earn at least as much as they earned from forest encroachment. The villagers were employed in planting trees and grasses on blank patches. Planting was scheduled to take place during the low-employment season. The government arranged for outside sources to provide fuelwood and construction poles to the villagers at cost. In addition, through a revenue-sharing agreement with the Forest Department, the villagers received 25 percent of the selling price of mature trees in cash. The responsibility of protecting the forest from encroachment was also entrusted to the villagers. Institutional arrangements were made for the election of representatives from among the villagers to monitor the work and to collect and distribute payments.

Following these changes, the villagers enforced total protection of the forest, and they themselves refrained from illegal cutting. They imposed and enforced a reduction of firewood cutting and introduced watching and patrolling by villagers. After 15 years, the degraded forests were rehabilitated, the villagers were markedly better off, and their relations with the Forest Department improved. Gradually the experiment was expanded to more villages and by 1989 there were more than 700 groups, or Village Protection Committees, protecting more than 70,000 hectares of degraded lands that were planted to forests in West Bengal. "The will to do so developed as these groups believed in the assurance of sustained benefits."[1] Similar success with small user groups has been reported in Nepal, Indonesia, and Niger.

These success stories show that for collective action to succeed, the following conditions must be met:

1) A link must be created between a well-defined small group and a well-defined piece of forest land;

2) The group members must perceive a clear correlation between their contributions and their returns;

3) Both authority and benefits flowing from resource management must be restricted to members of the group to the exclusion of outsiders and free riders;[2] and

4) Group cooperation must be established according to the particular communities' degree of social cohesion and experience with collective action.

. . . .

[1]A.K. Banerjee, *A Case of Group Formation in Forest Management*, Mimeo, June 1989.
[2]M.M. Cernea, *User Groups as Producers in Participatory Afforestation Strategies*, Development Discussion Paper No. 319 (Cambridge, MA: Harvard Institute for International Development, 1989).

BOX 3. KENYA: A COMMUNITY RESPONDS TO ENVIRONMENTAL DEGRADATION

In 1973, soil erosion had reached nearly intolerable levels in Katheka, Kenya, which has an annual rainfall of 400 to 600 millimeters. Tree removal was rampant and soil conservation efforts were nonexistent. Voluntary women's groups known as *mwethya*, or self-help groups, had been organized for centuries in times of need. During colonial times, however, the tradition had all but disappeared. For unknown reasons, the *mwethya* witnessed a resurgence in the mid-1970s. Within a few years the groups—predominantly women—were actively working and results were beginning to show.[1]

Since the early 1980s, volunteer self-help groups in Katheka have contributed significantly to controlling soil erosion, improving water catchment, and increasing food production. Fifteen volunteer groups, including 12 women's groups, meet twice weekly to work on a group member's farm and to carry out community projects.[2] Projects, which are often self-funded, have included terracing land, digging cut-off drains, and installing check dams.

The *mwethya* have led to increased environmental awareness among women. Respondents to a village survey almost unanimously commented that soil conservation increases water retention and, consequently, food production. They also agreed that terracing is critical to sustaining and increasing yields. This awareness leads to more efficient farming practices and more sustainable food production.

Decisionmaking and implementation are solely the responsibility of the groups. As a result, the women are invested with a strong sense of leadership and responsibility. It is they who benefit from the more efficient practices they choose to adopt. The groups are organized with incentives for participation. If, for example, a member misses two or three work sessions, the group skips that person's farm during the course of the rotation.

Katheka residents have practiced effective resource management within the confines of the *mwethya*, but they do not have the management capabilities or access to economic resources to combat external forces. Indeed, whenever external forces become involved, trouble seems to arise. For example, Nairobi businesses often send trucks to dig sand from the dry riverbeds. As a result of the sand removal, less water can be stored for the dry season. Dams built by the *mwethya* are rendered useless, and the riverbed lining is removed, increasing the rate of water flow during rainstorms and raising the rate of soil being carried away.

Despite these problems, the *mwethya* of Katheka remain mobilized to institute effective resource management. When such groups are invested with the ultimate responsibility for success or failure, the results are often positive. As farmers witness sustainable increased yields due to more efficient practices, they learn the value of resource management and conservation.

. . . .

[1]Program for International Development, Clark University, in cooperation with National Environment Secretariat, Ministry of Environment and Natural Resources, Government of Kenya, *Resources, Management Population and Local Institutions in Katheka: A Case Study of Effective Natural Resources Management in Machakos, Kenya* (Worcester, MA: Clark University, 1988).
[2]As of July 1987, there were 15 groups with 400 members, all but 40 of whom were women.

by growing neighboring communities or migration among rural areas has contributed to the degeneration of communal property into an open-access resource. For example, in Côte d'Ivoire, massive upland immigration of Saharan farmers into open-access forests has resulted in deforestation, land disputes, and diminished incentives for land conservation and management.[20]

ACCOMMODATING POPULATION GROWTH WITHIN THE NATIONAL ECONOMY

In a closed and stagnant economy with fixed natural resources, no capital accumulation, and no technological change, population size determines the standard of living as well as the state of natural resources and the environment. In such an economy, population growth translates into a roughly proportional decline in social welfare and depletion of natural resources. Even with zero population growth, economic growth is only sustainable if current resource use is at or below the maximum sustainable yield of renewable resources. Even this assumes maximum efficiency in the harvest and use of such resources. Nonrenewable resources, on the other hand, can make only a temporary contribution to the economy, since they are by definition depletable. A steady state is determined by the natural productivity of forests, fisheries, and agricultural land. Harvesting in excess of the maximum sustainable yields leads to a reduction in future resources and yields, and hence to a reduction in future consumption levels to a lower steady state.

Even in a closed economy without technological change, efforts will be made to accommodate population growth and economize on dwindling natural resources. As long as resource commodity prices reflect the true scarcity of resources, the increased demand from a larger population will lead to higher resource prices and efforts to economize by improving efficiency, reducing waste, and substituting depleting natural resources with more abundant human and capital resources (Figure 1). This means that population growth need not result in proportional depletion of natural resources, although without growth in productivity, living standards are likely to be affected since substitution is not costless. Moreover, without trade and technological progress, substitution possibilities are severely limited. In such a closed economy, population interventions have a direct bearing on natural resources, the environment, and the population's standard of living.

In a more open economy with trade, technological change, and economic growth, there is no simple and direct relationship between population growth on the one hand and resource depletion and environmental degradation on the other. The maximum sustainable yield of renewable natural resources no longer determines the economy's production possibilities or the maximum level of consumption available to be shared among the population.

International trade provides access to natural resources and the environment of other countries, both directly and indirectly. Importing natural resource commodities can result either in the conservation of domestic resources or in a higher level of consumption. It also eliminates the environmental costs of resource extraction at home. Importing final products eliminates the environmental costs of resource processing and industrial production; only the environmental cost of consumption remains. Of course, the other side of international trade is the greater depletion rates and increased environmental degradation experienced by exporting countries than would have been the case in the absence of trade. However, as long as international trade is based on comparative advantage *inclusive* of depletion and environmental costs, both importing and exporting countries are better off. Additionally, a higher standard of living is possible for a larger population than in closed economies. Thus, in the presence of international trade, population growth in a country no longer implies increased resource depletion or heightened environmental degradation in that country, although in the absence of technological change it might imply this for resource exporting countries and the world as a whole.

Technological change further breaks the link between population growth and the environment. On the one hand, technology improves resource recovery and use efficiency and expands substitution possibilities in both production and consumption, and thus conserves scarce natural resources. On the other hand, technology has two potential further effects: it develops new materials, products, and production processes that generate pollutants such as toxics that harm the environment more profoundly and persistently than traditional biodegradable pollutants do, while simultaneously providing the means to treat and safely dispose of both new and traditional pollutants. The key to the role of technology in both resource conservation and pollution control is the extent to which market prices reflect resource scarcities and environmental costs and benefits. Population growth may induce technological change if the increased demand for natural resources results in higher prices and hence incentives for innovation. There will be little technological response and efficiency improvement if population growth is at the expense of common property or unpriced resources, or if the consumption of natural resources is subsidized. In such a case, increased resource depletion and environmental degradation are certain to result from population growth. Under circumstances of open-access, underpricing, or subsidized use of resources, however, depletion, degradation, and unsustainable development is inevitable even with no population growth (Figure 1).

Analytically, the linkage between population growth and the environment can be divided into two separate effects: 1) the effect of population growth on economic growth, poverty, and income distribution, and 2) the effect of the latter three on the environment. The first effect has been discussed in detail elsewhere in this volume (e.g., the Overview and Chapter 3). This chapter focuses on the second part of the linkage—the effect of economic growth, poverty, and income distribution on the environment.

Population Growth, Economic Growth, and the Environment

As discussed by Cassen, Kelley, and McGreevey in this volume, rapid population growth, in some countries and time-periods at least, may be associated with downward pressure on wages and worsening distribution of income, if not actual negative effects on income per capita. This is mainly due, where it occurs, to spreading of capital over a larger number of workers or difficulties in raising the quantity and quality of investments in education and health. On the positive side, population growth may afford economies of scale and specialization. Some positive effects operate through the age-distribution of the population: when the proportion of people of working age is high relative to the number of dependents (children and old people), the presence of larger numbers of people is more likely to be beneficial. For this reason, when fertility is declining, the effect of past high fertility working its way through to the labor-force age-group can be positive. At a later stage, continuing fertility decline will make for an aging population, and the effect can turn negative again (though this stage is inevitable if populations are not to grow indefinitely).

The positive stage is exemplified by the recent history of Thailand, which experienced rapid population growth in the 1950s and 1960s and steep fertility decline in the 1970s and 1980s, and is now enjoying the dual benefit of high population participation in the labor force, and a growing savings rate and rising educational expenditures per child. A number of micro-level studies suggest that these demographic and behavioral changes are having an increasingly positive effect on economic growth.[21] More research is needed at the macro level.

If it is true that continuous rapid population growth is detrimental to the growth of per capita incomes, while past population growth is beneficial to the economy once fertility decline sets in, then the ultimate impact of population on the environment depends on the impact made by economic growth. The relationship between economic growth and the environment is therefore neither simple nor unidirectional.

In a closed economy with a limited resource base and static technology, continuous economic growth inevitably results in natural resource depletion and environmental degradation because the opportunities for improved efficiency and substitution are limited. In an open economy, especially one small enough not to influence the rest of the world by its behavior, economic growth can be beneficial or destructive to the domestic resource base and the environment depending on the prevailing institutional arrangements for costing resource use and environmental "externalities."[22] If there are secure, exclusive, and transferable property rights to all natural resources,[23] if environmental externalities are accounted for and internalized, and if economic growth is equitably distributed, then the effects of economic growth on the environment are likely to be beneficial for several reasons.[24]

First, the opportunity for international trade has several beneficial impacts on domestic natural resources and the environment once these resources are efficiently priced: 1) Scarce resources can be imported from countries where they are more abundant and hence less costly, thereby conserving domestic resources for the future and as sources of environmental amenities at higher levels of income; imports of required natural resources eliminate the environmental damage from resource extraction. 2) New technologies can be imported enabling improved resource recovery, higher use efficiency, and greater scope for substitution. 3) The country, if not rich in natural resources, can specialize in non-resource-intensive production such as electronics and services, while under closed economy conditions it is forced to produce all commodities regardless of comparative advantage. 4) Imports of resource-intensive or pollution-intensive intermediate and final products spare the country the environmental pollution generated during the production process. (The argument that trade simply shifts resource depletion and environmental costs to other countries is not valid if resource prices reflect true scarcities and social costs in the exporting countries; if they do not, it is not the responsibility of the importing country to make sure that they do.)

Second, economic growth occurring in the context of efficient and fairly complete markets that *fully reflect resource scarcities and social costs* is derived from specialization, improved efficiency, and increased productivity rather than from liquidation of natural resource assets; increasingly scarce resources are economized and more

FIGURE 1. POLICY AND MARKET SUCCESSES AND FAILURES IN RESPONDING TO RESOURCE SCARCITY AND ENVIRONMENTAL DEGRADATION

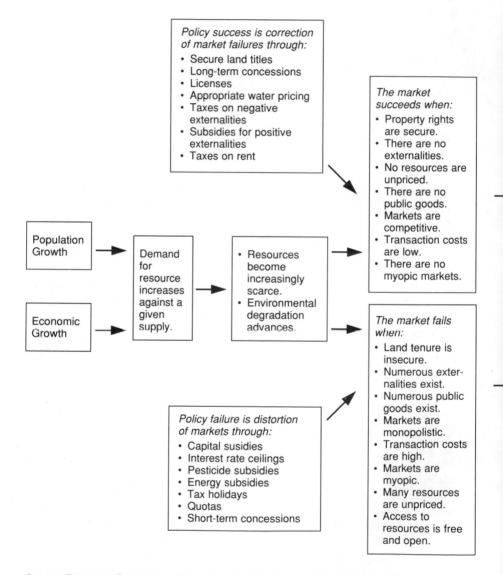

Source: Theodore Panayotou, *Green Markets: The Economies of Sustainable Development* (San Francisco: Institute for Contemporary Studies Press, 1993).

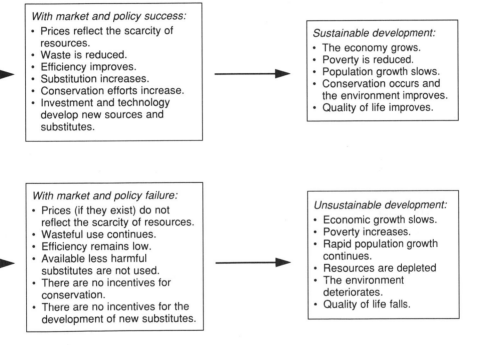

With market and policy success:
- Prices reflect the scarcity of resources.
- Waste is reduced.
- Efficiency improves.
- Substitution increases.
- Conservation efforts increase.
- Investment and technology develop new sources and substitutes.

Sustainable development:
- The economy grows.
- Poverty is reduced.
- Population growth slows.
- Conservation occurs and the environment improves.
- Quality of life improves.

With market and policy failure:
- Prices (if they exist) do not reflect the scarcity of resources.
- Wasteful use continues.
- Efficiency remains low.
- Available less harmful substitutes are not used.
- There are no incentives for conservation.
- There are no incentives for the development of new substitutes.

Unsustainable development:
- Economic growth slows.
- Poverty increases.
- Rapid population growth continues.
- Resources are depleted
- The environment deteriorates.
- Quality of life falls.

abundant resources are substituted. Under such conditions economic growth becomes a continuous process of structural transformation from natural-resource-intensive sectors to human-capital-and-technology-intensive sectors. This has been the experience of the United States and other developed countries.[25]

Third, as incomes grow the demand for environmental amenities rises; an efficient market and public sector would respond by increasing supplies of these amenities through conservation, increased pollution abatement, and investment in environmental assets and services. One difficulty with natural environments, especially in the tropics, is irreversibility. If an environmental resource (e.g., a rain forest) is destroyed during earlier stages of development when the demand for environmental amenities does not justify its preservation, it cannot later be recreated. While efficient markets are likely to anticipate this future demand and capitalize it into their current portfolio of assets, the market response is certain to be suboptimal because of higher private than social discount rates, and the public-good nature of many environmental amenities. This suggests a critical role for the public sector to discourage irreversible destruction of fragile environments and to augment the provision of environmental amenities through public investments.

Economic growth under conditions of efficient markets, full environmental costing (mitigated market failures and minimized market distortions), and free trade help conserve the natural environment. In contrast, economic growth in the presence of pervasive market failures and policy distortions is a sure prescription for environmental destruction. Under such conditions, liquidation of natural resources and conversion of private costs into social costs, rather than efficiency, productivity, and innovation, is the shortest route to profits and growth; population interventions and demographic shifts that contribute to economic growth could turn out to be detrimental to the environment. Extending and improving education, however, is almost always beneficial to the environment because it enlarges people's opportunities beyond dependence on natural resources and is likely to enhance environmental awareness.

The absence of economic growth, or economic decline, on the other hand, has detrimental effects on the environment because it limits people's opportunities to natural-resource-based activities, increasing their dependence on a limited resource base, and because it makes conservation and environmental protection an ill-afforded luxury. The experiences of Africa throughout the 1980s and of the Philippines during the mid-1980s are cases in point. Rapid population growth and chronic economic stagnation have brought about unprecedented environmental degradation that now constrains economic recovery. In fact, during the 1980s the Philippines and part of Sub-Saharan Africa experienced reverse structural change, with people moving back into primary resource sectors, including shifting cultivation, hunting, and gathering of resource products for subsistence.[26] The failure of distorted markets to reflect the true cost of mismanaged resources is as central to a stagnant economy as to a growing one. The experience of Eastern European countries, which experienced both economic and environmental mismanagement, is instructive. Of course, with regard to carbon dioxide emissions, western nations have not performed any better. This is to be expected since the global environmental costs are a "pure" case of a market failure.

Are There Limits to Growth?

Population cannot continue to grow exponentially forever. This is a truism, since the space on earth is finite and mass interplanetary migration is unlikely. It is also virtually impossible that population will grow to levels that would trigger Malthusian famines as an automatic population control mechanism. Despite predictions to the contrary, the world has been able to expand food production faster than population growth. Famines occur periodically, but they have been mostly isolated cases due to bad weather, civil war, destruction of livelihood, lack of infrastructure, or poor food distribution systems—not limits to production. Malthusian famines are extremely unlikely to materialize, since the world can bring to bear enormous technological, institutional, economic, and social innovation and infrastructure to address such impending catastrophes.

What will prevent the world's population from coming perilously close to a Malthusian catastrophe? Demographic transition from high to low population growth is a regular feature of economic and social development. From an environmental perspective, it is preferable that this transition takes place earlier rather than later. However, this requires three interrelated facets of development: 1) an economic growth rate that exceeds the population growth rate and allows improvement in living standards; 2) steady reduction of poverty, with particular emphasis on the education and employment of women; and 3) enhanced household, community, and economy-wide responsiveness to population growth. All three conditions, in turn, require removal of distortionary and discriminatory policies, institutional reform, and correction or mitigation of market failures.

These prescriptions raise three questions. The first question can be stated as follows: *Is exponential economic growth as impossible as exponential population growth, since the physical stock of resources is finite and the environment's capacity to assimilate wastes is limited?*

Unlike population growth, economic growth can continue indefinitely despite finite resources, without despoiling the environment. If *all* economic activities are charged the *full* cost of the resource depletion (scarcity value) and of the environmental damage they cause, there would be 1) less depletion and damage; 2) more resources to deal with residual problems; and 3) induced institutional and technological innovation to economize on scarce resources and to minimize environmental damage.

In the short run, growth would slow down and even stop if such additional costs are imposed on economic activity, especially if the costs of resource depletion and environmental damage are imposed suddenly. If, however, these costs are introduced gradually, allowing time for adjustment, the most likely result would be slower growth, but significant structural change away from capital- and resource-intensive, highly polluting industries to cleaner, resource-saving, labor-intensive and/or information-based industries and services. Long-term economic growth would be increased rather than reduced, since damages would be lower, and real resources otherwise expended on defensive and remedial measures would be saved and used to increase productivity and growth. Moreover, well-being would be enhanced even if growth did slow down. The finiteness of the earth's resources presents no absolute limit to economic growth as long as scarcity is fully reflected in prices, while technology and institutions are free to respond.

Technology, through increased efficiency, improved recovery, and new discoveries as well as substitution has so economized on resources such as energy and minerals, whose prices reflect scarcity, that their real price today is lower than 30 years ago despite the tripling of the world's real economic output. Technology has performed less well with products such as tropical timber, water, and other unpriced environmental resources. Had the price of fossil fuels reflected not only their scarcity but also environmental damage, cleaner alternatives would have been available at competitive cost. Even without the impetus of full-cost pricing, photovoltaics and thermal-solar power are almost competitive with fossil fuels.

It may be argued that sustainable use of natural resources is not the same as expanded use; many resources cannot be expanded beyond a certain point (one cannot, for example, make fish populations grow exponentially). While this is true, it misses the point. Economic growth can continue despite resource limits because of improvements in recovery and use efficiency and the development of substitutes. Only in the case of resources such as biodiversity, for which there are no substitutes and the loss is irreversible, can technology not play a direct role; but it still can have an indirect role through the development of products and processes that have minimal impact on resources. For example, tropical forests can be preserved through the development of alternative non-resource-based economic activities. But this can only happen if the subsidies on logging, ranching, and agricultural conversion are removed, and if these activities are charged for the loss of biodiversity and ecological functions of the forest.

Global environmental impacts such as climate change and ozone depletion can be addressed by including global environmental damage in the price of such products as fossil fuels and by phasing out other products such as chlorofluorocarbons (CFCs). The opposition of sovereign states and the absence of a "global government" make progress on the concept of internalizing global environmental costs difficult; yet the experience of the last two years, during which a number of environmental agreements have been reached, including the Montreal Protocol, the Global Environmental Facility, the Biodiversity Convention, etc., is a ground for optimism. Carbon taxes and internationally tradable emission permits unthinkable only five years ago are being seriously considered today.

The second question raised is as follows: *Considering the institutional weaknesses in many developing countries, how likely are they to undertake the policy reforms and institutional changes needed to speed up social response and demographic transition?*

The question is not whether national and global policy changes will eventually take place, but whether they will happen fast enough to avoid large losses or irreversible changes to local and global ecosystems. The weak demand for policy reform and the institutional weakness in many developing (and some developed) countries pose the greatest threat to the environment through inefficiency, underdevelopment, and delayed demographic transition. A combination of wrong diagnosis of the problem, limited analytical and institutional capability, vested interests, and sheer inertia limit both effective demand for and supply of policy reform and institutional change. A low-level equilibrium results, perpetuating the vicious circle of underdevelopment, rapid population growth, and environmental degradation.

Even under these circumstances, prediction of a Malthusian outcome is unwarranted. Experience suggests that eventually misguided policies are exposed, market failures become apparent, real causes surface, vested interests shift, institutional capacity is strengthened, and the demand for policy reform grows. Yet the lost time is not without consequences. Countries find themselves with a larger population, a smaller resource base, and an obviously more difficult task.

The final question can be posed: *Is population growth itself one of the factors that limits responsiveness and makes reform more difficult? Would actively promoted family planning make sense to keep population growth at a low level until the country builds its capacity to reform?*

While population growth tends to complicate and exacerbate environmental problems, reduction of the growth rate in the absence of other measures may not result in reduced pressure on natural resources. There is certainly no justification for coercive measures of population "control," for several reasons. First, even if fertility declines immediately, it takes many years for the reduction in numbers to be large enough to make a major difference. Second, any reduction in fertility is unlikely to be sustainable in the long run without changes in the determinants of the demand for children; the presence of open-access resources can itself encourage low-income families to have more rather than fewer children. Third, if resources remain underpriced, any reduction in pressure on them resulting from slower population growth may be taken up by others, especially commercial interests that stand to profit from underpricing. Fourth, population pressure on limited resources may be the lever that induces much-needed policy reform, institutional change, and technological innovation; relieving the pressure could extend the life of unsustainable policies.

Actions to reduce population and to protect the environment must therefore go hand-in-hand and should consist of the following measures: 1) as far as the environment is concerned, the emphasis of outside assistance and pressure should be primarily on policy reform and capacity building; 2) to accelerate the demographic transition, family planning services should be made available to those who want and need them; and 3) social and economic change that helps create demand for family planning should be emphasized; this should especially include education, health, and employment measures that benefit women, and appropriate reforms in environmental pricing.

Income Distribution, Poverty, and Environment

Patently inequitable distribution of income, even in a rapidly growing economy, means that a part of the country or a section of the population is not experiencing growth, but stagnation or economic decline. In most developing countries, this would mean that a large proportion of the population is experiencing persisting or worsening poverty. The negative impact of poverty on the environment is well established: 1) their future insecure, poor people tend to make decisions that meet current needs and discount the future heavily; 2) there is little demand for environmental amenities at subsistence levels and environmental expenditures are considered ill-afforded luxuries; 3) poor people lack the technology to exploit and use natural resources efficiently; 4) poor people lack access to institutional credit to invest in land improvements, perennial crops, and soil conservation; and 5) poor people's ability to save, educate their children, and obtain alternative employment is severely limited.

Studies in Thailand, the Philippines, and elsewhere have found that poverty (along with population density) is a major cause of deforestation. In Bangkok and Manila, poverty among slum dwellers, squatters, and workers in the informal sector is a major, albeit not the only, source of environmental problems, such as congestion, water pollution, and uncollected solid waste. To the extent that fertility decline has helped reduce poverty among the rural and urban poor, the environment has benefited. Interventions that help improve population quality would have further beneficial effects on the environment by enlarging people's opportunities, especially when combined with increased entitlements such as land titling and more access to formal employment.

However, not only absolute poverty, but also relative poverty is detrimental to the environment. Income levels throughout the country may improve with economic growth, but if the income gap between rural and urban areas, or between agriculture and industry, or between one region and another is chronically widened, the environment is likely to suffer. Rising expectations, fueled by general economic growth, the mass media, and changing consumption patterns in urban areas within an environment of vastly diverging opportunity costs and limited mobility may encourage exploitative behavior toward the resource base and the environment. Examples include shortening the fallow cycle, premature tree harvest, and diverting conservation expenditures to the acquisition of consumer durables such as vehicles and modern housing. Widening income disparity also may accelerate migration (further overwhelming urban infrastructure), expand urban slums, and exacerbate social tensions. Reduction in the size and adverse age distribution of the population, brought about by fertility decline, may help narrow the widening income gap and thereby lessen the pressure on the environment. Qualitative population interventions such as educational upgrading and training, increased environmental awareness, and local participation in environmental improvement could reinforce the underlying trends brought about by quantitative demographic changes.

EMPIRICAL EVIDENCE OF THE POPULATION–ENVIRONMENT LINK

Much of the empirical evidence of the relationship between population density (or growth) and environmental degradation is found in studies that attempt to explain variations in deforestation among locations and over time, with most finding that population density (or growth) contributes significantly to deforestation, either directly or through interaction with other determinants of deforestation such as poverty and government policies. Soil erosion and pollution provide additional evidence.

Deforestation

A 1992 econometric study of the causes of deforestation in northeast Thailand during the period 1973 to 1982 found that population density was the most important factor leading to deforestation, followed by wood price and poverty.[27] Other determinants were low farm yields and location. The dominance of population as a cause of deforestation should be expected in Thailand's poorest and most populous region; both population density and population growth are relatively high, non-farm activities are scarce, and soil fertility is poor. While there is a large flow of seasonal and permanent migration out of the northeast, clearing forest to acquire agricultural land continues to be the most attractive alternative for most new entrants into the labor force, as it requires no cash outlay or special skills.

Another channel through which increasing population density was found to contribute to deforestation in northeast Thailand is the shortening of the fallow cycle from 10 to 15 years to 4 to 6 years, a process that inhibits forest regeneration and gradually converts the swidden lands into grasslands. In response, shifting cultivators move on to clear new plots of forest land, leading to increased deforestation. Since newly opened lands tend to be of lower quality and more fragile, they may require longer fallow cycles to regenerate; instead, increasing population density forces even shorter fallow cycles.

Furthermore, farmers, who account for 90 percent of the northeast population, prefer the use of fuelwood over other sources of energy, such as kerosene, that require a cash outlay. The higher the kerosene price, the higher the rate of deforestation, other things being equal.

The stagnation and absolute decline of rural incomes in parts of northeast Thailand during the 1970s and early 1980s were also found to be important contributors to forest loss. A 10 percent decline in real incomes per capita was found to result in a 4 percent decline in forest cover, reflecting an increased demand for farmland and fuelwood.

A second study on the causes of deforestation in northeast Thailand extending the study period to 1988 had similar results.[28] Again, population emerged as a significant contributor to deforestation, with a 10 percent increase in the rate of population growth resulting in a 3.3 percent increase in deforestation. Poverty, crop prices, and location were also statistically significant contributing factors.

It is tempting to conclude that, at least for northeast Thailand during the 1970s and 1980s, population was a significant cause of deforestation. However, four other factors prevented people from responding to growing population density in alternative ways: 1) the open-access status of forest resources combined with stagnating or falling real rural incomes; 2) the insecurity of land tenure and corresponding lack of access to credit for productivity-raising investments in land improvement; 3) scarcity of off-farm employment in rural northeast Thailand; and 4) low levels of education and skills, limiting mobility. Indeed, a household level analysis confirmed the importance of education and security of land ownership to rural income in northeast Thailand and, indirectly, their importance in stemming forest encroachment and deforestation.[29]

A number of studies have attempted analysis of cross-section data at the country level. The results are mixed. One study, using data from 38 Sub-Saharan African countries, found a weak relationship between population growth rate and deforestation.[30] However, panel data for another study of the same set of countries using 1980 to 1989 data did not confirm a relationship between population and deforestation. Yet another study found a strong relationship between population growth and deforestation in four tropical developing countries;[31] however, it was the interaction between population and income per capita, rather than simply population density, that was a significant determinant of deforestation. This suggests that population density affects the environment differently at each stage of economic development. Indeed a rerun of the model with the addition of 27 developed countries reduced substantially both the magnitude and the significance of the extent to which population accounted for deforestation.

Another study used simple correlation and graphical analysis of cross-sectional national data to explore the relationship between population, land use, and the environment in developing countries, concluding that the relationship between population growth and deforestation is weak and dependent on the exclusion of particular "outlier" countries.[32] Analysis by this author using cross-sectional national data suggests a strong relationship between population density and loss of wildlife habitat, a weak relationship between population density and forest cover, and no relationship at all between cropland expansion and deforestation. However, there may be a relationship between *rates* of population growth and agricultural expansion: countries with population growth rates between 1.0 and 1.5 percent per annum have experienced a decline in agricultural area, while the reverse is true for countries with higher population growth rates.[33] Similarly, agricultural area expansion was positively related to population growth in another study after other factors such as agricultural trade, yield increases, and the degree of closure of the land frontier were controlled for.[34]

One analysis recommended that further studies focus on the sub-country or district level, or even better, at the household or farm level, for "that is the level at which resource use decisions are made, and households and farm units are the immediate actors whose behavior must be much better understood."[35] One such household-level study, using data from 419 households in two provinces in the Amazon in northeastern Ecuador, found that household size, land area, location, and length of residence are significant determinants of deforestation.[36]

Soils, Water, and Marine Pollution

Other manifestations of environmental degradation such as soil erosion and pollution have also received attention from studies seeking to test the population-environment nexus. Repetto, for example, found that increasing population density and limited economic opportunities in the urban areas of Java maintained pressure on the land, resulting in increased soil erosion and declining soil fertility (Box 1).

A substantial literature exploring the complex interactions of population and related food production on the environment describes mixed results. Increasing population density can go hand-in-hand with improving or worsening ecological conservation; environments can be degraded as a result of inappropriate prices and policies without increasing population density. In countries where there is no further high-quality land to be brought into cultivation, intensification of agricultural production can bring problems of rising environmental and economic costs, often related to increased use of chemical fertilizers and pesticides. Studies find both rising and falling costs. There is no inevitable tendency to worsening problems; much depends on the role of technology and appropriate incentives.[37]

A recent study of 42 rivers found a close correlation between the level of marine pollution from nitrates and the level of population in the watershed and predicted a 55 percent increase in river nitrate export as a result of doubling of population. While correlation does not imply causation (nor does simple regression analysis when several important variables are omitted), the results are fully consistent with the thesis of this chapter.[38] Given the absence of effective mechanisms to internalize the environmental costs of fertilizer use, sewage discharge, industrial and automotive emissions, and watershed disturbance (and the direct or indirect subsidization of the activities), it is not surprising that the larger the population, the larger the nitrate pollution. Yet the level of development (or at least the level of per capita income) and the strictness and enforcement of environmental regulations do play a role. However, since they are correlated and influence emissions in opposite directions, their omission biases the results in favor of a stronger population-nitrate emissions relationship than under a more complete specification. Again, population growth can be decoupled from increasing nitrate emissions if the associated damage is fully internalized to the offending activities.

A related study found that growth in the use of nitrogen parallels worldwide population growth, although there are significant variations by country depending on land availability and quality, on level of development, dietary habits, etc.[39] Because as much as 50 percent of the applied nitrogen finds its way into freshwater bodies and the sea and because no viable substitutes exist at present, the author is concerned that the probable increase of the world population by 1.9 billion over the next 20 years would result in a proportional increase in the use of synthetic nitrogen fertilizers and associated pollution problems. However, the facts that 50 percent of applied nitrogen leeches off into water bodies and that recovery efficiency varies from 20 to 70 percent suggest that there is enormous scope for increased efficiency and reduced application and associated waste. This indeed has taken place in Japan, where applications of nitrogen were reduced by 10 percent between 1960 and 1980, while agricultural production increased.[40] Nor does the use of fertilizer always lead to pollution problems. Lower groundwater in Japan has not been affected by one of the world's highest fertilization rates. With full cost pricing, proper application, and related land use management, the growth of agricultural production (whether population driven or not) can be decoupled from increased fertilizer use, which in turn can be decoupled from increased nitrogen leeching and loading on water systems.[41]

The situation with water resources is no different. While water faces competing demands from agriculture, industry, and urban growth, most countries, regardless of the degree of scarcity of water, continue to subsidize water for irrigation and other uses, and in many cases supply it free of charge. Even Indonesia, with one of the world's highest freshwater endowments per capita, faces water shortages that are invariably addressed through supply rather than demand management. India, Pakistan, Egypt, Jordan, Yemen, and Tunisia face severe water shortages concurrently with waterlogging and salinization due to overirrigation that has much to do with water subsidization and little to do with population growth. Water-use efficiency can at least be doubled, reducing water shortages and environmental problems related to overirrigation and agrochemical runoff, thereby accommodating both population and economic growth without bumping into near-term ecological thresholds.

SUMMARY AND CONCLUSIONS

In principle, population growth and rising density, within limits, need not lead to resource depletion and environmental degradation. The relationship between population and environment is neither immutable nor direct. It is mediated by mobility, access to markets, distribution of wealth, institutions, and government policies. Where these factors promote rapid and flexible responses, population growth can be combined with, or even promote, agricultural intensification, industrialization, and technological change culminating in sustainable development. Where markets are not functioning, mobility is restricted, land and wealth are skewedly distributed, and government policies counter or block the avenues of individual and social response, a low-level trap is artificially created where diminishing returns to land lead to resource depletion and degradation, rather than to investment and innovation.

Experience in Africa, Asia, and Latin America shows a variety of results from the interaction of population and the environment. Some countries—Korea, Taiwan, Chile, Mexico, Botswana, Kenya, Mauritius, and Zimbabwe—have to varying degrees broken the link between population growth and resource degradation through a combination of sustainable agricultural productivity growth (with favorable crop prices, security of land tenure, and availability of credit) and job creation outside agriculture. Other countries—India, the Philippines,

Honduras, Nicaragua, Peru, and much of Sub-Saharan Africa—have experienced slow agricultural growth, generally because of adverse policies (sometimes compounded by war, civil disturbance, and droughts); surplus labor has not been able to move out of agriculture due to the slow growth of employment elsewhere, itself often the result of misguided policies favoring capital-intensive industry.

Population has had its greatest impact on local ecosystems in poor, agrarian societies with undeveloped or incomplete markets, poor governance, distortionary policies, barriers to mobility, skewed distribution of income and assets, and severely limited economic opportunities. Even where the rate of population growth has declined quite rapidly, as in Sri Lanka and Thailand, environmental degradation has been comparable to that in other countries whose populations have been growing rapidly. The critical factor is whether or not the costs of environmental degradation have been brought into the decisionmaking of individuals and communities by suitable definition of property rights, pricing policies, and (where necessary) regulation; often the opposite has been the case, with price policies, taxes, and subsidies encouraging environmentally destructive behavior.

Population growth is most likely to put pressure on resources in the early stages of the demographic transition and reduce the capacity of economies and individuals to pay for environmental safeguards. Accelerating the demographic transition, by voluntary family planning programs and socioeconomic measures that make large numbers of children less desirable, is therefore thoroughly warranted. But it will not resolve environmental problems by itself; indeed, the presence of open-access resources is one of the factors that encourages large families.

To make local ecosystems sustainable as development proceeds, governments must pursue policy reforms that raise agricultural productivity and labor mobility. Such measures include secure and transferable land titles, liberalized interest rates and encouragement of rural credit, incentive crop-prices, and investment in rural infrastructure. At the same time, off-farm employment should be encouraged by removing protection and subsidies to capital-intensive industries; promoting export growth, especially in labor-intensive products; and spreading and improving education and training, particularly for women.

When women are better educated and have greater scope for employment, family income is increased, and large numbers of children limit mothers' earnings. Their children's nutrition and survival prospects improve, which also helps fertility to decline. Also, since women bear much of the burden of fuelwood, fodder, and water collection and the management of household and land resources, increasing their education and incomes is likely to lead to better resource management. Many of the policies needed for development, for population, and for preserving the environment are the same.

Notes

I am grateful to Robert Cassen for valuable suggestions, J.R. Seshazo for assistance with the research, and the Overseas Development Council for financial support. However, I do take sole responsibility for the views expressed, and for any errors or omissions.

[1] P.R. Ehrlich and A.H. Ehrlich, *The Population Explosion* (New York: Simon and Schuster, 1990).

[2] J. Simon, *Population Matters: People, Resources, Environment, and Immigration* (New Brunswick, NJ: Transaction Publishers, 1990).

[3] C.L. Jolly, *Four Theories of Population Change and Environment*, paper presented at meetings of the Population Association of America, Washington, DC, March 1991.

[4] R.P. Shaw, "The Impact of Population Growth on Environment: The Debate Heats Up," *Environmental Impact Assessment Review*, Vol. 12, Nos. 1 and 2 (1992), pp. 11-36.

[5] I use the terms "open-access" and "common property" interchangeably to refer to resources subject to free and open access by the general public. These terms are not to be confused, but contrasted, with "communal property," to which access and use is regulated by the community through customs and traditional rights.

[6] It is not necessarily optimal for individual members of the household either. As Cynthia Lloyd notes in Chapter 6 in this volume, individual children may be better off with fewer siblings.

[7] Of course, a large number of children is desired for other reasons as well. In a cash-scarce household with no access to capital markets, children are a source of family labor during planting and harvesting; in the absence of social safety nets such as social security and retirement, children serve as insurance and retirement assets. These factors, combined with high child mortality and the low status of women, serve to explain the strong preference for large families in some poor countries.

[8] E. Boserup, *The Conditions of Agricultural Growth: The Economics of Agrarian Change Under Population Pressure* (Chicago: Aldine, 1965).

[9] Gershon Feder, Tongroj Onchan, Yongyuth Chalamwong, and Chira Hongladarom, *Land Policies and Farm Productivity in Thailand* (Baltimore, MD: Johns Hopkins University Press, 1988).

[10] K.M. Cleaver and G.A. Schreiber, *The Population, Agriculture, and Environment Nexus in Sub-Saharan Africa*, Agriculture and Rural Development Series, No. 9 (Washington, DC: World Bank, 1993).

[11] M.C. Cruz, C.A. Meyer, R. Repetto, and R. Woodward, *Population Growth, Poverty, and Environmental Stress: Frontier Migration in the Philippines and Costa Rica* (Washington, DC: World Resources Institute, 1992).

[12] Shaw, op. cit.; and S.D. Mink, *Poverty, Population and the Environment*, World Bank Discussion Paper No. 189, (Washington, DC: World Bank, 1993); and Cleaver and Schreiber, op. cit.

[13] T. Panayotou, *Green Markets: The Economics of Sustainable Development* (San Francisco, CA: Institute for Contemporary Studies Press, 1993).

[14] Timothy Dyson, London School of Economics, personal communication.

[15] This was demonstrated with respect to watershed destruction in Java in R. Repetto, "Soil Loss and Population Pressure on Java," *Ambio*, Vol. 15, No. 1 (1986), and more generally in R. Repetto, *Economic Policy Reform for Natural Resource Conservation*, Environment Working Paper (Washington, DC: World Bank, May 1988).

[16] T. Panayotou, *Getting Incentives Right: Economic Instruments for Environmental Management in Developing Countries*, working paper (Cambridge, MA: Harvard Institute for International Development, 1992); T. Panayotou, *Green Markets: The Economies of Sustainable Development* (San Francisco, CA: Institute for Contemporary Studies Press, 1993); Mink, op. cit.; Cleaver and Schreiber, op. cit.

[17] Cleaver and Schreiber, op. cit.

[18] Sopin Tongpan and T. Panayotou, *Deforestation and Poverty: Can Commercial and Social Forestry Break the Vicious Circle* (Bangkok: Thailand Development Research Institute, 1990).

[19] M. Tiffen, M. Mortimore, and F. Gichuki, *More People, Less Erosion: Environmental Recovery in Kenya* (Chichester: Wiley and Sons, 1994).

[20] Cleaver and Schreiber, op. cit.

[21] Jere Behrman, with Chalongphob Sussangkarn, *Population and Economic Development in Thailand: Some Critical Household Behavioral Relations*, report for The Human Resources and Social Development Program, Thailand Development Research Institute, January 1989, revised July 1989; Jere Behrman, with Chalongphob Sussangkarn, *Do the More Wealthy Save Less?* (Bangkok: Thailand Development Research Institute, July 1989).

[22] Externalities in economics are effects—good or bad—which result from individual actions but are not taken into account in individual decisions (commonly because there is no cost, incentive, or price to the individual). In such cases there are discrepancies between "private" and "social" costs and benefits. Externalities are "internalized" when pricing, taxes and subsidies, or regulation, bring individual decisions in line with what is socially desirable (see Chapter 9 in this volume).

[23] Where environmental externalities (spillovers or offsite effects) are widespread, secure property rights over resources are necessary but by no means sufficient conditions for the elimination of "excessive" environmental degradation. For example, secure property rights have not eliminated the topsoil loss in U.S. agriculture for two reasons: 1) part of the environmental damage from soil erosion, e.g., sedimentation of rivers and reservoirs is external to the farmer and hence he has no cause to consider it; and 2) farmers, like other individuals, tend to use a higher discount rate than what the society at large considers appropriate. Both of these reasons are failures of the market call for public sector interventions to regulate land use or preferably to internalize the external cost to the private farmer. But even then, no one should expect zero topsoil loss; such an outcome would be economically and ecologically unrealistic and unwarranted.

[24] T. Panayotou and Chalongphob Sussangkarn, "Structural Adjustment and the Environment: The Case of Thailand," in D. Reed (ed.), *Structural Adjustment and the Environment* (Boulder, CO: Westview Press, 1992).

[25] T. Panayotou, *Empirical Tests and Policy Analysis of Environmental Degradation at Different Stages of Economic Development*, Working Paper for the International Labour Office (Geneva: World Employment Programme Research, 1993).

[26] Cruz et al., op. cit.

[27] T. Panayotou and Somthawin Sungsuwan, *An Econometric Study of the Causes of Tropical Deforestation: The Case of Northeast Thailand*, Development Discussion Paper No. 284 (Cambridge, MA: Harvard Institute for International Development, 1992).

[28] Tongpan and Panayotou, op. cit.

[29] Ibid.

[30] Cleaver and Schreiber, op. cit.

[31] Panayotou, *Empirical Tests and Policy Analysis*, op. cit.

[32] R.E. Bilsborow and M. Geores, *Population, Land Use, and the Environment in Developing Countries: What Can We Learn from Cross-National Data*, paper presented at the NAS Workshop on Population and Land Use, Washington, DC, 4-5 December 1991.

[33] Mink, op. cit.

[34] D. Southgate and D. Pearce, "Agricultural Colonization and Environmental Degradation in Frontier Developing Economies" (Washington, DC: World Bank, October 1988).

[35] Bilsborow and Geores, op. cit., p. 27.

[36] R. DeShazo, *Household Determinants of Deforestation*, Masters Thesis, University of North Carolina at Chapel Hill, Department of City and State Planning, 1993, p. 27.

[37] For some evidence of rising costs, see K.N. Ninan and H. Chandrashekhar, "The Green Revolution, Dryland Agriculture and Sustainability: Evidence from India," in G.H. Peters and B.F. Stanton (eds.), *Sustainable Agricultural Development*, Proceedings of the 21st International Conference of Agricultural Economists (Aldershot, UK/ Brookfield, VT: Dartmouth Publishing Company, 1992); C.L. Delgado and P. Pinstrup-Andersen, "Agricultural Productivity in the Third World: Patterns and Strategic Issues," paper to the AAEA/IFPRI Workshop, Orlando, Florida, July 1993, especially pp. 20-21. For a contrasting, positive experience, see M. Tiffen et al., op. cit.

[38] J.J. Cole, B.L. Beierls, N.F. Caraco, and M.L. Pace, "Nitrogen Loading of Rivers as Human-Driven Process," in M.J. McDonnel and T.A. Pickett (eds.), *Humans as Components of Ecosystems: The Ecology of Subtle Human Effects and Populated Areas* (New York: Springer-Verlag, 1993).

[39] Mink, op. cit.

[40] V. Smil, "The Critical Link Between Population Growth and Nitrogen," *Population and Development Review*, Vol. 17, No. 4 (December 1991).

[41] R. Rajagopal and R.L. Talcott, "Patterns in Groundwater Quality," *Environmental Management*, Vol. 7, pp. 465-474.

Chapter Six

Investing in the Next Generation: The Implications of High Fertility at the Level of the Family

Cynthia B. Lloyd

The human potential for future economic and social progress rests with today's generation of children. The family and the state contribute to the development of children's potential through support for their daily needs and through investments in their health and education. In countries where the state is relatively weak and has limited enforcement powers, families control children's access not only to their own family resources but also, to a greater or lesser extent, to public resources such as those provided through government-funded health and education systems. Because children are dependent on their parents (and other members of their families), it is difficult for them to seek health care or attend school without their family's concurrence or support.

High fertility at the national level is associated with a rapidly growing younger population; this has implications for the overall quantity and quality of public services available to children (see Chapter 3 in this volume). Furthermore, the fertility level is directly linked with the proportion of families that are large and the proportion of children growing up in large families; this has implications for the incidence of poverty among children (see Chapter 4 in this volume).[1] Within families, high fertility means more siblings per child; this has implications for the burden of parental responsibilities and for the level and distribution of family support for, and investment in, children. Not only do the structure and function of families shift with declines in fertility but so do the divisions of responsibilities and resources among family members—between parents and children, between mother and father, and between boys and girls.

The implications of high fertility are not gender-neutral. In all societies, women's special reproductive function lies at the heart of the sexual division of labor and the socialization of children for adult roles.[2] High fertility could not occur without a significant proportion of women's lives being devoted to childbearing, with all its attendant risks and responsibilities. Lower fertility in the context of improved child survival would imply, on the one hand, a shorter period of childbearing and, on the other hand, a longer period of healthy adult life to devote to fewer children and other roles.

This paper, written with the interests of the next generation in mind, provides an up-to-date review of the evidence, primarily from developing countries, on families' experiences with fertility and family size and their implications for investments in young people.[3] It looks at the experience of children collectively as well as individually and explores the ways in which boys' and girls' experiences differ. It goes beyond the more familiar effects of high fertility on children's health and educational opportunities—mothers' nutritional depletion as a result of frequent pregnancy and pressure on family resources—to explore its implications for children's access to opportunities beyond the home and for their socialization into adult roles. The links between fertility, the extent to which children are wanted, and equity among siblings are also explored.

The chapter first outlines the conventional wisdom on the relationship between "family size" and child investment and offers a context for analyzing four influences on the family size-child investment relationship: 1) the level of socioeconomic development, 2) the role of the state, 3) the culture of the family, and 4) the phase of the demographic transition.[4] It then reevaluates the conventional wisdom and explores potential positive implications of fertility decline for increased child investment.

THE CONVENTIONAL WISDOM: FAMILY RESOURCE CONSTRAINTS

Children with many siblings or closely spaced siblings are generally assumed to fare less well than children with fewer siblings in terms of such human development indicators as mortality, nutrition, and educational attainment. This is considered to be the result of family resource constraints that cause each child to get a smaller share of family resources, including family income, parental time, or the mother's physiological and nutritional resources—all of which are important to an infant's and young child's development. First-born children are seen to be initially advantaged; later-born children start life having to share family resources with more siblings. Although family income can be saved for use in the future to equalize resources among children, parents are not expected to have a similar ability to save other essential parental resources, such as their time and physical energy. Therefore, they are likely to find it more difficult to shield later-born children from the consequences of constraints on their resources.[5]

This conventional wisdom, although intuitively appealing, is based on a particular view of the parent-child family as a bounded economic unit in which children consume parental resources but do not contribute to them. It further assumes that parents of similar means allocate the same proportion of the family budget to their children collectively regardless of their number—a somewhat surprising assumption, given the widely accepted image of parents as unselfish caretakers of their children who are willing to adjust their own resources to meet their children's needs. The following brief review of the empirical evidence drawn from a broad range of developing countries lays out what we know about maternal depletion and family resource dilution as they relate to family size from existing data, leaving for a later discussion the potential implications of these findings for children currently living in countries where fertility rates remain high.

Child Mortality

Underlying the familiar message about the health benefits of family planning—"better health for mothers and children with family planning"—is the notion that fewer and more widely spaced births will reduce maternal mortality and increase children's survival chances. An extensive analysis of fertility surveys from a range of developing countries conducted from the mid-1970s to the late 1980s shows that the average relative risk of child death for children born less than a year and a half after the previous birth is roughly double the risk of death for children born two years or more after the last child. Children born to very young mothers (less than 18 years of age) also suffer increased mortality risks.[6] Several possible mechanisms may explain this relationship, each one related to constraints on parental resources that affect the nutritional status of the child.[7] The first mechanism is a physiological effect—maternal depletion—which is tied to the effects of pregnancy and breastfeeding on a mother's nutritional status, with implications for a newborn's birth-weight and later development. The second mechanism relates to competition among siblings for nutritional resources, partially but not entirely explained by early termination of breastfeeding.[8]

As fertility declines, reproductive patterns change in ways that are likely to have implications for the survival chances of an individual child. These include reductions in higher-parity births and in births to very young or much older women; these reductions, in turn, reduce the number of newborns facing heightened mortality risks.[9] However, other changes in reproductive patterns that sometimes accompany fertility decline—most importantly, a shortening of birth intervals as a result of declines in the duration of breastfeeding and of post-partum abstinence—can have the opposite effect.[10] When these changes occur, the advantages of smaller family size for an individual child's survival chances may be substantially lessened or even eliminated. Indeed, it is possible that the commonly observed negative statistical relationship between child survival and birth order may be largely explained by the closer birth spacing of women who give birth to more children.[11] Thus the implications for children's survival chances of declines in fertility in countries where fertility remains high will depend on other changes in reproductive patterns.

Child Health and Nutrition

Data from many parts of the developing world provide evidence that young children with more young siblings have poorer long-term nutritional outcomes[12] than children who have fewer young siblings, even after differences in birth order and birth spacing are accounted for.[13] Evidence from the Philippines suggests that these effects are not as strong for current (or short-term) nutritional status.[14] Although parents allocate current household resources equitably among children, they are unable to compensate later-born children for the cumulative disadvantage they suffer from having to share household resources (not only financial, but also parental time and attention) with more siblings than their earlier born sisters and brothers. In particular, mother's time may be one of the most important constraints. In settings where extended support systems are weak, this often leads to poorer care when young siblings are put in charge.[15]

Educational Attainment

Parental investments in children are highly interdependent. Good health is a prerequisite for effective learning; it is also strongly linked to productivity and future work roles. For example, a study of primary-school-age children in Nepal found a close link between a child's long-term nutritional status and primary school enrollment.[16] In Nicaragua, children's nutritional status was found to be strongly linked to mean years of educational attainment.[17] The number of siblings has the potential to affect children's schooling not only directly but also indirectly through its effects on nutrition and health.

The effects of family size on a child's progress through school, in terms of years of schooling attained, completion of critical levels, and educational quality, have been investigated in a variety of developing-country settings, most particularly in Asia. Out of a sample of 14 studies of children's current school enrollment, 28 separate sets of empirical results on educational attainment, and 7 studies of dropout or completion rates, measures of children's educational participation or progress in school, as well as the level of parental investments in schooling (in terms of expenditures), were found to be usually, but not always, negatively associated with numbers of siblings.[18] The size and the statistical significance of these effects varies substantially across countries and across groups within countries.

Parents influence children's learning and retention in school not just by relieving them of other family obligations, spending time with them, and helping them learn, but also through financial contributions to their children's school. High levels of expenditures represent a greater investment in complementary educational inputs such as books and tutors and better quality private schools. The few studies that looked at the relationship between numbers of siblings, parental expenditures, and school quality found consistently negative effects.[19] This is supported more generally by evidence from the Philippines and Thailand showing greater declines in expenditures per child than in expenditures per adult as household size increases.[20]

THE CONTEXT AND WHY IT MATTERS

The link between high fertility and lower levels of child investments, while generally in evidence, does not appear to be universally true or necessarily quantitatively important except in certain contexts or for certain groups. The studies mentioned above suggest that the level of socioeconomic development, the level of social expenditures by the state, the culture of the family, and the phase of the demographic transition are critical determinants of the relationship between fertility and the level of child investment.

The Level of Development

Some level of development is required before family size can have an impact on child investment. In an environment without schools or health clinics, parents have few ways to impact materially on their children's health or schooling, whether their resources are spread among few or many. According to one analyst, "The issue of sibling competition only becomes relevant if a moderate addition to parental resources directed toward the child is sufficient to bring about substantial improvement in child well-being."[21] Furthermore, the potential returns to parents and their children from health and educational investments in children are closely related to parental assessments of the quality of health and educational services available to their children and of their children's future opportunities in the labor market, both of which tend to improve with development.

The importance of level of development in determining the relationship between fertility and the level of child investment is substantiated by a recent comparative analysis of the impact of family size on children's nutritional status in 15 developing countries. The author found that the negative impact of family size on children's nutritional status increased as greater proportions of the population had access to safe drinking water and health services. Furthermore, the negative relationship between family size and educational attainment is more likely to occur and be statistically significant in urban than rural settings and in the more developed countries of Southeast Asia and Latin America than countries of South Asia and Sub-Saharan Africa.[22] Further evidence of the importance of development to the relationship between family size and child investment can be found in comparisons across generations in Taiwan, Nicaragua, and Malaysia. In each case, parents' education did not appear to be affected by their number of siblings, whereas negative effects of family size emerged in the current generation of children.[23]

The Role of the State

At any particular level of development, the greater the extent to which child services are subsidized by the state, the less important parental resource constraints are for child investment. For example, the probability that a child will enter school is largely unaffected by the number of other siblings in a variety of relatively poor settings (Egypt, Ghana, and Pakistan).[24] Most governments are committed to free universal access to primary school,[25] and the youngest school-age children (those 5 to 8 years of age) have relatively low labor value. The most important determinants of *entry* into school are parents' education and the accessibility of a school nearby. Educational *attainment*, on the other hand, is more likely to be related to family size because of the increasing expense and opportunity costs.[26]

Evidence for this point is drawn from the previously cited comparative analysis of family size and child nutrition and from a comparison of ethnic differences in Malaysia. For a group of 15 developing countries, the amount of assistance to the agricultural sector (a measure of government food subsidies) is strongly associated with a reduction in the negative impact of family size on child growth.[27] In Malaysia, the major proportion of government educational scholarships (beyond primary school) and government and private sector jobs are reserved for the Malays. Although family size appears to have no negative impact on educational achievement among the Malays, a negative relationship is apparent among the Chinese and Indians.[28]

The Culture of the Family

While the sharing of resources is a central feature of family life in all cultures, the size and composition of the family unit within which exchanges take place and the pattern of resource flows between mothers and fathers and between adults and children varies across cultures. The family circle within which resources are shared can extend laterally as well as vertically. Furthermore, children can participate actively in household chores and make an important economic contribution starting at a relatively young age.

More traditional settings tend to emphasize the welfare of the corporate family over the welfare of the individual—possibly because the family plays a central role in the redistribution of income. In such an environment, child investments may be motivated more by the needs of the corporate family than by the individual needs of the child, with greater specialization likely among children in larger families, often according to sex and birth order. This is not to say that parents are necessarily unwilling to invest in their children, but only that they are less likely to do so if there are no clear prospects of economic returns for the family as a whole in terms of improved job prospects for educated youth and a reasonable certainty of remittances.

Furthermore, mothers and fathers may have different incentives and abilities to invest given their very different economic circumstances. Although there is much evidence that mothers are more child-oriented in their expenditures than fathers, the implications of these differences for the allocation of resources between parents and children will depend on women's relative earnings, their personal autonomy, and their role in decisions about the allocation of other family resources.[29] Families in more traditional high-fertility societies may be less child-oriented in their expenditures because of the greater authority of males within the household and the greater authority of the parental generation in relation to the child generation.

Moreover, in some cultures, responsibilities for child support extend beyond children's own parents to encompass grandparents, aunts and uncles, and older siblings. For example, in Sub-Saharan Africa, where child fosterage is common and where other related adults share responsibility for children's upkeep, the number of siblings is less important in determining a child's future.[30] A comparison between three Latin American and three Sub-Saharan African countries of the relationship between family size and children's long-term nutritional status showed that being born in a large family had a large and statistically significant negative impact on children's nutrition status in Brazil and Colombia and to a smaller extent in the Dominican Republic. Among the African countries, there was no consistent relationship between family size and child nutrition. In Ghana, there was a small negative effect and in Mali and Senegal a positive but insignificant effect.[31] In these societies, child fostering, which increases in likelihood with family size,[32] breaks down household economic boundaries and spreads the impact of additional children on family resources across a wider kin network.

Further evidence of the importance of extended family support comes from studies of children's educational attainment by family size in Israel and Kenya.[33] Among Moslem Arabs in Israel, where the extended family is important to child support, the size of the nuclear family does not affect educational attainment. By contrast, family size is important to the educational attainment of Israeli Jews, who function largely within a nuclear economic circle. The potential importance of older siblings as a source of educational support for the youngest in the family is supported by evidence from both rural and urban samples in Kenya, which show the oldest and the youngest children in large families (over eight people) fare better in terms of educational attainment than middle children.

It appears that values associated with sharing among family members are changing over time as development occurs under the influence of today's developed countries.[34] The introduction of mass education undermines the traditional extended family's economic structure, weakens the authority of the old over the young and of men over women, and puts greater emphasis on the conjugal unit within the larger family.[35] Such changes reduce the larger family's control over the disposition of the financial gains accruing from investments in children, while bringing about a greater concentration of parents' investment in their own biological children. In settings where the extended family provides an important source of child support, this can reduce the competition for a share of those investments. At the same time, a growing individualism increases the value attached to self-actualization and, as a consequence, the value that parents attach to children's well-being as an end in itself rather than as an instrument for family solidarity and support.

Phase of the Demographic Transition

The stage of a country's transition from high to low fertility ("the demographic transition") represents a final historical dimension that brings texture to the interpretation of results. The link between improvements in child survival and the adoption of deliberate fertility regulation has implications not only for the relationship between fertility and family size but also for parental motivation to invest in children.

Fertility is directly linked to family size only when children's risk of death is very low. Family size may even increase initially as mortality falls, and then may remain stable for some time until fertility decline begins to outstrip mortality decline. As population growth rates accelerate before declines in fertility fully match declines in mortality, the number of children per woman increases by an average of 0.5 children, and then begins to fall first to, and then below, previous levels.[36]

Figure 1 shows the relationship between fertility and the mean number of living siblings per child (aged 0 to 15) for a group of 19 developing countries in Africa, Asia, and Latin America in the late 1980s, with the phase of demographic transition as well as region emerging as important. First, there appears to be a threshold of roughly 4 births per woman that must be reached before declines in fertility translate into declines in family size as experienced by children. Second, the pattern and timing of the link between fertility and family size is distinct in Sub-Saharan Africa where countries appear to have a lower than expected number of siblings per child for their level of fertility, probably due to higher child mortality.

The transition from "family building by fate" to "family building by design," brought about through improved child survival[37] and greater knowledge and education, involves the development of a sense of personal agency, a growing consciousness of the availability of choice and the possibility of personal betterment and, in settings where extended family support networks are important, a greater sense of obligation to one's own children than to the children of other

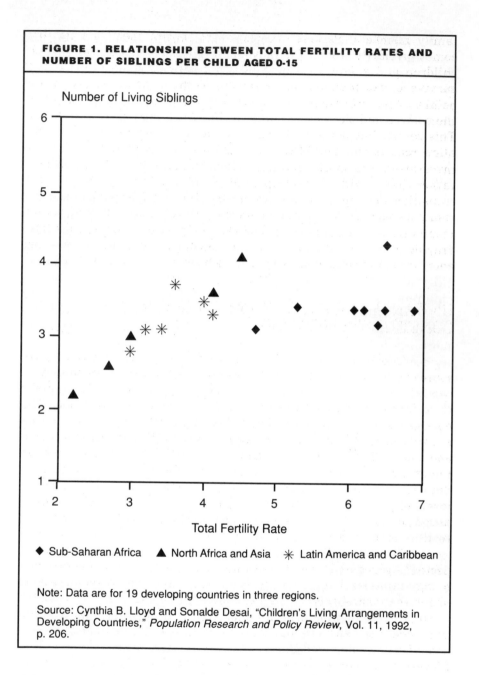

FIGURE 1. RELATIONSHIP BETWEEN TOTAL FERTILITY RATES AND NUMBER OF SIBLINGS PER CHILD AGED 0-15

Number of Living Siblings

Total Fertility Rate

◆ Sub-Saharan Africa   ▲ North Africa and Asia   ✳ Latin America and Caribbean

Note: Data are for 19 developing countries in three regions.

Source: Cynthia B. Lloyd and Sonalde Desai, "Children's Living Arrangements in Developing Countries," *Population Research and Policy Review*, Vol. 11, 1992, p. 206.

family members. Parents' motivation to control their own fertility comes primarily from a desire to make greater investments in their children and a growing confidence that both parent and child will survive long enough to reap the returns on the investment. It is at this point that parents can begin to imagine the alternative possibilities for themselves and their other children that fewer children would allow. This cannot happen until levels of social and economic development allow reasonable rates of return to child investment and the costs of investments are substantial and primarily borne by a child's parents rather than a wider kin group or the state. During this phase of the transition, declines in family size can be expected to be associated with rising levels of child investment on the part of parents. Indeed, recent results from Thailand, which has just completed a very rapid demographic transition, show a strong relationship between family size and entry into lower and upper secondary schools.[38]

UNWANTED FERTILITY: FAMILY RESOURCE CONSTRAINTS REVISITED

The boundaries of the family, the scope and direction of resource sharing within the family, and the costs and returns to human capital investment are all factors influencing parental motivation for child investment as well as the practice of fertility regulation. The emergence of "unwanted fertility" is symptomatic of parents' rising aspirations and their increasing awareness of alternatives to their own and their children's present condition. High fertility is likely to have the greatest negative impact on levels of child investment when children are unwanted. Unwanted fertility, in conjunction with prevalent levels of per child investment, thus becomes a measure of the unrealized potential for parental investment in children within a particular socioeconomic and cultural context.

To what extent is high fertility unwanted, unplanned, or unexpected? Aggregate levels of "unwanted fertility" for a number of developing countries have recently been estimated, based on questions about the desirability of the next birth in demographic and health surveys.[39] Over 30 percent of births appear to be unwanted in countries where fertility rates average between 4 and 6, with only 16 percent of births unwanted in countries with higher levels of fertility and 25 percent unwanted when average levels of fertility fall below 4. In other words, as fertility begins to decline in high fertility regions such as Sub-Saharan Africa, the Middle East, and South Asia, an increasing percentage of births will be unwanted, implying the possibility of a growing "underinvestment" in children directly attributable to excess fertility.

A review of the anthropology literature suggests evidence of excess mortality due to poor nutrition, poor health, and parental neglect among children whose parents have too many children or among girls whose parents would prefer boys.[40] When son preferences are strong, parents may have to exceed their preferred number of children just to achieve their desired number of sons. Thus to the extent that high fertility is partially motivated by preferences for sex rather than family size, there are important implications for selective under-investment in girls.

It is difficult to measure unwanted fertility directly at the family level because of parents' understandable reluctance to report existing children as unwanted. In one of the few attempts identified in the literature, the wantedness of a birth was found to be an important independent factor explaining variations in a child's probability of survival to the first birthday in rural Thailand.[41] Two recent attempts to estimate unwanted, unexpected, or "excess" fertility for individual women in India and Malaysia indirectly found that the arrival of unplanned or unexpected births had negative effects on child invest-ment.[42] However, general conclusions cannot be drawn from these two studies alone because results were based on a small sample in the case of India,[43] and on indirect statistical techniques in the case of Malay-sia.[44] The potential importance of being unwanted for a child's future cannot be denied; future research will need to give this issue special attention.

AN EXPANDED FRAMEWORK

The discussion to date has focused on the relationship between fertility levels and average levels of family investment in children, known as the *resource dilution effect*. This effect has been seen to be heavily conditioned by the overall level of fertility and the socio-cultural context, with the level of unwanted fertility serving as an indicator of the potential importance of this relationship in specific settings. However three additional dimensions of the relationship between fertility and child investment may be of greater importance in the long term: 1) the *opportunity effect*, i.e., the effect of fertility on the access parents are willing to provide their children to public invest-ment resources; 2) the *equity effect*, i.e., the effect of fertility on the distribution of family resources among siblings; and 3) the *intergenera-*

tional effect, i.e., the effect of fertility on assumption of nontraditional roles and the transmission of opportunities across generations.

The Opportunity Effect

The division of work roles varies within families according to family size because of differences in the amount of work to be done and the number of family members available to do it, as well as because of differences in bargaining power between men and women and between adults and children within the household, and differences in the nature and functions of the household unit. Parents act as their children's gatekeepers to the world of opportunities that lies outside the family, deciding on their behalf how their time will be used and where it will be spent. If children are needed for work at home or on the family farm, they will be less able to take advantage of opportunities provided through public investment, such as health services or schooling. As a result, public resources, even when distributed equitably by the state in terms of geography and costs, are utilized unevenly. A family's labor needs dictate the amount of publically available resources children are able to access and benefit from.

Although greater numbers of young children increase the workload of all adult members of the household, mothers' work burden increases disproportionately.[45] Indeed, time devoted to children is largely responsible for differences in total work time between the sexes. The consequences for older children of the mother's increased burden are directly related to the availability of extended family support and to the roles that children themselves are expected to take up in larger families. Older siblings are a primary source of childcare for younger siblings in the household. Indeed, in growing families, mothers who take up greater economic responsibilities will often rely on their daughters to serve as mother substitutes for their younger children, with direct consequences for their daughters' progress in school.[46]

A review of studies of the family factors associated with children's work roles suggests that children with more siblings are likely to work longer hours on average, particularly when they are among the oldest, than children with fewer siblings.[47] Moreover, girls are more strongly affected than boys. In rural Maharashtra, working children with more siblings worked longer hours than working children with fewer siblings, largely because of greater time devoted to housework.[48] In the Philippines and Botswana, children's domestic work time was found to be greater in households with more children, and in Brazil, older children (aged 10 to 14) with young siblings (aged 0 to 4) were more likely to be in the work force with negative implications for school attendance.[49]

The Equity Effect

The resources available to a particular child are not the same as average family resources per child because siblings arrive in the family sequentially and therefore experience childhood differently both from the point of view of family resources and sibling composition. The relationship between the number of siblings, family resources for children, and investments in a particular child is influenced by a child's individual characteristics, particularly sex and birth order. Even the most egalitarian parents will have difficulty equalizing resources among children over time, given the situational advantage of first- and last-born children with respect to the availability of parental time. Sex can also be an important differentiating factor. If parents have rigid notions about sex roles or perceive different opportunities available to boys and girls, they will treat boys and girls differently. The latitude for such differentiation increases along with the number of siblings and, therefore, children with fewer siblings are likely to receive more equal treatment.

Comparisons of family size effects by sex and birth order provide evidence of greater inequality among children with many siblings. However, whether later-born or earlier-born children are favored depends on the cultural context as well as the particular dimension of child investment under consideration. For example, later born children appear to have poorer long-term nutritional status than their earlier born siblings.[50]

In the case of education, the pattern of inequity varies according to the system of family support. In Africa, the first born is often favored in terms of educational access and attainment relative to his/her proximate siblings in the hopes that the oldest sibling will ultimately be able to support the education of the youngest in the family. The effectiveness of this strategy requires a large age spread between the oldest and youngest siblings, which is most likely to occur in large families. A dramatic example of this is provided in a study of educational attainment in Kenya that shows the youngest children in large families of six to eight children achieving much higher levels of education than their immediately older siblings.[51] On the other hand, in Asia—where fertility is lower and characterized by a narrower age spread between oldest and youngest sibling—oldest siblings often have to interrupt their education to help care for younger children at home.[52]

The Intergenerational Effect

Adolescence is the period of children's lives when they prepare for adult roles. During this period, a child's same sex parent or other significant adult family member becomes a role model in shaping expectations and a mentor in teaching specific skills. Not only family size per se, but also the spacing and sex distribution of siblings, will affect the extent to which children within a family experience adolescence in the same way or differently. The smaller the number of children in a family, the less the opportunity for differentiation and specialization among children. Smaller families are less likely to include both boys and girls. Differentiation by sex in the socialization process is likely to be less intense where children have the opportunity to undertake tasks traditionally assigned to the opposite sex. Conversely, in large families with children of both sexes, boys and girls are likely to specialize in sex-segregated tasks; this will have implications for their educational attainment, living arrangements, and, in the case of adolescent girls, for the timing of sexual initiation and marriage as well as the arrival of the first child.

Because of the chance that one sex will be underrepresented or unrepresented, children with fewer siblings may have more opportunities to transcend traditional gender roles in terms of specific work tasks.[53] However, the potential benefits for girls of greater equalization of work roles by gender will depend on whether girls are able to benefit personally in terms of greater access to and control over resources for the future. Where women's status is low and sex discrimination within the family is pervasive, girls will not benefit from greater freedom to take on new roles. In rural Maharashstra, for example, girls do not appear to share with their brothers in the extra family resources available for children's education in smaller families. Instead, greater educational attainment of boys with fewer siblings is made possible through the increased time contributed by their sisters to the family farm. Thus while girls with fewer siblings are more likely to take up the work traditionally reserved for boys, their educational attainment is no greater than that of girls growing up with many siblings because of the family's continued need for help on the farm.[54]

Girls learn to become mothers by helping their mothers care for their siblings. By early adolescence, girls have the potential to become mothers themselves. Early marriage or motherhood for a girl may relieve her parents of some economic responsibility while at the same time depriving them of her assistance. Early marriage usually means girls end up dropping out of school, as in most developing societies pregnant girls and young mothers are not welcome in the classroom.[55] Indeed a particular risk to pregnant school girls and their babies is the young mother's attempt to hide the pregnancy, leading her to neglect her own nutritional needs and those of the baby.[56]

When families are large, the early marriage of older girls is an effective way of making the natal family smaller. In Taiwan, for example, the oldest daughters in large families often marry early, thus truncating their education.[57] An alternative approach in West African settings is child fosterage, which involves sending a teenage girl to the family of relatives to help care for their children. In Ghana, the proportion of teenage girls living apart from their mothers is higher than the proportion of teenage boys living away. For rural girls in particular, the proportion dropping out of school and the proportion living away from home increase significantly with each additional younger sibling, a pattern not observed for teenage boys; these same girls are also likely to be younger at the time of marriage and of their first birth.[58]

In most parts of the world, parents with more children tend to discriminate against their female children in the allocation of schooling and other forms of investment more than parents with fewer children (perhaps because their desired family size is indeed smaller than the family size required to achieve their desired number of sons). When these girls reach adulthood they have been socialized to perform more traditional roles, are less knowledgeable about the world around them, have fewer remunerative skills, and are less able to access resources on their own. As a result, they are more reliant on their children, less likely to practice methods of modern contraception, and likely to have more children than young women with fewer siblings. Thus high fertility perpetuates high fertility, shortening the space between generations and increasing the momentum of population growth.

THE NEXT GENERATION: REPEATING THE PATTERN OR BREAKING THE CYCLE?

The aspirations and capacities of children in developing countries are shaped by their families, teachers, and peers. Although their lives are touched by modernization, traditional values and expectations remain strong. Today's children face opportunities that were unavailable to their parents as children. At the same time, families face new risks as higher levels of schooling and more modern job opportunities take young adults farther away from their aging parents. Families, in particular parents, serve as the gatekeepers for their children, regulating their access to opportunities that lie outside the family and its immediate surroundings.

Within this environment, children growing up with many siblings are increasingly at a disadvantage in many parts of the world. There is less absorptive capacity within the present economic and environmental climate for successively larger cohorts of children than in the past, particularly in Sub-Saharan Africa, South Asia, and the Middle East, where population growth is proceeding at unprecedented rates. These growth rates result in a rapid increase in the proportion of the population that is under the age of 15. Many countries with rapid population growth also experienced sharp economic downturns in the 1980s, often accompanied by structural adjustment. Social sector budgets—in particular, health and education—have been cut back. As a result, the cost to parents of education and health for their children has risen at the same time that the level and quality of publicly provided services has been cut back. This combination of rapid population growth and economic adjustment can have extremely negative implications for family resources and overall levels of child investment.

In larger, more traditional families, the authority structure within the household is more likely to be male-dominated and less child-oriented in its expenditure pattern. Parental time and resources are more constrained, limiting the resources available for investments in each child and reducing parents' ability to assist their children in taking advantage of new opportunities. These family resource constraints have negative implications for children's health and educational attainment and increase children's current and future obligations to their families.

In addition, differentiation and specialization among children —in particular between girls and boys—is more prevalent when parents have many children. Parents who need to gain access to a more modern world at the same time that they need to maintain the traditional one, have no alternative but to treat their children unequally. Although some children with many siblings are clearly able to pursue their education to the extent of their abilities, this is usually at the expense of their mothers and other siblings who will work harder on their behalf. Girls, in particular, may be asked to make the greatest sacrifices in terms of longer work hours, foreshortened education, and early marriage. Thus higher fertility leads to inequality among children between families as well as among siblings within families.

These inequalities within families have long-term consequences, particularly inequalities between boys and girls. If girls become adults with little education, they will be likely to begin childbearing at a young age, will have limited earning opportunities, and will have little control over resource allocation decisions within their households. As a result the cycle of disadvantage will be repeated and fertility is likely to remain high into the future. On the other hand, a child with fewer siblings is more likely to be a wanted child, likely to be granted greater access to public resources by her/his parents, more likely to receive equitable treatment in relation to her/his siblings, and more likely to take on nontraditional roles that will lead to lower fertility aspirations in the next generation.

The link between high fertility, sibling inequality, and gender role differentiation suggest some possibilities for breaking the intergenerational cycle that persistent high fertility engenders. Prominent among these would be the following measures: 1) the universal provision of high quality family planning and safe abortion services to both women and men regardless of age and marital status; 2) the enforcement of compulsory primary school for all children; 3) the adoption of explicit measures to reduce the costs and increase the acceptability of schooling for girls in a culturally appropriate way including the provision of female teachers, transportation, free uniforms, etc.; 4) the enforcement of children's rights to the economic support from both biological parents; and 5) the elimination of all forms of discrimination against women, in particular in matters relating to equal access to and control over resources. Such measures would reduce the number of unwanted births, increase the desirability of smaller families, and strengthen the positive impact of fertility decline on the level of child investment, thus postponing the start of childbearing and reducing its pace among the next generation of young adults.

Notes

The author acknowledges with much appreciation the important contribution of Niev Duffy to the preparation of this paper. She assembled, reviewed, and summarized a vast amount of literature from a variety of different disciplinary traditions that the author used to broaden the scope of the paper and enrich the treatment of the material. The author also thanks many valued colleagues for helpful comments on earlier drafts: Mark Montgomery, Robert Cassen, Niev Duffy, Judith Bruce, John Bongaarts, Susan Cochrane, Monica DasGupta, Sonalde Desai, Carolyn Makinson, and Timothy Dyson.

[1] The average number of children per mother is actually smaller than the average number of siblings per child because there are more children from large families than there are mothers with large families. Therefore as family size declines, the proportional decreases in mean number of siblings per child will be even greater than the proportional decline in fertility. Mary Jo Bane, *Here to Stay* (New York: Basic Books, Inc., 1976), p. 10.

[2] Cynthia B. Lloyd, "The Division of Labor Between the Sexes: A Review," in *Sex, Discrimination, and the Division of Labor* (New York: Columbia University Press, 1975), pp. 1-24.

[3] The most recent review of the empirical literature was a paper prepared for the National Research Council's Working Group on Population Growth and Economic Development. See Elizabeth M. King, "The Effect of Family Size on Family Welfare: What Do We Know?" *Population Growth and Economic Development: Issues and Evidence*, D. Gale Johnson and Ronald D. Lee (eds.), (Madison: University of Wisconsin Press, 1987), pp. 373-412.

[4] Throughout this paper, the term "family size" will be used to describe the number of siblings sharing the same parent. In common usage, the expression "family size" can imply other things such as the number of adults and children in a family or a household but in this context the term will be used exclusively as it relates most directly to fertility and number of surviving children.

[5] Peter H. Lindert, "Sibling Position and Achievement," *Journal of Human Resources*, Vol. XII, No. 2 (Spring 1977), pp. 198-219; David Heer, "Effects of Sibling Number on Child Outcome," *Annual Review of Sociology*, Vol. 11 (1985), pp. 27-47; and Brian Powell and Lala Carr Stellman, "Beyond Sibship Size: Sibling Density, Sex Composition and Educational Outcomes," *Social Forces*, Vol. 69, No.1 (September 1990), pp. 181-206.

[6] John Hobcraft, "Fertility Patterns and Child Survival: A Comparative Analysis," *Population Bulletin of the United Nations*, Vol. 33 (1992), pp. 1-31.

[7] These mechanisms are more fully discussed in Working Group on the Health Consequences of Contraceptive Use and Controlled Fertility, *Contraception and Reproduction: Health Consequences for Women and Children in the Developing World* (Washington, DC: National Academy Press, 1989), pp. 63-65.

[8] Obviously the existence of this competition requires that the preceding children are still alive.

[9] There has been much controversy in the literature about the implications of an increasing proportions of first order births (which are high risk) on overall mortality rates as fertility falls. John Bongaarts has shown that because of shifts in the distribution of births by parity, a fertility decline may have little effect on infant mortality rates. This point is less important here, however, because we are focusing on the family's and the child's experience and we are comparing larger vs. smaller families all of whom have had a first birth. John Bongaarts, "Does Family Planning Reduce Infant Mortality Rates?" *Population and Development Review*, Vol. 13, No. 2 (1987), pp. 323-334.

[10] John Hobcraft, "Child Spacing and Child Mortality," *Proceedings of Demographic and Health Surveys World Conference*, Vol. II (Columbia, MD: IRD/Macro International, Inc., 1991), pp. 1157-1182.

[11] Working Group on the Health Consequences of Contraceptive Use and Controlled Fertility, op. cit.

[12] The measure used in the nutrition literature to measure stunting or long term chronic malnutrition is a child's height for age measured as a standard deviation from the means for children of the same sex and age in a North American reference population.

[13] Sonalde Desai, "The Impact of Family Size on Children's Nutritional Status: Insights From a Comparative Perspective," *Fertility, Family Size, and Structure: Consequences for Families and Children*, C.B. Lloyd (ed.), (New York: The Population Council, 1993); Peter S. Heller and William D. Drake, "Malnutrition, Child Morbidity and the Family Decision Process," *Journal of Development Economics*, Vol. 6 (1979), pp. 203-235; Richard Lalou and Cheikh S.M. Mbacké, "The Micro-Consequences of High Fertility on Child Malnutrition in Mali," in Lloyd, *Fertility, Family Size, and Structure*, op cit.; Barbara Wolfe and Jere Behrman, "Determinants of Child Mortality, Health and Nutrition in a Developing Country," *Journal of Development Economics*, Vol. 11 (1982), pp. 163-193; and Carol A.M. Clark, "Demographic and SocioEconomic Correlates of Infant Growth in Guatemala," Rand Note N-1702-AID/Rf, September 1981. The results of these studies are summarized in Cynthia B. Lloyd, "Investing in the Next Generation: The Implications of High Fertility at the Level of the Family," Population Council Working Paper No. 63 (New York: The Population Council, 1994), Appendix Table 1.

[14] Measured as weight for height, Susan Horton, "Child Nutrition and Family Size in the Philippines," *Journal of Development Economics*, Vol. 23, No. 1 (1986), pp. 161-176.

[15] Susan Joekes, "Women's Work and Social Support for Child Care in the Third World," Joanne Leslie and Michael Paolisso (eds.), *Women, Work and Child Welfare in the Third World* (Boulder, CO: Westview Press, 1989); and Alaka Malwade Basu, "Family Size and Child Welfare in an Urban Slum: Some Disadvantages of Being Poor but 'Modern,'" in Lloyd, *Fertility, Family Size, and Structure*, op. cit.

[16] Peter R. Moock and Joanne Leslie, "Childhood Malnutrition and Schooling in the Terai Region of Nepal," *Journal of Development Economics*, Vol. 20, No.1 (1986), pp. 33-52.

[17] Wolfe and Behrman, op. cit.

[18] All these studies are summarized in Appendix Tables 2-4 in Cynthia B. Lloyd, "Investing in the Next Generation," op. cit.

[19] Nancy Birdsall, "A Cost of Siblings: Child Schooling in Urban Colombia," *Research in Population Economics*, Vol. 2 (1980), pp. 115-150; Andrew Mason, "Demographic Change, Household Resources, and Schooling Decisions," in Naohiro Ogawa, Gavin W. Jones, and Jeffrey G. Williamson (eds.), *Human Resources in Development Along the Asia-Pacific Rim* (Oxford: Oxford University Press, 1993); Basu, op. cit.; Zeba A. Sathar and Cynthia B. Lloyd, "Who Gets Primary Schooling in Pakistan: Inequalities Among and Within Families," Population Council Working Paper No. 53 (New York: The Population Council, 1993); and Cynthia B. Lloyd and Anastasia J. Gage-Brandon, "Does Sibsize Matter? The Implications of Family Size for Children's Education in Ghana," in Lloyd, *Fertility, Family Size, and Structure*, op. cit.

[20] John Bauer and Andrew Mason, "Equivalence Scales, Costs of Children, and Poverty in the Philippines and Thailand," in Lloyd, *Fertility, Family Size, and Structure*, op. cit.

[21] Desai, op. cit.

[22] See Appendix Tables in Lloyd, "Investing in the Next Generation," op. cit.

[23] Albert T. Hermalin, Judith A. Seltzer, and Ching-Hsiang Lin, "Transitions in the Effect of Family Size on Female Educational Attainment," *Comparative Education Review* (June 1982), pp. 254-270; Sudha Shreeniwas, "Family Size, Structure, and Children's Education: Ethnic Differentials Over Time in Peninsular Malaysia," in Lloyd, *Fertility, Family Size, and Structure*: op. cit.; Jere Behrman and Barbara L. Wolfe, "Investments in Schooling in Two Generations in Prerevolutionary Nicaragua: The Roles of Family Background and School Supply," *Journal of Development Economics*, Vol. 27 (October 1987), pp. 395-419; and William Parish and Robert Willis, "Daughters, Education, and Family Budgets: Taiwan Experiences," *Journal of Human Resources*, Vol. 28, No. 4 (1993), pp. 863- 898.

[24] Relatively few studies have focused particularly on the determinants of school entry and none have found an important effect. See, for example, Sathar and Lloyd, op. cit.; Lloyd and Gage-Brandon, "Does Sibsize Matter?" op. cit.; and Susan H. Cochrane, Kalpana Mehra, and Ibrahim T. Osheba, "The Educational Participation of Egyptian Children," in *Demographic Responses to Modernization*, Awad M. Hallouda, Samir Farid, and Susan Cochrane (eds.), (Cairo: CAPMAS, 1988). Nepal is an exception; see Dean T. Jamison and Marlaine E. Lockheed, "Participation in Schooling: Determinants and Learning Outcomes in Nepal," *Economic Development and Cultural Change*, Vol. 35, No. 2 (1987), pp.279-306.

[25] Even in Pakistan, where the government is not noted for its commitment to education, 82 percent of urban girls, 95 percent of urban boys, 79 percent of rural girls, and 91 percent of urban boys live within one kilometer of a primary school. See Sathar and Lloyd, op. cit.

[26] See Lloyd, "Investing in the Next Generation," op. cit., Appendix Table 4.

[27] Desai, "Impact of Family Size on Children's Nutritional Status," op. cit.

[28] Shreeniwas, op. cit.

[29] See Judith Bruce and Cynthia B. Lloyd, "Finding the Ties That Bind: Beyond Headship and Household," in L. Haddad, J. Hoddinott, and H. Alderman (eds.), *Intrahousehold Resource Allocation in Developing Countries: Methods, Models and Policy* (Baltimore, MD: Johns Hopkins University Press, 1994).

[30] Desai, "Impact of Family Size on Children's Nutritional Status," op. cit.

[31] Sonalde Desai, "Children at Risk: The Role of Family Structure in Latin America and West Africa," *Population and Development Review*, Vol. 18, No. 4 (1992), pp. 689-717.

32 Cynthia B. Lloyd and Sonalde Desai, "Children's Living Arrangements in Developing Countries," *Population Research and Policy Review*, Vol. 11 (1992).

33 Yossi Shavit and Jennifer L. Pierce, "Sibship Size and Educational Attainment in Nuclear and Extended Families: Arabs and Jews in Israel," *American Sociological Review*, Vol. 56, No. 3 (1991), pp. 321-330; and Melba Gomes, "Family Size and Educational Attainment in Kenya," *Population and Development Review*, Vol. 10, No. 4 (1984), pp. 647-660.

34 John C. Caldwell, "Towards a Restatement of Demographic Transition Theory," *Population and Development Review*, Vol. 2, Nos. 3 and 4 (1976), pp. 321-366.

35 John C. Caldwell, "Mass Education as a Determinant of the Timing of the Fertility Decline," *Population and Development Review*, Vol. 6, No. 2 (1980), pp. 225-255.

36 John Bongaarts, "The Projection of Family Composition Over the Life Course with Family Status Life Tables," in J. Bongaarts, T. Burch, and K. Wachter (eds.), *Family Demography* (Oxford: Clarendon Press, 1987), pp. 189-212.

37 Cynthia B. Lloyd and Serguey Ivanov, "The Effects of Improved Child Survival on Family Planning Practice and Fertility," *Studies in Family Planning*, Vol. 19, No. 3 (1988), pp. 141-161.

38 John Knodel, Napaporn Havanon, and Wersasit Sittitrai, "Family Size and Children's Education in Thailand," *Population and Development Review*, Vol. 16, No. 1 (1990), pp. 31-62; John Knodel and Malinee Wongsith, "Family Size and Children's Education in Thailand; Evidence from a National Sample," *Demography*, Vol. 28, No. 1, pp. 119-132.

39 "Unwanted fertility" is calculated as the difference between actual fertility rates and "wanted" fertility rates—the portion of the total fertility rate that is attributable to births among women who want more children at the time of the survey. See John Bongaarts, "The Measurement of Wanted Fertility," *Population and Development Review*, Vol. 16, No.3 (1990), pp. 487-506.

40 Susan Scrimshaw, "Infant Mortality and Behavior in the Regulation of Family Size," *Population and Development Review*, Vol. 4, No. 3 (1978), pp. 383-404.

41 Paul D. Frenzen and Dennis P. Hogan, "The Impact of Class, Education, and Health Care on Infant Mortality in a Developing Society: The Case of Rural Thailand," *Demography*, Vol. 19, No. 3 (1982), pp. 391-408.

42 One approach has been the use of data on twins because we can be sure that one of the pair was unplanned or unexpected. Mark Rosenzweig and Kenneth Wolpin, "Testing the Quantity-Quality Fertility Model: The Use of Twins as a Natural Experiment," *Econometrica*, Vol. 48, No. 1 (1980), pp. 227-240. An alternative approach has been to estimate a reproductive function and approximate the component of fertility that is not under the couple's control. Mark Rosenzweig and Paul Schultz, "Fertility and Investments in Human Capital: Estimates of the Consequences of Imperfect Fertility Control in Malaysia," *Journal of Econometrics*, Vol. 36, Nos. 1 and 2 (1987), pp. 163-184.

43 Rosenzweig and Wolpin, op. cit.

44 Rosenzweig and Schultz, op. cit.

45 Elizabeth King and Robert E. Evenson, "Time Allocation and Home Production in Philippine Rural Households," in Mayra Buvinic, Margaret A. Lycette, and William P. McGreevey (eds.), *Women and Poverty in the Third World* (Baltimore, MD: Johns Hopkins University Press, 1983); and Nancy Folbre, "Household Production in the Philippines: A Non-Neo-Classical Approach," *Economic Development and Cultural Change*, Vol. 32, No. 2 (1984), pp. 303-330.

46 Basu, op. cit.; and Lloyd and Gage-Brandon, "Does Sibsize Matter?" op. cit.

47 Shireen J. Jejeebhoy, "Family Size, Outcomes for Children, and Gender Disparities: The Case of Rural Maharashtra," in Lloyd, *Fertility, Family Size, and Structure*, op. cit.; Deborah DeGraff, Richard E. Bilsborrow, and Alejandro N. Herrin, "The Implications of High Fertility for Children's Time Use in the Philippines," C.B. Lloyd (ed.), (New York: The Population Council, 1993); and Eva Mueller, "The Value and Allocation of Time in Rural Botswana," *Journal of Development Economics*, Vol. 15 (1984), pp. 329-360.

48 Jejeebhoy, op. cit.

[49] Deborah Levison, "Family Composition and Child Labor: Survival Strategies of the Brazilian Poor," paper presented at the Annual Meeting of the Population Association of America (1989).

[50] Jere Behrman, "Nutrition, Health, Birth Order and Seasonality: Intrahousehold Allocations Among Children in Rural India," *Journal of Development Economics*, Vol. 28, No. 1, pp. 43-62; Susan Horton, op. cit.; and Benjamin Senauer and Marito Garcia, "Determinants of the Nutrition and Health Status of Preschool Children: An Analysis with Longitudinal Data," *Economic Development and Cultural Change*, Vol. 39, No. 2 (1991), pp. 371-389.

[51] Gomes, op. cit.

[52] William Parish and Robert J. Willis, op. cit.

[53] Cynthia B. Lloyd and Anastasia J. Gage-Brandon, "High Fertility and the Intergenerational Transmission of Gender Inequality: Children's Transition to Adulthood in Ghana," paper presented at the Seminar on Women and Demographic Change in Sub-Saharan Africa, Dakar, Senegal (March 1993).

[54] Jejeebhoy, op. cit.

[55] Dominique Meekers, Anastasia J. Gage, and Li Zhan, "Preparing Adolescents for Adulthood: Family Life Education and School Expulsion in Kenya," Working Paper No. 1993-09 (University Park, PA: Population Research Institute, Pennsylvania State University, 1993).

[56] Thomas K. LeGrand and Cheikh S.M. Mbacké, "Teenage Pregnancy and Child Health and Mortality in the Urban Sahel," in Lloyd, *Fertility, Family Size, and Structure*, op. cit.

[57] Parish and Willis, op. cit.

[58] Lloyd and Gage-Brandon, "High Fertility and the Intergenerational Transmission of Gender Inequality," op. cit.

Chapter Seven

Risk, Reproduction, and Rights: The Uses of Reproductive Health Data

Deborah Maine, Lynn Freedman, Farida Shaheed, and Schuyler Frautschi

> The woman can, if she strives against her own temper-
> ament and natural physical structure, carry out with
> some success all the duties assigned to man by nature,
> but man in no way can make himself fit to bear and
> rear children.
> —S. Abdul A'la Maududi (1903-1979)[1]

> And even if [women] bear themselves weary—or ulti-
> mately bear themselves out—that does not hurt. Let
> them bear themselves out. This is the purpose for
> which they exist.
> —Martin Luther (1483-1546)[2]

Reproductive health is not now, and never has been, simply a matter of preventing disease. This is because a woman's ability to bear children is linked to the continuity of families, clans, and social groups; the control of property; the interaction between human communities and their environment; the relationship between men and women; and the expression of sexuality. It is therefore valuable currency in every society and so has been regulated by families, religious institutions, and governmental authorities. In fact, for centuries, societies have assigned the work of reproduction to women as their sole or primary duty and accepted the often disastrous health consequences of that assignment; this has been explained by reference to specific understandings of "nature" and has been enforced and legitimated through the rules and laws of religion and custom.

Less apparent, but equally longstanding, is women's resistance to such external regulation. A woman may consider the ability to bear children to be the source of status in her life, her key to economic survival, the origin of her power in her family and society, or the source of deep emotional satisfaction; *or* she may see it as the root cause of her oppression by laws and social structures, the barrier to her participation in the affairs of her community, the obstacle to personal fulfillment, or the cause of intense pain and anxiety. However she views her reproductive capacity at a given moment in her life, for almost every woman, it is an intimate, basic part of her physical existence and sense of self. Control over fertility is therefore critical to a woman's ability to be an active agent in her own life and in the world around her. Indeed, throughout history, women have assessed their own needs and developed ways to control their own fertility, whether openly or surreptitiously, through contraception and abortion.[3]

From both the societal and the individual perspectives, then, sex, pregnancy, and childbirth have always entailed something else as well—*risk*. Most obviously, there is the risk of disease or bodily harm that can result from sex, pregnancy, and childbirth—and from the means used to facilitate, prevent, or control them. But because reproduction is a socially and culturally embedded activity, it entails an array of other risks as well: most fundamentally, sex, pregnancy, and childbirth—and their regulation—pose risks to the social order and to the role of women in it. In an important sense, "reproductive health" is about the management of those risks: what they are, how to assess them, and how to and who should control them.

In this paper, we review the epidemiological data in several key areas of reproductive health, as well as some of the policies and programs that have been developed from and/or justified by such data. In the process, we discuss ways that risk data influence reproductive health policies and programs, and the role that rights principles should play in supporting or mediating that influence.

REPRODUCTIVE HEALTH AND THE ROLE OF RISK

The concept of risk is used at four different levels in the health field. First, at the *population level*, epidemiological research is used to quantify risk by examining correlations between "risk factors" (e.g., maternal age) and outcomes (e.g., maternal mortality). Such correlations may be evidence of, but are not proof of, causation.

Second, at the *clinical level*, health professionals translate epidemiological risk measurements into guidelines for counseling or treating individual patients. This is a process fraught with uncertainty because, while such data can tell us which kinds of people are most likely to experience a given outcome, they cannot tell us whether a particular individual will experience that outcome.

Third, at the *individual level*, risk is a personal issue for each patient or client. Sandra Gifford, writing about the many ways that risk is understood and experienced in the case of benign breast disease (a risk factor for developing breast cancer), has described this as "lived risk," which is "qualitative, subjective, and highly ambiguous."[4] The way a woman processes, understands, and acts on information that the clinician gives her about her statistical risk can only be understood within the wider circumstances of her life and her own personal experiences. Thus "subjective probabilities emerge from the interaction of personal and social values about the costs of uncertain futures."[5]

These first three kinds of risk have obvious implications for reproductive health programs. For example, epidemiological studies tell us that, as a group, women in their forties are at "high risk" for maternal mortality. A health provider with this information might therefore counsel a 40-year-old woman that it is "dangerous" for her to become pregnant, and so might advise her about the possible costs and benefits of different methods of avoiding pregnancy. The woman must then weigh these specific health risks together with a whole spectrum of social risks that stem from her roles as a wife, sexual partner, and mother. For example, what consequences will the use of contraception have on relations (sexual or otherwise) with her husband; what consequences will having or not having an additional child have on her present economic circumstances, her future security, her status in her community, or her power in her family?

Finally, at the *political level*, risk data can be used for many different purposes. For example, they can inform decisions about resource allocation within the health field. But risk data also have great rhetorical power and so have been effectively used to support, and even to disguise, what are fundamentally political agendas. As reproductive health becomes an increasingly important and accepted goal in the international health field, it is crucial that we begin to examine how health research informs—and sometimes obscures—the goals of politicians, service providers, and women's health activists as they debate the directions that population and reproductive health policies will take.

RISK AND THE ROLE OF RIGHTS

Epidemiological data play a critical role in the health field, not just because they elucidate biological processes, but because they shape the way we think about health and disease and guide the choices we make about programs and policies. Such choices can never be value-free, as they inevitably require *someone* to weigh the risks and benefits that the data describe and *someone* to make policy and program decisions that influence *who* will assume the risks and *who* will reap the benefits. That such value-laden choices are indeed being made is not always obvious, in part because risk data, expressed through the seemingly neutral language of statistics and science, can obscure what is at stake. Yet even a decisionmaker operating in good faith with the sole purpose of improving women's reproductive health will wittingly or unwittingly—but unavoidably—make such choices.

The 40-year-old, high-risk woman described above illustrates the point. If the sole criterion guiding the decision about this woman's reproductive health were her physical, biological well-being, then she should neither become pregnant nor use most available contraceptive methods since there is always a risk of side effects and contraceptive failure. Indeed, given the chance of contracting a sexually transmitted disease (STD), she should not engage in sexual intercourse at all. Although celibacy might help ensure that she remains free of disease, from almost every point of view this would be an absurd outcome: In the area of reproductive health, physical well-being simply cannot be separated from the social, cultural, and political context of a woman's life.

Risk data, therefore, can inform choices about women's health, but they cannot provide a basis or a principle for weighing the factors they describe. For that task, "reproductive rights" have a critical role to play. The fundamental dignity of women as human beings requires that they be regarded not simply as childbearers or rearers, but as full individuals entitled to dominion over their own physical being, and as moral agents capable of understanding and making decisions about their own lives. This principle is drawn from multiple provisions in specific human rights documents signed by scores of countries from every continent on the globe.[6] Such legal documents are sometimes criticized as being "western" in origin and style. But in fact, the essential principles to which they give expression have resonance in many non-western traditions throughout the world.[7]

For the purpose of understanding the health implications of risk data, three specific guidelines can be derived from this basic human rights principle. First, if a woman is to be more than a means to reach some externally defined goal that she may or may not share—e.g., having male heirs, lowering fertility rates, satisfying another's sexual needs—then reproductive health itself must be understood from a woman's point of view. By this we mean that the biological factors illuminated by epidemiological data must be understood as only one element of the reproductive process. Biological and other elements of the reproductive process should be understood from the perspective of how they are experienced by women. Second, the weight that a particular risk or benefit is accorded in the entire decisionmaking process should be determined, first and foremost, by the woman, based on her own understanding of her particular circumstances. Health providers and policymakers must credit and trust a woman's determination of what is "good" for herself, even when that determination seems "wrong" or "incorrect" from their outsider's perspective. Third, a woman's view of her reproductive health and the decisions she makes are influenced by many factors—including the health system itself. Thus, the health system should give priority to creating conditions that give positive meaning and support to a woman's right to make informed decisions about her reproductive life.

The sections that follow review the data in three specific areas of reproductive health—maternal morbidity and mortality, contraceptive morbidity and mortality, and sexually transmitted diseases—and then examine their implications for health policies and programs in light of reproductive rights principles.

THE RELATIONSHIP BETWEEN FERTILITY AND REPRODUCTIVE HEALTH

Whether or not women get pregnant and bear children—and when, how often, and under what circumstances they do so—has a significant impact on their health. This has long been known by people around the world.[8] Our understanding of this relationship, however, continues to evolve. Although being pregnant and giving birth have definite risks, so do the various means of avoiding conception. Maternal mortality and morbidity, and contraceptive risks and benefits are the major ways in which fertility affects reproductive health.

Maternal Morbidity

Relatively little is known about morbidity related to childbearing in developing countries. One reason may be the nearly universal low priority given to women's health issues.[9] There are also technical reasons for the scarcity of information. For example, most non-fatal complications, such as bleeding and infection, clear up without any outward sign. Other complications, such as prolapsed uterus (in which a woman's uterus protrudes into her vagina), are difficult to detect without a gynecological examination. Including such examinations in surveys—in order to measure prevalence—is expensive and often can be culturally objectionable.

Indeed, the shame associated with gynecological problems is a major barrier to their treatment. Obstetric fistula is a good example. This condition is usually caused by prolonged labor and difficult delivery, during which an opening is torn between the urethra or anus and the vagina, resulting in chronic incontinence. Fistulae are most likely to occur in populations where sexual activity and childbearing begin very young (under 16 years of age) and access to obstetric care is limited.[10] They have been best documented in northern Nigeria, where there are long waiting lists for surgical repair of fistulae.[11] Nevertheless, it is assumed that even more women with this condition do not seek medical care because it is considered shameful—so shameful, in fact, that many women with fistulae are abandoned by their husbands and families.[12]

In short, although it may not be possible to estimate with any precision how common it is for women to have chronic health problems related to pregnancy and childbirth, there is sufficient information to state that these health problems cause a great deal of suffering in developing countries.

Maternal Mortality

The most dramatic way in which fertility affects women's health is through maternal mortality.[13] Deaths due to pregnancy, abortion, and childbirth—now extremely rare in developed countries—are still everyday events in developing countries. The World Health Organization (WHO) estimates that at least 500,000 maternal deaths occur worldwide every year, nearly all in developing countries.[14] The discrepancy between developed and developing countries is greater for maternal deaths than for any other health indicator. Only one out of every 10,000 women in Northern Europe dies of maternal causes, whereas it is estimated that one out of every 21 women in Africa will die due to pregnancy or childbirth.[15] The United States has about 300 maternal deaths each year, while Bangladesh (with a population less than half as large) has an estimated 28,000 maternal deaths each year.[16]

Three risk factors for maternal mortality are discussed—the age and parity of the woman, the spacing of her pregnancies, and the wantedness of the current pregnancy.

MATERNAL AGE AND PARITY. Numerous studies have shown that a woman's chances of dying as a result of pregnancy and delivery are affected by her age and parity.[17] These effects are found in both developing and developed countries. Typically, maternal mortality is lowest among women giving birth at 20 through 24 years old, and among women having their second or third birth (parity 1 and 2).[18]

Although age and parity are connected, each has an independent effect on mortality. In other words, among women aged 30 through 34, those having their fifth birth are more likely to die than those having their second birth. These relationships are probably due to a combination of social and biological factors. For instance, very young women are particularly likely to develop obstructed labor because their pelvic bones are not fully grown. They are also more likely to die of complications of abortion because they are more frequently unmarried and so are more likely both to choose abortion and to lack the money needed to obtain a safe abortion.

The concept of *relative risk* of dying a maternal death refers to the likelihood of members of one group dying compared with that of another group (e.g., relative to women in their early twenties, other women face higher risks). Relative risk is one way to describe the data, but there are other ways that are also valid. The method of presenting data that is most appropriate depends on how the data are being used. Table 1 shows relative risk, as well as other ways of presenting mortality data by age group for Matlab, Bangladesh. To calculate relative risk, one compares the maternal mortality ratio (number of deaths per 1,000 live births) of various age groups to that of women with the lowest ratio (in this case, women aged 20 through 29). For example, maternal mortality was nearly four times higher in the age group 10 through 14 years than among women aged 20 through 29.

Another way to look at the same data is by showing *absolute risk*. For every 1,000 young women aged 10 through 14 who gave birth, 17.7 died of maternal causes. Thus their absolute risk of maternal death was about 18 per 1,000. Or, to look on the bright side, their chances of survival were 982 out of 1,000.

Yet another way to analyze the same data is to look at the *age distribution of the deaths*, which gives quite a different picture. The ten-year age group with the largest *number* of maternal deaths is actually the same as the age group with the lowest relative risk, i.e., women aged 20 through 29. Forty-three percent of all maternal deaths

TABLE 1. MATERNAL MORTALITY AND FERTILITY BY AGE IN MATLAB, BANGLADESH, 1968–1970

Age	Maternal Mortality Ratio[a]	Relative Risk of Maternal Death[b]	Live Births per Year	Number of Maternal Deaths
10–14	17.7	3.9	509	9
15–19	7.4	1.6	3,907	29
20–29	4.5	1.0	11,286	51
30–39	5.8	1.3	4,667	27
40–49	6.7	1.5	447	3

[a]Number of maternal deaths per 1,000 live births.
[b]Relative risk is the ratio of disease in those with a particular risk factor to those without it. It is calculated for each age group by dividing the maternal mortality ratio of that group by the lowest maternal mortality ratio (in this case, women aged 20 to 29).

Source: Lincoln C. Chen et al., "Maternal Mortality in Rural Bangladesh," *Studies in Family Planning*, Vol. 5, No. 11 (November 1974), p. 337.

were among women in this age group. The reason for this seeming paradox is that there were many more births in this age group than in any other. So, even though their risk was relatively low, this group of women had more deaths than any other.

It is important to acknowledge the different ways of interpreting the same set of data because the mode of interpretation can affect the program and policy implications one draws. Relative risk is most appropriate for two purposes. The first is to study causation at the population level; finding a high relative risk (e.g., for lung cancer among heavy smokers) strengthens arguments of a causal relationship. The second is to guide clinical practice; physicians are interested in relative risk because it can help them tailor advice and treatment to individual patients.

Relative risk is generally less appropriate for other purposes. For example, from the point of view of the woman herself, it may be that the likelihood of her own survival—not her chances *compared to* other women—is most pertinent. Relative risk may not be appropriate at the population level either; if one were designing a program to reduce maternal deaths, targeting the high-risk women younger than 20 and older than 40 would mean neglecting the majority of women who die.

SPACING OF PREGNANCIES. The spacing of pregnancies has a strong effect on child survival.[19] It is often said that birth interval affects the mother's health as well. However, we know of no clear evidence that mortality is significantly higher among women having closely spaced births. Unfortunately, the effect on morbidity has not been adequately studied, although it certainly would make sense for closely spaced pregnancies to have some impact on women's health, even if it is not fatal.

That this lack of documentation is seldom noted illustrates the tendency to assume automatically that women and children have the same health needs.[20] What is good for the mother's health is usually good for the child, but the reverse is not always true. For example, increasing the birth weight of newborns will increase their survival but may also increase the number of women who cannot deliver normally.[21] Without access to emergency obstetric care, many such women will develop obstructed labor and be maimed or die.

WANTEDNESS OF PREGNANCIES. Whether or not a particular pregnancy is wanted is usually not included in the list of risk factors for maternal death. Yet where women do not have access to safe abortion services, this may in fact be the most powerful risk factor of all. It is worth noting that where safe, legal abortions are available, case-fatality rates are extremely low; the United States, for example, has a rate of 0.4 deaths per 100,000 induced abortions, or less than one-tenth its risk of childbirth.[22]

Because of legal and social sanctions, data on induced abortions are difficult to obtain in many countries. Even so, there is ample evidence that it is one of the leading reproductive health problems of women in developing countries. Community studies in Bangladesh, Cuba, Ethiopia, and India found that 14 to 24 percent of all maternal deaths were due to abortion.[23] The number of women coming to Kenyatta Hospital in Nairobi for treatment of complications of illicit abortion has increased over time; by the late 1980s, about 10,000 women were being treated each year.[24]

Improving access to modern contraceptive methods can reduce the number of deaths from illicit abortion, but it can not eliminate them. One reason for this is that even low rates of contraceptive failure result in substantial numbers of pregnancies. For example, a one-percent contraceptive failure rate in a method being used by a million women results in a thousand unwanted pregnancies every year. Moreover, there are various social, financial, practical, and psychological factors that contribute to unwanted pregnancies. So there will always be a demand for abortion, whatever the level of contraceptive use. Consequently, any serious attempt to reduce deaths from abortion must go beyond simply improving access to contraception; it must also improve access to safe abortion services.

It is commonly assumed that better family planning and ante-natal care programs are the best solution to maternal mortality. This is not supported by the literature. For example, it has often been said that family planning programs will reduce maternal deaths by preventing high-risk pregnancies. A 1988 study in Matlab, Bangladesh by Koenig et al., showed that increased use of modern contraceptive methods did in fact substantially reduce maternal deaths in the population.[25] Per 100,000 women of reproductive age, the maternal mortality rate declined from 121 in 1976 to 66 in 1985. But the family planning program reduced maternal deaths "solely by reducing the numbers of pregnancies and births."[26] Consequently, although there was a substantial decrease in the number of maternal deaths in the population, there was no significant change in the risk of death among *pregnant* women (deaths per 100,000 live births). Once women became pregnant, they were just as likely as before to die a maternal death.

Thus, family planning can reduce the total number of maternal deaths in the population, but it is only a partial solution to the problem of maternal mortality because it does little to reduce deaths among pregnant women. Therefore, it does not help ensure that the woman who chooses to have a child can do so safely. In fact, the most reliable way to dramatically change the chance that a woman will survive childbirth is to make emergency obstetric care widely available.

The key to understanding this is to recognize two facts. First, as the Matlab data and many other studies show, the greatest number of maternal deaths actually occur in women who are "low risk."[27] This means that risk data do not enable us to predict most maternal deaths. Second, the majority of cases of serious obstetric complications are not only unpredictable, they are also unpreventable. This was clearly shown by a prospective study conducted in a rural area of The Gambia. In this study, Great Britain's Medical Research Council provided exemplary prenatal care to pregnant women: risk screening was done twice during pregnancy; urine tests were performed to detect toxemia; each woman was visited once a month; and any illness detected was treated. There was, however, no medical facility nearby at which obstetric complications could be treated. Despite the prenatal care, the level of maternal mortality was astronomically high—the equivalent of more than 2,000 maternal deaths per 100,000 live births. In reviewing the data, the researchers found that risk factors were not helpful in identifying which women were most likely to die.[28]

Even though we may not be able to predict or prevent most obstetric complications, we certainly know how to treat them. If women with complications obtain prompt, adequate emergency obstetric care, the vast majority of maternal deaths can be prevented. It is access to such care, rather than just the generally higher standard of living, that accounts for most of the difference in maternal mortality ratios between developed and developing countries.[29]

Contraceptive Mortality and Morbidity

In 1979, an article by Beral in the *British Medical Journal* discussed the concept of "reproductive mortality," which includes not only maternal deaths but deaths due to contraceptive side effects as well.[30] By 1975, she stated, more than half of reproductive deaths in England and Wales were attributable to contraceptive side effects.

This was a startling announcement. To understand it properly, however, one needs to understand what might be called "the paradox of prevention." If a preventive intervention (e.g., pertussis vaccine) has any fatal side effects, no matter how rare, then some of the deaths related to the condition it is meant to prevent (pertussis) will be due to the intervention. The more effective in preventing the original condition (pertussis) the intervention is, and the more widespread its use, the higher the proportion of deaths due to the preventive intervention (vaccine) will be. Of course the total number of deaths will be lower.

As applied to modern contraceptive methods, the paradox of prevention produces just the kind of finding Beral reported. The more effective contraceptive methods are, and the more widespread their use, the higher the proportion of reproductive deaths that will be related to contraceptive side effects. Of course, the total number of reproductive deaths will have been greatly reduced.

This is not to dismiss the hazards of contraception. They deserve serious attention and, at least in the research community, they have received it. The side effects of contraceptive methods have been best studied in developed countries, where it is sometimes possible to follow large groups of women over long periods of time—e.g., through the British National Health Service or the Kaiser-Permanente health service organization in California. In analyzing and publicizing these data, the choice of *relative* rather than *absolute* risk has caused some confusion and misunderstanding.

A study by Harlap et al. did an excellent job of reviewing the literature and putting the findings into perspective.[31] For example, oral contraceptive use increases deaths from cardiovascular disease among older women and women who smoke, but it also saves many lives, as Table 2 shows for the United States. The number of deaths associated with various regimens reflects not only their side effects, but also the risk of death during unplanned pregnancies. It is for this

TABLE 2. ESTIMATED ANNUAL DEATHS BY AGE AND CONTRACEPTIVE REGIMEN IN THE UNITED STATES
(deaths per 100,000 women)

Contraceptive Regimen	20–24 Years Old	30–34 Years Old	40–44 Years Old
No Method	5.4	6.3	20.6
No Method and Abortion	2.0	1.9	5.3
Diaphragm/Cap	1.1	0.9	3.1
Intrauterine Device	0.2	0.1	0.6
Oral Contraceptive	1.3	1.8	1.9
Long-Acting Hormonal	0.6	0.8	0.6
Tubal Sterilization	1.2	1.1	1.3

Source: S. Harlap, K. Kost, and J. Darroch Forrest, *Preventing Pregnancy, Protecting Health: A New Look at Birth Control Choices in the United States* (New York: Alan Guttmacher Institute, 1991) pp. 98–99.

reason that some deaths are credited to methods that have no known serious side effects—e.g., the diaphragm.

The intensive research that has been done also sheds light on morbidity caused and prevented by various contraceptive methods. In terms of side effects serious enough to cause hospitalization, oral contraceptive use is expected to be associated with an extra 133 hospitalizations in the United States each year per 100,000 users aged 15 to 44.[32] Most of these hospitalizations (93) will be related to gallbladder disease, seven to invasive cancer, and four to cardiovascular disease. On the other hand, it is estimated that more than 1,500 hospitalizations will be averted each year in the same population due to oral contraceptive use. Most of these hospitalizations would be for cesarean sections (1,075), spontaneous abortions (265), and ectopic pregnancies (139), which would have taken place during pregnancies averted by oral contraceptive use. In addition, in this same population, oral contraceptive use would prevent hospitalizations for ovarian cysts (87 per year), benign breast disease (23), and cancer of the ovary and endometrium (5), among other conditions.

Unfortunately, there is much less information from developing countries, although researchers have not found evidence of additional serious side effects or higher mortality as a result of contraceptive use. Parallel studies of reproductive mortality in Bali, Indonesia, and Menoufia, Egypt were conducted in the early 1980s by Fortney and her colleagues.[33] The findings were generally consistent with findings from studies in developed countries. In both sites, users of oral contraceptives aged 30 or older had twice the risk of death from cardiovascular disease as nonusers. Even so, the absolute risk of death due to contraceptive use was low: four deaths in Menoufia and two in Bali per 100,000 users per year. By comparison, pregnancy and delivery were 120 times more dangerous than using contraceptives for a year in Bali, and 48 times more dangerous in Menoufia.

Thus, when the literature on contraceptive risks and benefits is viewed as a whole, what emerges is the conclusion that, at the population level, pregnancy is almost always more dangerous than contraceptive use.

SEXUALLY TRANSMITTED DISEASES

Unlike maternal mortality, sexually transmitted diseases are a serious public health problem in both developed and developing countries. According to the World Health Organization, in 1990 alone there were 250 million new cases of STDs among men and women, including 120 million of trichomoniasis, 25 million of gonorrhea, 20 million of genital herpes, 3.5 million of syphilis, 2.5 million of hepatitis B, 2 million of chancroid, and 1 million of human immunodeficiency virus (HIV), the virus that causes AIDS.[34] Although there are serious deficiencies in reporting systems,[35] it does appear that incidence and prevalence of many STDs are increasing. Moreover, there appears to be a synergistic effect between infection with the HIV virus and some other STDs, especially those which cause genital lesions (thus providing portals of entry for HIV).

The health consequences of hundreds of millions of new STD cases contracted every year are staggering. They include chronic abdominal pain in women, discomfort and possibly genital erosion and infertility in men and women, and pneumonia or blinding eye infections in infants infected at birth. Even though many of these conditions can be controlled with treatment, many others cannot. AIDS has received the most attention, but STDs can lead to other fatal complications as well. These include stillbirths, ectopic pregnancies, and cervical cancer.[36]

STDs can also affect fertility. The most pronounced impact is infertility associated with scarring of the fallopian tubes. This occurs most often with pelvic inflammatory disease (PID), which often stems from gonorrhea and chlamydia infection. The best measure of the effect of STDs on fertility includes not only infertility, but also the subfertility associated with "pregnancy wastage" (e.g., miscarriages caused by syphilis) and STD-associated infant mortality (e.g., deaths caused by herpes or AIDS). The cumulative problem of childlessness is especially severe in parts of Sub-Saharan Africa. In Gabon, 32 percent of couples are involuntarily childless; in the Congo and Zaire, the proportion is 21 percent.[37] In comparison, less than 5 percent of couples in the United States suffer this problem.[38]

By almost any standard, health problems of the magnitude of those associated with STDs deserve serious attention from the health care system; when the social and psychological damage resulting from STDs is added to the physical misery they cause, the case for increased attention becomes even more compelling. That STDs have been relatively neglected is perhaps evidence of the problems in program development and policy formation that we examine in the following sections.

IMPLICATIONS FOR PROGRAMS AND POLICIES

The overwhelming emphasis in reproductive health programs as they have developed over the last several decades has been on promoting family planning and delivering antenatal care. In part, this emphasis is due to the influence of policy objectives not directly related to women's health per se—most significantly, population growth reduction and child survival. In recent years there has been a serious effort to demonstrate that family planning and antenatal care programs are also important for women's health and to use the promotion of women's health as another, important rationale to support them. And, indeed, the epidemiological data do show that family planning can be extremely important to women's health.

But the rights principles presented earlier require a rather different emphasis in reproductive health programs and policy. Perhaps the best way to express the distinction between the more traditional approach and the approach advocated here is this: we do not begin by asking whether a particular type of program improves women's health, but rather by asking what is the nature of women's health problems, and then asking what kinds of programs will best address *those* problems.

This means starting with a view of health—and particularly of sexuality and reproduction—as it is experienced by women. From this starting point, it is not enough to demonstrate through epidemiological studies that a given intervention by the health care system is associated with improvements in women's health. From a woman's point of view, that a particular intervention could improve her health may be irrelevant or unimportant if the measure ignores what she perceives her real health problems to be. In fact, it may be worse than irrelevant, because a health care system that is heavily oriented to goals (whether expressed in health terms or in other, such as demographic, terms) that do not coincide with a woman's priorities in her life can actually work against the strategies she has developed to ensure her own and her family's survival, and possibly even undermine her efforts to gain control over her sexual and reproductive existence.

This dissonance between a woman's perception of her health and well-being and the system's perception of what is "good" for her or her wider society may even be partly responsible for the troubling gap between women's knowledge of family planning combined with their desire to regulate their fertility, on the one hand, and contraceptive prevalence on the other.[39]

Pakistan provides a good example. Despite having one of the first official family planning programs in the world (the Family Planning Association of Pakistan was established in 1953), contraceptive prevalence remains extremely low (12 percent) and fertility remains extremely high. The total fertility rate (the total number of births an average woman would have at current fertility levels) is 6.8.[40] Attempts to analyze what has gone wrong with Pakistan's program point first to the supply-side strategies and "contraceptive inundation" programs of the 1960s and early 1970s. Such programs clearly suffered from mismanagement and other technical problems and failed to recognize that high fertility was socially desirable and perceived to be economically rational for many families.[41] In subsequent years, the program switched strategies to emphasize demand creation and social marketing of certain contraceptives. Yet contraceptive prevalence rates have barely budged.

Recent surveys of women showing an "unmet demand" of 58 percent and a contraceptive knowledge of over 50 percent hint at the real problem. Women in Pakistan are caught in a double bind. Laws, customs, and policies severely restrict their ability to obtain the education, skills, or jobs that would change the pattern of economic dependence that stifles their ability to make autonomous choices about their lives and that continues to make high fertility the surest route to social and economic security. And to make matters worse, Pakistan's family planning program fails to address these pressing issues, leaving women as disempowered as before.

Driven, first and foremost, by demographic goals, the program makes virtually no attempt to determine what its clients need and want.[42] Moreover, the program is shaped by social attitudes that deny women full agency (for example, by imposing family and spousal consent requirements for contraceptive services, particularly abortion).

Consequently, services hardly begin to address sexual and reproductive health issues with the same priorities that women bring to them. Caught between social structures that deny them basic rights and health services that show little concern for their social, physical, or psychological needs, it is little wonder that even women who want to find ways to control their fertility have not made use of the government's family planning services.

Thus, a reconceptualization of which issues are relevant to reproductive health is a precondition for developing programs and policies that will enable women to achieve a greater measure of control over their lives. But simply saying that the system should frame health issues as women perceive and experience them is only the first step. The epidemiological data make it abundantly clear that in the area of reproductive health, the choices are not straightforward; they invariably require weighing risks and benefits.

An important question in service programs, then, is whose view of risk should govern choices that will be made about an individual woman's life with respect to pregnancy and childbirth? The answer should be clear: a woman should be provided with the best possible information about the risks and benefits of available options; she should be permitted to weigh that information in the context of her own life; and she should be permitted to make decisions about her own sexuality and about pregnancy and/or childbirth based on her own calculus of relevant factors.

A woman's basic right to make these decisions needs to be respected by health programs, not only because that right exists in law,[43] but also because it relates fundamentally to health. A woman's ability to have control over and to make decisions about her own reproductive and sexual life can itself have implications for her overall health and well-being.[44] Put simply, choice has "health value" in its own right. Consequently, even in societies where women's lives are constricted by a broad range of laws and customs, trusting and respecting women's choices can and must have an explicit, conscious, and affirmative place in reproductive health programs.

A growing body of data supports the view that programs that fail to respect a woman's ability to assess the entire range of circumstances affecting her own life will not be successful in the long run. The problem in family planning programs is not lack of demand—women want to be able to control their fertility.[45] The shocking number of deaths from clandestine abortions certainly attests to this fact. The problem in family planning is poor quality programs. Experience has shown that where family planning programs are dominated by demographic goals, and where services are delivered in a manner that is dismissive or disrespectful of women's views of their own health and well-being, women will ultimately refuse to "comply" with providers' recommendations about what is "good for them."

Conversely, numerous studies demonstrate that family planning programs that are oriented to the realities and pressures of women's lives—that make physical access easy, provide usable information, offer a variety of methods, and treat women and their choices with respect—will be more successful.[46] Studies have shown that the larger the variety of methods that are available, the more couples will utilize some method. With data from 36 countries, Lapham and Mauldin found that contraceptive prevalence increases by about 12 percent for each additional method offered; in general, countries offering five or six readily accessible methods had more than twice the contraceptive prevalence as those offering only one or two methods.[47]

Family planning is undeniably good for women's health, but even the best family planning programs cannot be the entire answer to women's health needs; women who are pregnant may need emergency obstetric care, and women who have STDs need treatment.

In other respects as well, the relationship between family planning programs and STDs has not been an entirely comfortable one. For example, the current reliance on techniques for STD prevention that are also contraceptives represents a serious limitation in the choices available to women, especially because the most common and effective technique for STD prevention—condoms—is controlled by men. More research is needed to find ways for women to get pregnant without becoming infected. Stein and others have called for the development of microbicides that would allow conception but prevent infection.[48] Currently a large number of women risk exposure to STDs while trying to become pregnant; it is arguable that resources dedicated to developing technologies to ameliorate this issue have not been concomitant with the scale of the problem.[49]

Similarly, family planning can decrease maternal deaths, but it cannot help women give birth safely. Only access to emergency obstetric care can do that. Yet, such care rarely gets the priority that it surely deserves. All too often, "safe motherhood" programs devote their resources to screening programs designed to identify high-risk women. Such programs are not justified on either health or cost effectiveness grounds. Program planners often state that emergency obstetric care is too expensive. However, some developing countries (such as India and Bangladesh) already have a health infrastructure consisting of hospitals, health centers, doctors, nurses, and paramedical personnel. The government and the people are paying for these health services, but the systems are not functioning well. What could be less economical than paying for something that you don't receive?

In other countries the infrastructure is much weaker. Even then, providing emergency obstetric care may be economical if measured in terms of cost effectiveness. For example, training traditional birth attendants (TBAs) may be inexpensive per TBA, but TBAs cannot prevent or treat most obstetric complications. Therefore, per maternal death averted, training TBAs is much more expensive than upgrading health centers to provide basic emergency obstetric care and upgrading district hospitals to provide comprehensive emergency care. A cost-effectiveness exercise exploring this subject found that training TBAs and providing antenatal care were more than three times as expensive per maternal death averted as either providing family planning or upgrading health centers and district hospitals.[50]

The principle advocated here—that family planning programs should be designed to support women's control over their reproductive lives—need not be understood to exclude men from reproductive health programs. Clearly programs that address male resistance to contraception and family planning will help women to implement the choices they make. Although it is also important that men's role in, and responsibility for, sex, contraception, and family planning be recognized, care must be taken to ensure that involving men does not limit women's autonomy, as has been reported to be the case, for example, with programs in Pakistan targeting men.[51] Undoubtedly this means that there is no one "right" way to involve men in reproductive health programs; many decisions, such as whether to integrate or separate programs for men and women, will certainly depend on local cultural and practical considerations.

Moreover, in every environment, men will also have physical and psychological health needs related to reproduction, such as controlling fertility and avoiding STDs. Where high quality programs with few barriers to access have addressed men's reproductive health needs, the results have been positive. The Family Planning Association in Honduras, for example, has created popular clinical services specifically for men. In New York City, Columbia University runs a Young Men's Clinic, catering to the special needs of male adolescents; the program engages men in the earliest stages of sexual activity and has struggled to keep up with expanding demand. In some settings, programs that work with men and women as couples appeal to other segments of the populations they serve.[52]

THE USES AND LIMITATIONS OF DATA

Distinguishing risk at the population, clinical, and individual levels can help clarify which view of the data is most appropriate for addressing the problems faced by different decisionmakers. This paper has demonstrated, for example, that the use of relative risk is usually not appropriate for designing reproductive health programs because it does not help identify priorities from either the population (public health) perspective or the individual woman's perspective. Even in the clinical setting, emphasis on relative risk can be problematic because it reflects the clinician's point of view, not the woman's. In the end, which point of view should govern decisionmaking is less a scientific question of health, than it is an ethical and policy question of rights.

The reproductive rights principles that we have begun to elaborate can help answer these questions. Keeping rights at the forefront of the discussion about health can bring a needed perspective to the use of epidemiological data at the broader, political level as well. Two specific issues related to the risk data we have discussed here help illustrate the point. The first relates to the political uses of contraceptive risk data. The second relates to perceptions of risk groups in the history of attempts to control the spread of STDs.

The data demonstrating that contraception almost always presents a lower risk of death than does childbirth justify—even mandate—making contraceptives available and accessible to all women. But the same data have been used to justify population programs in which women are given little or no contraceptive choice. This is the case, for example, in Vietnam (where family planning programs offer intrauterine devices, or IUDs, almost exclusively), and in parts of India (where family planning programs still focus on sterilization).[53] As Dixon-Mueller and Germain discuss in an essay criticizing reliance on narrow concepts of relative risk, such policies not only ignore different levels of risk among different groups of women, they fail to acknowledge a wide range of other health and non-health concerns and the way such concerns might be valued by a given woman in the context of her own life.[54]

At their worst, such programs can border on coercion by denying women information or options with respect to contraception, while simultaneously instilling fear by exaggerating the risks of childbirth. Indeed, service delivery programs that focus on achieving the patient's compliance with the provider's recommendations and ignore issues that may be critically important in an individual woman's life tend to feed condescending attitudes—viewing women as incapable of making the "right" choices about their health.[55] Where population policies include "contraceptive acceptor" targets that health care providers must achieve or be subject to penalties, the situation is ripe for abuse.[56]

The use of health data to justify poor quality, even coercive, family planning programs has drawn fire from many health and rights activists. Yet the same data have been used by foes of such policies to exaggerate the risks of contraceptives and, on that basis, to advocate policies that would ban certain contraceptives altogether or make access to them unduly complicated. For example, some groups of women's health activists in the United States and elsewhere are working to ban Norplant outright, rather than working on improving services for client counseling and removal of the device on demand.[57]

The question of what level of safety should be proven and what quality of services should be available before a contraceptive should be distributed is a complex and difficult one. But the failure to acknowledge the existence of wide variations in the needs and safety/risk perceptions of individual women—and their right to the information and means to make informed choices about controlling their own reproduction—can be just as dismissive of the realities of women's lives when it comes from health activists as when it comes from advocates of population control. What these different attempts to influence contraceptive policies have in common is the underlying conviction that the proponent of the policy knows what is best for women. That conviction should be recognized and rejected; it should not be permitted to hide behind the supposed neutrality of data.

There are other, perhaps even more insidious, ways that risk data have been manipulated to promote social and political agendas. The use of seemingly objective scientific evidence to justify, in the guise of improving health, measures designed to regulate the behavior of individual women whose lives—whether by choice or by necessity—defy conventional norms of wifehood and motherhood, has a long tradition in law and policy.[58] Nowhere is this more apparent than in the area of STD regulation, where women's reproductive health has suffered a combination of neglect and blame, which often becomes institutionalized through programs based on inaccurate representations of risk.[59]

The history of venereal disease control efforts is replete with misadventures,[60] yet many current policies do not appear to be informed by important lessons from the past. The epidemic of blame associated with the AIDS pandemic provides a recent example.[61] Epidemiological studies in the early 1980s fueled the popular notion of high-risk groups, which became a trampoline for discrimination against unpopular minority groups, such as Haitians and gay men in the United States.

Despite evidence from other countries of the risk of HIV to women, it was not adequately studied in the United States—largely as a result of the perception that AIDS was a gay male syndrome.[62] Official agencies such as the Centers for Disease Control and the WHO Global Programme on AIDS, which helped shape the global response to AIDS, have now redefined the clinical symptomology of AIDS to include opportunistic infections suffered uniquely by women so that they may now be counted. They have also shifted away from the rubric *high risk groups* to focus on *high risk behavior*. In many ways, however, these reactions to the data came too little, too late. For, in fact, in many parts of the world, prostitutes are singled out in AIDS prevention programs as carriers of infection.[63] Numerous studies show that large proportions of prostitutes are HIV positive, but few note that most HIV positive women are not prostitutes.[64]

Here, the genealogy of targeted prevention is doubly complicated. Not surprisingly, women have been targeted because they are viewed as uniquely responsible for the reproductive function, especially where perinatal HIV transmission is a growing problem. But additionally, women are targeted because they are perceived to be a main vector for AIDS transmission in the adult population, mostly through prostitution. Thus HIV-positive women risk incarceration in many countries, including the United States.[65] Although it is sometimes noted that women are more likely to be infected during a single exposure with men than vice versa,[66] heterosexual transmission of AIDS has somehow become a call to target prostitutes, but not their male clients who carry infection home to their families. We do not mean to imply that special programs to address commercial sex workers are misguided or irrelevant; we do, however, object when these are the main focus of national programs or are publicized in a way that blames sex workers or downplays other sources of risk.

CONCLUSION

This chapter has attempted to illuminate the ways the results of epidemiological studies are used and misused as guides to policies and programs that affect women's reproductive health. It suggests that relative risk is usually not the appropriate measure of risk, since it reflects neither the client's perspective nor the possible public health implications. Policies and programs need to be guided first and foremost by respect for fundamental dignity and the rights of women as human beings. The core of these rights is respect for women's decisions, which are based not just on health considerations, but on a variety of personal, economic, and practical considerations as well. Programs that claim to promote reproductive health cannot be fully successful unless they supply women with the information and means to implement their own risk/benefit calculations.

Notes

[1] S. Abdul A'la Maududi, *Purdah and the Status of Women in Islam* (Lahore: Islamic Publications LTD., Ninth Edition, 1987, first published in 1993 in Urdu and translated into English in 1972), p. 121. Maududi, an internationally recognized scholar of Islam, was the head of the right-wing, fundamentalist political party in Pakistan, the Jamaat-e-Islami.

[2] M. Luther, "The Estate of Marriage," (1552) in Volume 45 of Luther's Works, *The Christian in Society II* (Philadelphia, PA: Muhlenberg Press, 1962), p. 46.

[3] L. Gordon, *Woman's Body, Woman's Rights*, revised edition (New York: Penguin Books, 1990); and A. McLaren, *Reproductive Rituals* (New York: Methuen & Co., 1984).

[4] S.M. Gifford, "The Meaning of Lumps: A Case Study of the Ambiguities of Risk," in C.R. James, R. Stall, and S.M. Gifford (eds.), *Anthropology and Epidemiology: Interdisciplinary Approaches to the Study of Health and Disease* (Dordrecht, Holland: D. Reidel, 1986), p. 220.

[5] Ibid., p. 233.

[6] R.J. Cook, *Human Rights in Relation to Women's Health* (Geneva: World Health Organization (WHO), 1993).

[7] Abdullahi Ahmed An-Na'im, *Toward an Islamic Reformation: Civil Liberties, Human Rights, and International Law* (New York: Syracuse University Press, 1990); and R. Thandabantu Nhalapo, "International Protection of Human Rights and the Family: African Variations on a Common Theme," *International Journal of Law and the Family*, Vol. 3, 1989, pp. 1-20.

[8] A.R. Omran and C.C. Standley (eds.), *Family Formation Patterns and Health: An International Collaborative Study in India, Iran, Lebanon, Philippines, and Turkey* (Geneva: WHO, 1976).

[9] In the United States, this problem is receiving attention in the Women's Health Equity Act, an omnibus legislative package consisting of 32 separate pieces of legislation now pending in the U.S. Congress (e.g., Pharmaceutical Testing Fairness Act, H.R.2795); and R.L. Kirschstein, "Research on Women's Health," *American Journal of Public Health*, Vol. 81 (1991), pp. 291-293.

[10] F. Tazhib, "Vesico-Vaginal Fistula in Nigerian Children," *The Lancet* (7 December 1985), pp. 1291-93.

[11] Ibid.

[12] M. Murphey, "Social Consequences of Vesico-Vaginal Fistula in Northern Nigeria," *Journal of Biosocial Science*, Vol. 13 (1981), pp. 139-150.

[13] According to the World Health Organization (WHO), maternal mortality is "the death of a woman during pregnancy or within 42 days of the termination of pregnancy, irrespective of the duration or site of pregnancy, from any cause related to or aggravated by the pregnancy or its management, but not from accidental causes." Since induced abortion is, in effect, a form of pregnancy management, abortion deaths are included. See WHO, *International Classification of Diseases 9* (Geneva: WHO, 1977).

[14] C. AbouZahr and E. Royston, *Maternal Mortality: A Global Factbook* (Geneva: WHO, 1991).

[15] R.W. Rochat, in *Preventing the Tragedy of Maternal Deaths: A Report on the International Safe Motherhood Conference, Nairobi, February 1987*, A. Starrs (ed.), (Washington, DC: World Bank, 1987), p. 13.

[16] U.S. Department of Health and Human Services, *Vital Statistics of the United States 1988* (Hyattsville, MD: U.S. Department of Health and Human Services, 1991); and R.C. Carriere, "Why the Other Half Dies—Maternal Mortality in Bangladesh," statement at the First International Conference on Obstetrics and Gynecology, UNICEF, Dhaka, 11 December 1992.

[17] D. Nortman, *Parental Age as a Factor in Pregnancy Outcomes*, Reports on Population/Family Planning No. 16 (New York: The Population Council, 1974).

[18] L.C. Chen et al., "Maternal Mortality in Rural Bangladesh," *Studies in Family Planning*, Vol. 5, No. 11 (November 1974), pp. 334-341.

[19] J. Hobcraft, J. McDonald, and S. Rutstein, "Child Spacing Effects on Infant and Early Childhood Mortality," *Population Index*, Vol. 49, No. 4 (1983), pp. 585-618.

[20] A. Rosenfield and D. Maine, "Maternal Mortality: A Neglected Tragedy: Where is the 'M' in 'MCH'?" *The Lancet*, Vol. 2 (15 July 1985), pp. 83-85.

[21] K.A. Harrison, "Predicting Trends in Operative Delivery for Cephalopelvic Disproportion in Africa," *The Lancet*, Vol. 335 (7 April 1990), pp. 862-862.

[22] S. Harlap, K. Kost, and J. Darroch Forrest, *Preventing Pregnancy, Protecting Health: A New Look at Birth Control Choices in the United States* (New York: Alan Guttmacher Institute, 1991), p. 95.

[23] D. Maine, *Safe Motherhood: Options and Issues* (New York: Center for Population and Family Health, 1991).

[24] F.M. Coeytaux, "Induced Abortion in Sub-Saharan Africa: What We Do and Do Not Know," in *Studies in Family Planning*, Vol. 19, No. 3 (May/June 1988), pp. 186-190.

[25] M.A. Koenig et al., "Maternal Mortality in Matlab, Bangladesh: 1976-85," in *Studies in Family Planning*, Vol. 19, No. 2 (March/April 1988), pp. 69-80.

[26] Ibid., p. 77. The reason is that increased use of contraceptives "led to a shift in the pattern of childbearing away from one high-risk group (older, high parity women) but toward another subgroup with equivalent or even higher mortality risks (younger, nulliparous women)."

[27] Kasongo Project Team, "Antenatal Screening for Fetopelvic Dystocias: A Cost-Effectiveness Approach to the Choice of Simple Indicators for Use by Auxiliary Personnel," *Journal of Tropical Medicine and Hygiene*, Vol. 87, No. 4 (August 1984), pp. 173-183. See also A.M. Greenwood et al., "A Prospective Study of the Outcome of Pregnancy in a Rural Area of The Gambia," *Bulletin of the WHO*, Vol. 65, No. 5 (1987), pp. 635-643.

[28] Ibid.

[29] I. Loudon, "On Maternal and Infant Mortality 1900-1960," *Social History of Medicine* Vol. 4, No. 1 (April 1991) pp. 29-73. This fact was further demonstrated by a study of maternal mortality in the Faith Assembly of God, a religious community in the United States whose members do not make use of modern medical care, even in emergencies. This community is prosperous, and its members are well educated and well fed. Yet, in 1982 alone, there were 872 maternal deaths per 100,000 live births in this community. This is about 100 times higher than the level of maternal mortality in the U.S. population as a whole, and even higher than the current level cited for Bangladesh (see note 14).

[30] V. Beral, "Reproductive Mortality," *British Medical Journal*, Vol. 2 (1979), pp. 632-634.

[31] Harlap et al., op. cit.

[32] Ibid., p. 89.

[33] J. Fortney et al., "Reproductive Mortality in Two Developing Countries," *American Journal of Public Health*, Vol. 76 (1986), pp. 134-138.

[34] WHO, "Sexually Transmitted Infections Increasing—250 Million New Infections Annually," *WHO Features*, Vol. 152 (December 1990), pp. 1-6.

[35] G.M. Antel, "The World Picture," in *Sexually Transmitted Diseases: Proceedings of a Conference Sponsored Jointly by the Royal Society of Medicine of the RSM Foundation 1975* (New York: Academic Press, 1976), pp. 25-31.

[36] Population Reports, "Controlling Sexually Transmitted Diseases," Series L, No. 9 (June 1993).

[37] A. Meheus, "Women's Health: Importance of Reproductive Tract Infections, Pelvic Inflammatory Disease and Cervical Cancer," in *Reproductive Tract Infections*, A. Germain et al. (eds.), (New York: Plenum Press, 1992).

[38] J.R. Wilkie, "Involuntary Childlessness in the United States," *Zeitschrift Fur Bevolkerungswissenschaft*, Vol. 10, No. 1 (1984), pp. 37-52.

[39] S.W. Sinding, J. Ross, and A. Rosenfield, "Seeking Common Ground: Unmet Need and Demographic Goals," *International Family Planning Perspectives*, Vol. 20, No. 1 (March 1994), pp. 23-27. For a critique of the definition of "unmet need" and "unmet demand," see also R. Dixon-Mueller and A. Germain, "Stalking the Elusive Unmet Need," *Studies in Family Planning*, Vol. 23, No. 5, (September/October 1993), pp. 330-335.

[40] United Nations, *World Population 1992* (New York: United Nations, 1992). A recent review of the demographic data on Pakistan concludes that estimates of the total fertility rate in the 1980s range from 6.0 to 6.9 and that "there is no consensus on the fertility levels in Pakistan." Z.A. Sathar, "The Much-Awaited Fertility Decline in Pakistan: Wishful Thinking or Reality?" *International Family Planning Perspectives*, Vol. 19, No. 4 (December 1993), pp. 142-146.

[41] W.C. Robinson, M.A. Shah, and N.M. Shah, "The Family Planning Programme in Pakistan: What Went Wrong?" *International Family Planning Perspectives*, Vol. 7, No. 3 (September 1981); and Z.A. Sathar, *Population Policy and Demographic Change in Pakistan*, Seminar on 8th Five-Year Plan, Planning Commission, Government of Pakistan, December 1991.

[42] Sathar, *Population Policy and Demographic Change in Pakistan*, op. cit.

[43] Article 16, "Convention on the Elimination of all Forms of Discrimination Against Women," 18 December 1979, U.N. Doc. A/RES/34/180; L.P. Freedman and S.L. Isaacs, "Human Rights and Reproductive Choice," *Studies in Family Planning*, Vol. 24, No. 1 (1993), pp. 18-30; and R.J. Cook, "International Protection of Women's Reproductive Rights," *New York University Journal of International Law and Politics*, Vol. 24 (1992), pp. 647-727.

[44] R. Dixon-Mueller, *Population Policy and Women's Rights* (Westport, CT: Praeger, 1993).

[45] Sinding, Ross, and Rosenfield, op. cit. See also Dixon-Mueller and Germain, op. cit.

[46] J. Ross, M. Rich, and J. Molzan, *Management Strategies for Family Planning Programs* (New York: Center for Population and Family Health, Columbia University School of Public Health, Columbia University School of Public Health, 1989) and the sources cited therein.

[47] R.J. Lapham and W.P. Mauldin, "Contraceptive Prevalence: The Influence of Organized Family Planning," *Studies in Family Planning*, Vol. 16, No. 3 (May-June 1985), pp. 117-137.

[48] Z. Stein, "HIV Prevention: The Need for Methods Women Can Use," *American Journal of Public Health*, Vol. 80 (1990), pp. 460-462.

[49] C.J. Elias and L. Heise, "The Development of Microbicides: A New Method of HIV Prevention for Women," Working Paper No. 6 (New York: The Population Council, 1993).

[50] Maine, op. cit., pp. 46-53.

[51] International Planned Parenthood Federation, Open File, November 1993, p. 8, citing Depthnews Women's Feature, August 1993.

[52] One example of a reproductive health program that includes both separate services for men and women *and* services designed to treat men and women as couples is the main STD/HIV clinic run by the Trinidadian government in Port-of-Spain.

[53] J. Allman et al., "Fertility and Family Planning in Vietnam," *Studies in Family Planning*, Vol. 22, No. 5 (September/October 1991), pp. 308-317.

[54] A. Germain and R. Dixon-Mueller, "Whose Life Is It Anyway? Assessing the Relative Risks of Contraception and Pregnancy," *Four Essays on Birth Control Needs and Risks* (New York: International Women's Health Coalition, 1993).

[55] J.A. Gupta, "People Like You Never Agree to Get It: Visit to an Indian Family Planning Clinic," *Reproductive Health Matters*, No. 1 (May 1993).

[56] Davidson Gwatkin, "Political Will and Family Planning: The Implications of India's Emergency Experience," *Population and Development Review*, Vol. 5, No. 29 (1979).

[57] B. Mintzes, A. Hardon, and J. Hanhart (eds.), *Norplant: Under Her Skin* (The Netherlands: Women's Health Action Foundation and WEMOS, 1993).

[58] See, for example, C. Smart, "Disruptive Bodies and Unruly Sex: The Regulation of Reproduction and Sexuality in the Nineteenth Century," in C. Smart (ed.), *Regulating Womanhood: Historical Essays on Marriage, Motherhood and Sexuality* (New York: Routledge, 1992); R. Hubbard, M.S. Henifin, and B. Fried (eds.), *Biological Woman: The Convenient Myth* (Cambridge, MA: Schenkman Publishing Co., Inc., 1982); V. Sapiro (ed.), *Women, Biology, and Public Policy* (Newbury Park, CA: Sage Publications, 1985); and S.J. Gould, *The Mismeasure of Man* (New York: W.W. Norton, 1981).

[59] The combination of blame and neglect is not confined to STD regulation. Wendy Chavkin has pointed out that there are relatively few drug treatment programs in the United States that will accept pregnant women. Yet rather than ensure that such women can get treatment, women are often demeaned and penalized for the potential harm to which they may be exposing the fetus, and in some instances are even imprisoned to prevent further drug use. See "Drug Addiction and Pregnancy: Policy Crossroads," *American Journal of Public Health*, Vol. 80, No. 4 (April 1990), pp. 483-487.

[60] A. Brandt, *No Magic Bullet: A Social History of Venereal Disease in the United States Since 1880*, exp. ed. (New York: Oxford University Press, 1987); and J.R. Walkowitz, *Prostitution and Victorian Society: Women, Class, and the State* (New York: Cambridge University Press, 1980).

[61] Renée Sabatier et al., *Blaming Other: Prejudice, Race, and Worldwide AIDS* (Washington, DC: Panos Institute, 1988).

[62] E. Fee and N. Krieger, "Understanding AIDS: Historical Interpretations and the Limits of Biomedical Individualism," *American Journal of Public Health*, Vol. 83, No. 10 (October 1993), pp. 1477-860.

[63] N. Ferenic, P. Alexander, G. Slutkin, and P. Lamptey, "Effectiveness and Coverage of Sex-Work Interventions in Developing Countries," *AIDS Health Promotion Exchange*, Vol. 1 (1992), pp. 14-16.

[64] Elias and Heise, op. cit., pp. 6-7.

[65] R. Bayer and A. Fairchild-Carrino, "AIDS and the Limits of Control: Public Health Orders, Quarantine, and Recalcitrant Behavior," *American Journal of Public Health*, Vol. 83, No. 10, pp. 1471-1476; and *AIDS and the Law*; see also M. Bruyn, "Women and AIDS in Developing Countries," *Social Science and Medicine*, Vol. 34, No. 3 (1992), pp. 249-262.

[66] European Study Group on Heterosexual Transmission of HIV, "Comparison of Female to Male and Male to Female Transmission of HIV in 563 Stable Couples," *British Medical Journal*, Vol. 304, pp. 809-813.

Chapter Eight

International Migration, Fertility, and Development

Michael S. Teitelbaum and Sharon Stanton Russell

International migration, long ignored in discussions of population and development, has recently become a major issue in domestic and international policy debates. Prospective trends in global economic and political conditions mean that the potential is high for continued increases in international population movements. This poses fundamental challenges:

■ to the "new world order" emerging in the post-Cold War period (or, perhaps, migrations are an integral part of this new order);

■ to the post-World War II system of sovereign states;

■ to the painfully built international refugee system, which is now threatened as never before; and

■ to the political survival of governments and democratic political parties committed to tolerance in countries such as France, Germany, and Belgium.

Although only a small minority of the world's people ever move across national boundaries as migrants, the potential impact on various aspects of population (e.g., demographic changes surrounding fertility, population size and growth, age structure, internal population composition) and on development is both significant and complex.

International migration may best be seen as a focal point of intersection among economic, demographic, and political differentials. As these disparities widen, so does the potential for (although not necessarily the actuality of) international migration.

This chapter explores the relationships among fertility, international population movements, and development. It reviews international migration patterns and trends and considers the range of forces creating increased potential for movement; discusses responses to these forces and trends; and examines the links among international migration, fertility, and underlying demographic change, as well as those between international population movements and economic development in emigration countries.

TRENDS IN INTERNATIONAL MIGRATION

Scale and Composition

International migration statistics are often inaccurate and incomplete and generally lag several years behind, making reliable worldwide estimates difficult. Using the most recent global numbers, which are based on the 1980 round of censuses and refugee data for the period, the U.N. Population Division estimates that approximately 100 million migrants lived outside their countries of birth or citizenship as of around 1985.[1] This figure includes those recorded in censuses as foreign born or foreign nationals, and some 12 to 13 million refugees as reported for that time by the U.N. High Commissioner for Refugees (UNHCR) and the U.N. Relief and Works Agency (UNRWA). The 100-million figure includes roughly 36 million in Asia, the Middle East, and North Africa; over 23 million in Eastern and Western Europe; over 20 million in the United States and Canada; 10 million in Sub-Saharan Africa; 6 million in Latin America and the Caribbean; and 4 million in Oceania (see Figure 1).[2]

"Guesstimates" at best, these numbers have undoubtedly grown in recent years as the result of both changing national boundaries and increasing international mobility. For example, they do not include the more than 70 million citizens of the former Soviet Union now living outside the bounds of their "own" ethnic polity;[3] nor do they include estimates for illegal migrants or externally displaced persons not reported in census or refugee sources.

International migrants are as diverse as their motivations to move. Some are settlers, whose migration—whether legal or illegal—is essentially permanent; others have moved (at least in the first instance) on a temporary basis. Some observers have begun to consider the role of environmental factors in generating a further category termed "eco-migrants." In general, migrants tend to be young adults. Between 40 and 60 percent of all international migrants worldwide—and over one half of refugees—are women and girls.[4] At the beginning

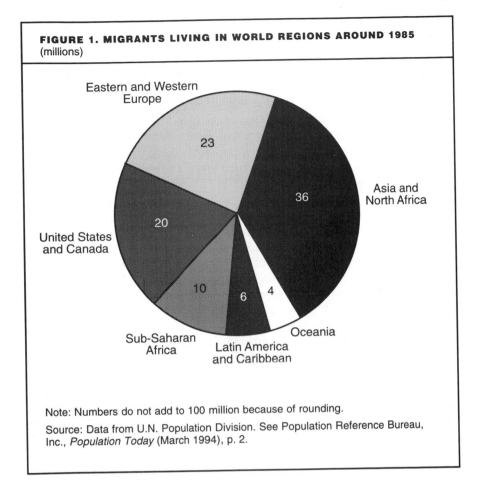

FIGURE 1. MIGRANTS LIVING IN WORLD REGIONS AROUND 1985
(millions)

Eastern and Western Europe — 23

Asia and North Africa — 36

United States and Canada — 20

Sub-Saharan Africa — 10

Latin America and Caribbean — 6

Oceania — 4

Note: Numbers do not add to 100 million because of rounding.

Source: Data from U.N. Population Division. See Population Reference Bureau, Inc., *Population Today* (March 1994), p. 2.

of 1993, approximately 19 million people were officially designated as refugees.[5] In addition, there are about an equal number of forced migrants in refugee-like situations.

Regional Patterns

Only some regional patterns and trends in international population movements can be highlighted in this brief chapter. However, two general points deserve emphasis. First, the bulk of the world's population, and of each country, never moves across international borders; only in the most extreme cases, such as Cuba, Afghanistan, Haiti, and El Salvador, has even as much as 10 percent of the population emigrated. Second, although international migration trends have attracted the most visible concern in Western industrialized countries, more than half of international migration is between developing countries (i.e., south to south), followed (in order of scale) by south to north and east to west movements.

Asia, with some 36 million migrants, has experienced large-scale and sudden population movements. In 1993, there were over 7 million refugees, including over 4.5 million Afghans and 2.7 million Palestinians.

Before the 1991 Persian Gulf War, a major feature of international migration to Western Asia was labor migration to the oil-rich Gulf states, which hosted approximately 7 million migrant workers and their dependents in the late 1980s.[6] There were three major trends in this migration stream over the past decade. First was the growing number of Asians, up from 12 percent of all migrants to Gulf states in 1970 to 63 percent in 1985. Second was the growing proportion of women among migrants for employment. Third, despite anticipation of a massive decline in labor migration in the 1980s, the number of migrants apparently remained stable or increased slightly. Some of these foreign workers, along with Kuwaitis, Iraqi Shiites, and Kurds, were among the 4 to 5 million people uprooted following Iraq's invasion of Kuwait.

Since the end of the Gulf War, Asian and some Arab workers (notably Egyptians) have begun to return to the Gulf, where the need for foreign workers is likely to continue. However, of possibly greater significance is increasing labor migration within East and Southeast Asia. These regions have become the most economically dynamic in the world, and international migration within Asia is to increasingly diverse destinations—notably to the newly industrializing economies of Hong Kong, Korea, Singapore, and Taiwan, as well as to Brunei, Malaysia, and Japan.[7] An increasing proportion of Asian migrants are women moving for jobs in domestic service and the entertainment industry.

Sub-Saharan Africa has the second largest concentration of refugees (after Asia), with an official count of 5.4 million at the end of 1992 and possibly as many externally displaced.[8] Most voluntary migration is to other countries within Sub-Saharan Africa, despite increasing flows to Europe. Labor migration is important throughout Africa, especially to some Central and Western African countries and to the Republic of South Africa. African migration flows tend to be highly volatile, changing suddenly in response to conflicts and natural disasters.

Within and from Latin America and the Caribbean, the most salient feature of international migration is the overwhelming attraction of a relatively few countries, notably the United States, Argentina, and Venezuela. Mexico has by far the largest number of emigrants, the vast majority of whom are in the United States; some 4.3 million Mexicans were enumerated in the 1990 U.S. census.[9] Colombia and Cuba are also major source countries, each with about 750,000 emigrants; roughly three-quarters of Colombians go to neighboring Venezuela, while for the balance—as well as for most Cubans—the United States is the favored destination. Migration among Latin American countries has been increasing; between the 1970s and 1980s, the number of Latin Americans in the region but outside their countries of origin grew from less than 1 million to nearly 2 million. Movements were principally to Argentina and Venezuela, but also to and from Brazil, and from El Salvador, Nicaragua, and Guatemala. The U.N. High Commissioner for Refugees (UNHCR) reports over 885,000 refugees in Latin America at the end of 1992; however, this figure includes 720,000 people reported by host governments as being in refugee-like circumstances. Excluding these, the number drops to 165,000.[10]

The *United States, Canada,* and *Australia* are distinctive in being traditional countries of immigration.[11] In each of the last several years, the United States has admitted between 700,000 and 850,000 permanent immigrants;[12] this does not include asylum seekers, people admitted on non-immigrant visas, and the 3.1 million illegal aliens legalized since the 1986 Immigration Reform and Control Act. About half of permanent immigrants originate from Asia and another 40 percent from the Western Hemisphere (mostly from Latin America and the Caribbean).[13] On the basis of changes enacted in the 1990 Immigration Act, these numbers are expected to rise to a range of 800,000 to 1 million during the 1990s.[14] In addition, as of 1993, there were an estimated 3.5 million illegal residents in the United States (with perhaps 300,000 added each year), the majority from Latin America.[15] Canada, under a new five-year immigration plan that took effect in 1991, expects "moderate controlled growth" in immigration, with annual levels rising from 200,000 in 1990 to 250,000 in 1993–95. Australia experienced rising net annual immigration during the latter half of the 1980s, peaking at 164,000 in 1989, followed by substantial declines to approximately 102,000 in 1992.[16] Both North America and Australia have experienced growing immigration from Asian countries, as well as rising numbers of asylum seekers.

Migration to *Western Europe* is predominantly—and increasingly—from outside the region, notably from the Maghreb, Turkey, and former Yugoslavia; in addition there are growing numbers from Eastern Europe, Sub-Saharan Africa, and Asia—many of whom enter as asylum seekers. While Germany and, to a lesser extent, France and

Switzerland, continue to receive the largest number of migrants, the countries of Southern Europe have become important new ports of entry to the European Union. Indeed, in recent years, Italy, Spain, and Greece were transformed from long-standing emigration countries to countries of net in-migration.

Dramatic political changes in the countries of *Eastern Europe and the former Soviet Union* have prompted concern over the prospects of large-scale migration to Western European countries. So far, massive and disorderly flows have not materialized; nevertheless significant population movements are associated with these changes. Most notably, selected ethnic groups (Germans, Jews, Armenians, Greeks) have emigrated from the countries of the former Soviet Union to external "homelands," and significant numbers have moved from Eastern European countries to the western part of Germany, to Austria, and to other destinations. Moreover, there are widespread speculations about much larger impending pressures for out-migration from the former Soviet republics, Yugoslavia, Romania, and elsewhere in Eastern and Central Europe. There are also population movements between Russia and other republics, as well as evidence of growing undocumented migration both into Poland from the east and out of Poland to the west.

UNDERLYING FORCES AND PRECIPITATING FACTORS IN INTERNATIONAL MIGRATION[17]

There is no single well-developed theory of international migration.[18] Rather, analysts use a variety of organizing concepts (often drawn from observations about internal migration) to discuss international population movements. One of the most classic is the "push-pull" formulation, which emphasizes "push" factors in areas of migrant origin and "pull" factors in areas of destination. Analyses that stress "supply" and "demand" are a variant of this approach. "World systems" theorists argue that migration results from the extension of the global capitalist system to "peripheral" developing areas. Neo-classical market economists of the human capital school tend to view migration as the result of individual cost-benefit calculations based upon differential wage rates and the probability of obtaining employment. Others emphasize the importance of the household as a decisionmaking unit and stress the role of migration as a strategy for reducing risk and smoothing variations in household income—even in the absence of wage differentials.[19]

Still others (especially sociologists) point to the important role not only of individual and household characteristics, but also of community characteristics and of family, ethnic, and kinship networks in shaping and perpetuating migration patterns. Some demographers, geographers, and historians regard geographically and economically related migrations in certain periods as "migration systems." Political scientists and other analysts stress that international migration is not simply the result of market forces or individual and family behaviors but rather is influenced by the role of governments, whether in creating the political and economic conditions that encourage (or force) emigration or in exercising their sovereign right to control entry.

Many of these perspectives are incorporated in this chapter's discussion of international migration. In addition, this discussion draws sharp distinctions between the various driving forces that underlie international population movements and the intermediating factors that can determine whether or not movement actually occurs.

The diverse forces underlying international population movements have been growing substantially over the past three decades and can be expected to continue to do so well into the next century. These forces include:

■ The dramatic demographic increase of the past three decades (documented elsewhere in this volume) has led (with a 15–20 year lag) to rapid labor force growth, especially in the young adult age groups known to have the highest migration propensities. In the two decades from 1970 to 1990, the economically active population of the developing world increased by 59 percent, or some 658 million people. By comparison, the economically active population of the developed countries increased by only 23 percent, or 109 million people (see Table 1);

■ Over the two decades from 1990 to 2010, labor force growth in the developing world is projected to be considerably larger in absolute terms (733 million) and somewhat smaller in percentage terms (41 percent) than over the prior two decades. Because fertility declines have not yet occurred in much of Africa, the economically active population could increase as much as 75 percent (excluding the unknown mortality impact of AIDS); and

■ Other things being equal, increasing economic differentials between countries—in real wages and standards of living—raise the incentives for international movement. Labor demand in receiving areas, and unemployment and underemployment in countries of origin, constitute important forces driving international migration.

These demographic and economic forces create only the *potential* for international migration. Whether or not migration actually takes place depends on intermediating factors that may or may not precipitate migration flows. Such "precipitating factors" include:

TABLE 1. ECONOMICALLY ACTIVE POPULATION, 1970–1990 AND 1990–2010
(millions and percentages)

	Economically Active[a] (millions)			1970–1990 Increase		1990–2010 Increase	
	1970	1990	2010	(millions)	(percent)	(millions)	(percent)
World	1,597	2,364	3,147	767	48	783	33
Developing	1,120	1,778	2,511	658	59	733	41
Developed	477	586	636	109	23	50	9
Latin America	91	158	246	67	74	88	56
Africa	148	243	425	95	65	183	75
South Asia	432	661	977	229	53	316	48
East Asia	501	776	921	274	55	145	19
Oceania	8	12	16	4	49	3	28
Soviet Union	117	147	167	29	25	21	14
Europe	204	232	239	28	14	7	3
North America	96	135	156	39	41	20	15

[a]Data for 1990 and 2010 are projections.

Source: *Economically Active Population 1950–2025* (Geneva: ILO, 1986), Vol. V, Table 2.

■ Technological advances, especially in transportation and communication, which have literally transformed life in industrialized countries since World War II and have increasingly begun to do the same in previously isolated areas of Asia, Africa, and Latin America;

■ Recruitment of migrants by employers in receiving countries, sometimes facilitated by actions of their governments;

■ The development over time of dense social networks across borders, creating a social infrastructure of international migration;

■ Increasing trade competition between the high-wage economies of the industrialized countries and the low-wage economies in much of the developing world;

■ Governmental decisions (whether explicit or implicit) to promote labor export or import as a matter of public policy; and

■ Increases in violence, repression, persecution, human rights violations, and ethnic tensions, which in addition affect many more people because of rapid population growth in many countries and regions.

International migration flows have become increasingly volatile and unpredictable, as much for political as for economic reasons. This is particularly evident in the increasing number of people officially designated as refugees; according to UNHCR, the number of refugees rose rapidly during the 1980s, from 8.2 million in 1980 to 19 million at the beginning of 1993. In addition, there are another 24 million people who are not officially recognized as refugees but who are in refugee-like situations or internally displaced, bringing the total number to approximately 43 million.[20]

Whether or not they are officially recognized as refugees, most forced migrants who cross international borders take refuge in developing countries, although large—and until recently—growing numbers have entered industrialized countries and then claimed refugee status or "political asylum."[21] The number of asylum seekers in European countries rose from 65,000 in 1983 to 690,000 in 1992, with Germany receiving the largest number.[22] Most asylum claims in the early 1990s have originated in Eastern Europe, but sizable numbers come from more distant countries, including Sri Lanka, Somalia, and Ghana. However, the liberalization of East European political systems, coupled with deteriorating economic conditions in Western Europe, has led many West European governments to question the validity of most asylum claims and to change their asylum policies. As a result, the number of asylum seekers is thought to have declined in 1993 by roughly 140,000. Determinations as to who qualifies as a "refugee" are increasingly difficult as the boundaries between "political" and "economic" reasons for movement become increasingly blurred.

ATTITUDES AND REACTIONS

Reactions in Countries of Origin

Out-migration has become a way of life in many developing countries, with some governments encouraging labor export. Governments of countries as diverse as Turkey, the Philippines, South Korea, India, Pakistan, Bangladesh, Sri Lanka, Jamaica, Cuba, Barbados, Mexico, El Salvador, and Nicaragua have pursued such policies at various times, in most cases implicitly rather than explicitly.

Governments of labor-exporting countries generally show considerable ambivalence about large-scale emigration of their citizens. On the one hand, emigration provides relatively well-paid employment, especially attractive for governments struggling to keep pace with rapid labor force increases. In some countries (such as Egypt, Sri Lanka, and India) educational systems are producing far more highly educated graduates than domestic demand can absorb; by providing employment for both unskilled and skilled workers, emigration provides an outlet for domestic frustration that might otherwise present serious political problems. Emigration also can produce large inflows of valuable hard currency remittances. In addition, some governments welcome, or even encourage, the emigration of selected ethnic groups and political dissidents.

On the other hand, origin-country governments express concern that emigration deprives countries of their best human resources, represents a transfer of educational investment from poor to rich countries, and leads to abuses or exploitation of their workers.[23] Out-migration can also pose the risk of rather serious and sometimes dramatic economic problems requiring sudden adaptations when migrants return unexpectedly and in large numbers. In the aftermath of the Iraqi incursion into Kuwait in 1990, governments of the nearly 1.5 million foreigners in Kuwait found themselves unexpectedly responsible for the protection, emergency transportation, and reabsorption of large numbers of their nationals, while simultaneously experiencing traumatic terminations of hard-currency remittance inflows. Jordan and Yemen were most seriously affected, but similar if smaller-scale problems arose for the governments of Bangladesh, India, Pakistan, and the Philippines.

Reactions in Receiving Countries

Attitudes in receiving countries vary widely and have changed dramatically over time, making it best to consider several categories of receiving countries. In the developing world, these include major oil-exporting countries, other countries that are regional "poles" of migration, and those receiving international refugee flows. In the industrialized world (not discussed in detail in this volume), a wide range of experiences and attitudes about international migration can be found.

Throughout the 1970s, many (though not all) major oil-exporting developing countries actively recruited international migrants to staff their rapidly growing economies (e.g., Saudi Arabia and Kuwait) or implicitly welcomed unauthorized migration by taking no action to deter it (e.g., Nigeria and Venezuela). More recently, attitudes toward migration have shifted. With the downturn in real oil prices and economic growth rates during the 1980s, these same countries became less positive about migration. Between 1983 and 1985, Nigeria, for example, expelled large numbers of migrants from other African countries (about half from Ghana; the balance involving at least eight other countries), whose unlawful residence had been tolerated under more favorable economic conditions. Following Iraq's invasion in 1990, most of Kuwait's foreign workers fled, while Saudi Arabia expelled some 750,000 Yemeni workers after their government openly supported Iraq. After the Gulf War, the Kuwaiti government took measures to force the departure of most remaining Palestinian/Jordanian migrants because the Palestine Liberation Organization (PLO) and Jordan had supported Iraq and because of evidence that some Palestinians in Kuwait had collaborated with Iraqi forces.

Some other developing countries are regional "poles" of attraction for migrants, because they have higher levels of prosperity or economic development, or lower land prices,[24] than the countries of emigration. Examples of regional "poles" include Côte d'Ivoire, Argentina, and Malaysia. Typically, such receiving governments initially view these regional migrations positively, or at least implicitly accept the movements by failing to enforce migration regulations. However, reversals are common when economic conditions deteriorate and the rising number of migrants becomes politically controversial.

Most of the world's 19 million refugees can be found in the developing world, usually in neighboring states. Attitudes among developing countries that receive refugees vary widely. In some cases, refugees are viewed positively, especially when the refugees are members of cognate ethnic or racial groupings (as in many Sub-Saharan African cases) or when they represent a pool of "refugee warriors"[25] arrayed against antagonistic neighboring governments (as in the cases of Cambodians in Thailand and Afghanis in Pakistan and Iran). In other cases, refugee flows into developing countries are most unwelcome, and are dealt with harshly (the "push-off" of Vietnamese boat people landing on the beaches of Malaysia is but one memorable example).

Attitudes in industrialized countries toward immigration vary widely, ranging from the few that have seen themselves historically as countries of large-scale immigration (e.g., the United States, Canada, and Australia) to those that have essentially followed a zero immigration policy (most notably Japan). International migration is increasingly controversial in nearly all industrialized countries. This is most obvious in Western Europe, where debates about immigration have contributed to the rise of far right political movements and to turbulence in efforts to further integrate the European Union.

LINKS TO FERTILITY AND OTHER FORCES OF DEMOGRAPHIC CHANGE

Despite the popular view that high fertility in developing areas, coupled with low fertility in industrialized countries, is a major cause of international migration,[26] the relationship between migration and other demographic factors—population size, population growth, age structure, and internal population composition among others—is far from simple. The patterns and changes in each of these spheres are heterogeneous and complex. The terms "fertility" and "population size and growth," for example, are shorthand for a wide range of demographic patterns and changes, including low fertility in Europe and Japan; the small population and high fertility of Kuwait; and high fertility in Africa. Similarly, the age structures of populations can be "young" (and migrants tend to be young adults), "old" (an easily misunderstood term often used to describe the age composition of many industrialized societies so concerned about international migration today), or in transition. Finally, "internal population composition" embraces a number of dimensions—ethnic, racial, religious, and political. Nevertheless, some cautious generalizations can be made.

The greatest volume of international migration is between developing countries, where both origin and receiving areas are characterized by high fertility and youthful age structures. Demographic differentials do little to explain these movements.

Demographic differentials may be of special importance, however, in South to North population movements. High in-migration to low-fertility countries from countries with high fertility rates poses a number of challenging questions. First, does high fertility in emigration countries serve as what Mexican researchers call an "expulsive force" impelling people to migrate internationally? Second, does low fertility in the receiving country serve as an "inducement" or "magnet" to increased in-migration? Third, to what extent is the fertility of international migrants itself affected by their mobility?

The "expulsive" force of high fertility rates in emigration countries can occur only after a substantial lag. Sustained high fertility in a context of declining rates of infant and child mortality produces a very youthful age structure, with the numbers at each age of childhood notably larger than the numbers at the next older age. Only after the passage of 15 to 20 years, as these successively larger groups of children reach the age of labor force entry, may the "expulsive" force of high fertility be felt. Unless job growth is sustained at exceptionally high levels, the labor market for young adults becomes saturated, and relative incomes decline for this segment of the population. Typically this is accompanied by substantial rural-to-urban migration and, if circumstances permit, by follow-on migration to more favorable labor markets in other countries. Even if high fertility in developing countries were to decline to moderate levels tomorrow, the demographic pressures for migration would continue for several decades. Indeed, there is evidence from Malaysia and Thailand that out-migration did not accelerate until fertility declines had already begun.[27] Such phenomena can be explained by the fact that the numbers of young adults are increasing at the same time that rising per capita incomes give more people the means to migrate.

It may also be that low fertility in receiving countries serves as a kind of magnet attracting international migration, if only indirectly and again with a long delay. In some countries with high in-migration, fertility rates are at extraordinarily low levels. In Germany, for example, the total fertility rate in 1993 was 1.4 children per woman; in Italy, 1.3. Of course, migrants themselves do not analyze fertility rates. Instead, the fact of low fertility can be highlighted and politically "amplified" by pressures on governments from employers worried about future "labor shortages," or from politicians expressing collective fears of population decline. Such concerns may produce explicit or implicit policies favoring in-migration. Such demographic considerations may have been at least implicit factors in the political decisions that produced large-scale migratory movements to Germany and Italy in the 1980s. The Canadian government was far more explicit, justifying expansion of its immigrant and refugee admissions partly on demographic grounds.[28]

The important demographic point is that the age composition of a population is determined primarily by its fertility rates—not by its mortality rates, as commonly believed. Other things being equal, a population with a high proportion of children and young adults produced by high fertility (what demographers call a steeply sloping age structure) has a higher propensity for internal and international population movements, since migration is almost always heavily concentrated among young adults, i.e., among those 20 to 35 years of age.

An understanding of fertility and age structure is useful for contrasting the propensities for emigration from developing countries with those from Eastern European countries. In developing countries, fertility rates tend to be high and age structures consequently steeply sloping, whereas in Eastern Europe fertility has been relatively low for several decades, with age compositions comparable to those of Western nations. Hence, controlling for economic and other differences, the propensity for emigration from the South is likely to be higher and longer-lived than from the East, even though wage differentials with the West are currently about the same for both the South and the East. The fact that there is significant migration from Eastern to Western Europe—both areas of low fertility—underscores the point that high fertility is neither a necessary nor a sufficient condition for international migration.

Another important issue is how international migration affects the fertility of migrants themselves. Migrants who move from higher to lower fertility settings generally have fertility rates lower than those of co-nationals who remain at home. It is not clear, however, whether this is a function of self-selection among the migrants, the years of spousal separation that often accompany long distance migration, or migrants' cultural adaptation to their new setting.

Second-generation offspring of immigrants tend to exhibit fertility rates closer to, if not convergent with, those of the society in which they live. Yet much remains unknown about the likely convergence of fertility rates between migrants and natives. Fertility data for foreign-born or foreign nationals are often weak; they are even weaker for second-generation offspring if data are not collected on their parents' place of birth (the relevant U.S. Census question was eliminated after 1970). Moreover, many findings about fertility convergence are based upon historical experiences of past immigration streams that did not continue and/or of migrant groups that did not bring with them powerful cultural commitments to traditional family and fertility behaviors (such as those held by some Muslim migrants). More generally, attempts to anticipate the future course of fertility behavior have not been notably successful. It remains to be seen, therefore, whether past patterns of fertility convergence will prevail in coming decades.

INTERNATIONAL MIGRATION AND DEVELOPMENT AT HOME

Historically and today, voluntary international migration is one means by which people in developing countries seek to improve their economic and social conditions. From the perspective of developing-country governments, international migration is a major source of foreign exchange (especially for poor countries that attract little foreign investment), a key element in the functioning of labor markets and trade in services, and a potentially powerful resource for the alleviation of poverty among migrant households. Ultimately, many governments hope that international migration will prove to be an engine for development. As noted earlier, a number of countries have explicitly or implicitly promoted emigration for these reasons.

Still, the relationship between international migration and development remains complex, poorly understood, and hotly debated. A number of questions remain unanswered: To what extent and in what ways does migration generate development in areas of emigration? And how does the development process itself influence international migration over time? Research findings on these issues are sparse and often conflicting, and it is difficult to generalize their conclusions. This section reviews evidence on the relationship between migration and selected aspects of development.

International Migration in Development Strategies

Most analysts agree that there is no automatic mechanism by which international migration and remittances result in development.[29] Few developing countries have systematically incorporated international migration into their development strategies, and even fewer have harnessed migration for rapid economic development. Some have found that reliance on international migration carries risks as well as benefits. Declining economic conditions in host countries, sudden political upheavals, and international wage competition all can make labor-supplying countries vulnerable to unexpected reversals.

On the other hand, there are clearly historical cases in which emigration has contributed to development (e.g., nineteenth century Sweden, Germany, and Britain), although the processes by which this occurred are long term (a matter of generations) and remain poorly understood. Much could be learned from more thorough analysis of recent "transition cases" such as Italy, Greece, South Korea, and Taiwan. All of these experienced substantial emigration, accompanied or followed by decades of rapid economic development; all subsequently became countries of in-migration. As the U.S. Commission for the Study of International Migration and Cooperative Economic Development put it, "Development and the availability of jobs at home is the only way to diminish migratory pressures over time"—by which it meant at least several decades.[30]

Paradoxically, successful and rapid economic development can serve to increase the propensities for emigration, at least in the short term (10 to 20 years).[31] Development often is profoundly destabilizing to the old social and economic order. Rural modernization is required if agricultural productivity is to be increased, but modernization can also promote an exodus toward urban areas by disrupting traditional economic and social relationships. Rapid urban growth, in turn, can result in saturated labor markets and increased inequality in income distribution. Urban dwellers, even those on the fringes of the economy, also experience rising expectations and increased access to the knowledge and resources necessary for international migration, while transportation and communication improvements accompanying development lower the barriers and costs of such movements.

The Remittances Debate

Remittances—the portion of earnings abroad that migrants send back to their home countries—constitute one of the most important potential links between migration and development. On a global basis, official remittance inflows are large, second in value only to crude oil: global remittance credits were $71 billion in 1990, up from just over $43 billion in 1980.[32] The real figures are probably even higher, since substantial fractions of remittances flow through informal channels and to countries that have not reported their balance of payments to the International Monetary Fund. Remittances are an increasingly important mechanism for the transfer of resources from developed to developing countries: net transfers (i.e., credits minus debits) to developing countries rose from $21 billion in 1980 to nearly $31 billion in 1989, almost two-thirds of the $51 billion in official development assistance provided in 1988.[33] (See Table 2.)

In both absolute and proportional terms, remittances are important sources of money supply and foreign exchange for developing countries. In some cases, remittance credits are 6 to 10 percent of GDP. As shares of merchandise imports and exports, remittances are even more significant, exceeding 30 and 50 percent, respectively, in a number of countries.[34]

TABLE 2. REMITTANCE FLOWS, 1980-1990 ($ millions)

	Net Global Remittances				
	1980	1984	1988	1989	1990
Net Global Credit	9,735	10,304	9,842	12,380	11,558
Global Credit	42,350	40,526	54,761	60,884	71,141
Global Debit	32,615	30,222	44,919	48,504	59,583
	Net Transfers				
	1980	1984	1988	1989	1990
Developing Countries	21,125	22,445	28,961	30,998	36,704
Developed Countries	(11,389)	(12,141)	(17,119)	(18,618)	(25,147)

Note: Numbers in parentheses indicate net outflows.

Source: Sharon Stanton Russell, "Migrant Remittances and Development," *International Migration*, Nos. 3/4 (1992), pp. 286–287, Table 3.

Yet the processes by which such vast amounts of money "percolate up" through developing economies—and how their effects may differ from "top down" development—are not well-researched, and the consequences of remittances for development remain the subject of debate.[35] One school of thought argues that the consequences are largely negative: that remittances are devoted primarily toward the purchase of land and housing, jewelry, and general household consumption, rather than productive investment; that remittances fuel inflation (as has been shown to be the case for land and housing prices in Yemen and Egypt and for construction materials in Greece);[36] and that they do little to stimulate development.[37]

The positive school of thought argues that migrants do save and invest; that expenditures for land, housing, and jewelry are rational (offering better rates of return or stores of value than available investments in agriculture or industry); and that expenditures on housing and consumption have multiplier effects in the wider economy and reduce the need for government spending on infrastructure, subsidies, and services.[38] Proponents of this view point to cases such as Turkey, where remittances may not have had the alleged inflationary impacts, because they served to increase the supply of as well as demand for goods by facilitating the importation of inputs that increased domestic production.[39] Similarly, Morocco, Tunisia, and Portugal all experienced low rates of inflation during the period 1977 to 1989, when these countries were notably successful in mobilizing remittances.[40]

There is ample (and conflicting) evidence to support both points of view.[41] In part, the continuing and inconclusive debate is fueled by the use of different methodological approaches. Many studies draw their conclusions based upon the proportional distribution of remittances among alternative uses at a given point in time. Too few analyze the expenditures of migrants in comparison with those of nonmigrants at the same income level, or consider the complex and diverse underlying factors that affect remittance flows and uses, or trace these patterns over time. Such factors include the characteristics of migrants (e.g., age, education, occupation, earnings, marital status, and location of family members); macroeconomic conditions in both migrant origin and receiving countries (e.g., exchange rates or relative interest rates); perceived political and economic prospects in the home country; and the ease and security of transferring funds.[42]

Poverty Alleviation and Income Inequality

The effects of migration on poverty depend on the extent to which the poor participate in the migration process. The poorest people in a society seldom have the means to migrate. Limited evidence, however, suggests that when the very poor do migrate, the results for them are positive—at least in the short term. For example, migrants' remittances have been credited with reducing absolute poverty in areas of Pakistan and Egypt and with enabling Sri Lankan migrants to provide for their families' basic needs at home.[43] However, these studies often are confined to sub-national areas of out-migration; it has proven difficult to demonstrate national-scale effects on poverty reduction.

The consequences of migration for income inequality depend greatly on the income-composition of a given migrant stream. In areas of Egypt where migrants are concentrated in upper-income households, increases in income inequality have been observed (although the contribution of remittances to inequality was less than that of agricultural income). In Pakistan, where migrants have been fairly evenly distributed across income levels, remittances have had a neutral effect on inequality.[44]

Employment and Human Capital

The employment and human capital consequences of out-migration depend on such factors as the age and education levels of migrants, job opportunities, relative wage rates, and entrepreneurial rates of return. In general, however, out-migration appears to have a positive effect on reducing potential or existing unemployment in emigration areas by absorbing some portion of annual labor force growth and (where migrants had been employed prior to departure) by creating vacancies for those remaining.

Absolute reductions in unemployment have proven difficult to demonstrate, in part because labor force growth continues to exceed employment growth; some observers argue that unemployment may rise if the departure of migrant workers affects complementary workers at home. Further, the theoretically expected fall in unemployment and rise in wages may not occur if there is a large labor pool from which to draw or if labor scarcity prompts employers to shift toward capital-intensive production.[45]

The benefits of migration in absorbing labor force *growth* are clearer. In Pakistan, for example, between 1978 and 1983 the number of emigrants was equivalent to about one-third of growth in the labor force in this period; in Egypt, taking into account new labor force entrants, unemployment may have been as much as 75 percent lower in the 1970s than it otherwise would have been.[46]

International migration has the potential to affect the stock of human capital in areas of origin either negatively or positively. Negative effects occur primarily through the loss of needed skills, frequently referred to as "brain drain." More recently, with the growing volume of migration between developing countries, the migration of skilled workers has been called "reverse transfer of technology" or "technical cooperation between developing countries" (TCDC). In some cases (Sudan, Nigeria, Zambia), migration of skilled workers results in manpower shortages, most notably in sectors—such as health and education—that are critical to human development. In many cases, however, skilled workers are in excess supply and hence unable to use their skills productively in their own countries; some describe this as "brain overflow," i.e., the brains that are "drained" might otherwise have been unemployed. Some highly skilled workers (e.g., scientists) may be employable but frustrated by a lack of facilities. Finally, in some countries, intellectual elites have been subjected to human rights violations and even persecution that motivate them to depart for more favorable environments.

In many instances, consequences of the loss of workers for the country of origin are difficult to discern. For example, although the emigration of skilled Turkish workers to Germany was publicly decried by the Turkish government and some employers, there is little, if any, research evidence of negative effects on output in farming or manufacturing.[47] On balance, whether emigration of skilled or other workers hinders the development process depends on the extent to which the human and other resources are available to fill the gap.

One frequently mentioned positive effect of emigration on human capital is the acquisition abroad of skills that will contribute to development when migrants return. This argument rests on four assumptions: that migrants actually return; that they will, in fact, acquire skills abroad; that those skills are appropriate to employment opportunities at home; and that returning workers will employ skills learned abroad.[48] Obviously, if migrants remain abroad permanently or accept jobs abroad requiring skill levels at or below the jobs they held prior to migration, the potential contribution to the country of origin is lost.

Whether or not international migration improves the skills of migrants themselves, there is mounting evidence that it improves the ability of migrants' families to educate and provide health care for their children. Remittances have been shown to be an important source of school fees, books and materials, and financing for expansion of educational facilities. Several studies suggest that migrants are more likely than non-migrants to educate their children and, when they do, to spend more than non-migrants on education.[49] There is also evidence that remittance income increases demand for health services and the probability of seeking modern care.[50]

Migration and Trade

Economic theory has long suggested that migration and trade are substitutes, but that view is changing; migration and trade are increasingly recognized as complements.[51]

Remittances have enabled many labor-exporting countries to finance a sizable share of their imports and thus to participate in world merchandise trade. In addition, international migration helps facilitate the expansion of trade in services. In the late 1970s and early 1980s, labor migration was central to South Korea's export of construction services to Western Asia, while in recent years, the Philippines has expanded banking services to serve migrants in the Middle East and Europe. In Turkey, the presence of migrants abroad has increased demand for transport, banking, and communication services, and stimulated tourist and business travel between Turkey and European Union countries. In a number of migration streams, complex networks of intermediaries (both legal and illegal) have developed around the process of recruiting and transporting migrants.[52]

Expanding the access of developing countries to trade in world markets is key to job creation, development, and reduction of migratory pressures in the long term. Yet many industrialized countries face domestic economic and political pressures to resist the removal of trade barriers. The resistance of European farmers to agricultural trade with Eastern European countries is but one example. Because of pressures from domestic lobbies, even preferential trade agreements such as the Caribbean Basin Initiative and the Lomé Conventions often exclude or limit labor-intensive products for which less developed countries have a comparative advantage.

CONCLUSIONS

The salience of international migrations has risen sharply in recent years as the number of migrants has increased, and their movements have become more volatile. The connections of migration trends to the high fertility and demographic growth rates of the past several decades are complex and indirect. So too are the linkages between international migration and economic development trends. Over the long term of generations, successful economic development can moderate the rising propensity to migrate; over the short-to-medium term of one to two decades, however, no such moderating impact of development should be expected, and indeed development over this time frame could increase migration propensities.

Notes

The authors wish to thank the several reviewers invited by the Overseas Development Council for their helpful suggestions.

[1] Hania Zlotnik, U.N. Population Division/DESD, personal communication, 17 November 1993. Determining the number of international migrants is complex and difficult, for a number of reasons. Census data are the most complete and comparable sources but are seldom timely; currently available census results date from the 1980s, for example. Further, some censuses report foreign born, while others report foreign nationals. Foreign birth is generally better than nationality for inferring migration, since nationality may or may not change as migrants settle and may or may not apply to the second generation.

[2] Estimates prepared by Zlotnik, op. cit. Asia, the Middle East, and North Africa here include regional groupings defined by the United Nations as South Asia, South East and East Asia, and North Africa and West Asia.

[3] Rogers Brubaker, "Political Dimensions of Migration From and Among Soviet Successor States," in *International Migration and Security*, Myron Weiner (ed.), (Boulder, CO: Westview Press, 1993), p. 48.

[4] United Nations, *World Population Trends and Policies: 1987 Monitoring Report*, ST/ESA/SER.A/103 (New York: United Nations, 1988), p. 240; and Susan Forbes Martin, personal communication, 8 November 1993.

[5] United Nations High Commissioner for Refugees (UNHCR), *The State of the World's Refugees: The Challenge of Protection* (New York: Penguin Books, 1993), p. 153. In this chapter, *refugee* refers to those officially recognized as such by the UNHCR, in keeping with the 1951 U.N. Convention Relating to the Status of Refugees, the 1967 Protocol Relating to the Status of Refugees, and the Organization for African Unity (OAU) Convention of 1969. The Convention defines a refugee in part as a person who, "owing to a well-founded fear of being persecuted for reasons of race, religion, nationality . . . is outside the country of his nationality and is unable or unwilling to avail himself of the protection of that country. . . ." The OAU expands the definition of a refugee to include those who, "owing to external aggression, occupation, foreign domination, or events seriously disturbing the public order . . . are compelled to leave . . . to seek refuge in another place." *Forced migrants* include refugees by these definitions, as well as others forced to flee across international boundaries from severe economic, political, and ecological conditions in their homelands.

[6] J.S. Birks, I.J. Seccomb, and C.A. Sinclair, "Labour Migration in the Arab Gulf States: Patterns, Trends, and Prospects," Round Table on International Migration in the Philippines and South-East Asia, Manila, 8-11 December 1987, mimeo.

[7] Nasra Shah, "Migration Between Asian Countries and Its Likely Future," paper prepared for the U.N. Expert Group Meeting on Population Distribution and Migration, Santa Cruz, Bolivia, 18-22 January 1993, p. 5.

[8] UNHCR, op. cit., p. 8. The figure for Sub-Saharan Africa excludes Algeria, Egypt, Libya, Morocco, and Tunisia.

[9] U.S. Department of Commerce, Bureau of the Census, *1990 Census of the Population: The Foreign Born in the U.S.* (Washington, DC: U.S. Government Printing Office, July 1993), Table 1.

[10] UNHCR, op. cit., pp. 152-153, Annex I.1.

[11] This paper focuses on *international* migration. Hence, the terms *in-migration* and *out-migration* (frequently used in discussions of internal migration) are used here only in reference to cross-border movements into and out of a country. These terms are broader than *immigration* and *emigration* in that the latter imply indefinite or permanent residence. The term *immigration*, which applies to entry by non-nationals, is defined differently in different countries: the United Nations definition, which is used only by the United Kingdom and New Zealand, includes those who intend to stay for one year or more; France includes those resident for three months or more; in the United States, *immigrant* is a legal category of admission to stay indefinitely, without reference to actual or intended length of residence. The term *emigrant* is used in reference to the exit of foreigners and nationals for residence or extended stay abroad (e.g., longer than one year). All these terms refer to flows, not stocks.

[12] Estimated from annual *Statistical Yearbooks*, U.S. Immigration and Naturalization Service (Washington, DC: Government Printing Office). Specifically, we took the number of immigrants admitted in each year, subtracted the number of refugee adjustments (which refer to refugees admitted in prior years), and then added in the numbers of refugees admitted in that year.

[13] Organisation for Economic Co-operation and Development (OECD), *Continuous Reporting System on Migration (SOPEMI): Trends in International Migration* (Paris: OECD, 1992), pp. 86-87.

[14] Robert Warren, Immigration and Naturalization Service, personal communication, 15 December 1993.

[15] U.S. Immigration and Naturalization Service, Office of Strategic Planning, Statistics Division, "Estimates of the Resident Illegal Alien Population: October 1992," unpublished, mimeo.

[16] OECD, op. cit., pp. 55-57; Australia, Department of Immigration, Local Government and Ethnic Affairs, Table 1.2 of 8 April 1993 Minute from Nick Lawry, Director, BIR Liaison and Program Evaluation Section.

[17] This section draws upon Sharon Stanton Russell and Michael S. Teitelbaum, *International Migration and International Trade*, World Bank Discussion Paper, No. 160 (Washington, DC: World Bank, 1992), pp. 4-7.

[18] For an informative discussion of contending theoretical approaches, see Douglas S. Massey et al., "Theories of International Migration: Review and Appraisal," *Population and Development Review*, Vol. 19, No. 3 (September 1993), pp. 431-466.

[19] Oded Stark, *The Migration of Labor* (Cambridge, MA: Basil Blackwell, 1991).

[20] UNHCR, op. cit., p. 25.

[21] UNHCR, op. cit., p. 153. For the definitions of refugees, see note 5 in this chapter.

[22] Intergovernmental Consultations on Asylum, Refugee, and Migration Policies in Europe, North America, and Australia, "Asylum Applications in Participating States 1983-1993," January 1994, mimeo.

[23] Algeria, for example, restricted emigration to France in 1973, following a series of anti-Algerian incidents; the Philippines government has periodically banned labor migration by Filipino women to Kuwait because of concerns about abuses.

[24] Attractively low land prices have been important in the migration of Bangladeshis to the Indian state of Assam, and of Salvadorans to Honduras before the 1969 "Football War" between these two countries.

[25] Aristide R. Zolberg, Astri Suhrki, and Sergio Aguayo, *Escape From Violence: Conflict and the Refugee Crisis in the Developing World* (New York: Oxford University Press, 1989).

[26] See, for example, Paul Kennedy, *Preparing for the Twenty-First Century* (New York: Random House, 1993), Ch. 2.

[27] Ronald Skeldon, "On Mobility and Fertility Transitions in East and Southeast Asia," *Asian and Pacific Migration Journal*, Vol. 1, No. 2, pp. 220-249.

[28] See, for example, Employment and Immigration Canada, *Annual Report to Parliament: Immigration Plan for 1991-1995* (25 October 1990), pp. 5 and 6 (tabled in parliament). A "backgrounder" released on 2 February 1994 by the Canadian Minister of Citizenship and Immigration, Sergio Marchi, states that current levels of immigration "help us to sustain an annual population growth rate of about 1.5 percent—higher than any other industrialized nation. . . ." *Backgrounder: A New Approach to Consultation for a New Vision of Immigration.*

[29] Demetrios G. Papademetriou and Phillip L. Martin (eds.), *The Unsettled Relationship: Labor Migration and Economic Development* (New York: Greenwood Press, 1991).

[30] U.S. Commission for the Study of International Migration and Cooperative Economic Development, *Unauthorized Migration: An Economic Development Response* (Washington, DC: U.S. Government Printing Office, 1990), pp. xiii and 35.

[31] Ibid.

[32] Official inflows (credits) are those recorded and published annually in the International Monetary Fund's *Balance of Payments Statistics* (Washington, DC: International Monetary Fund). Total inflows are the sum of three categories: worker remittances, which are the value of transfers from workers abroad for more than a year; migrant transfers, or the flow of goods and financial assets associated with an international move; and labor income, or the factor income of migrants working abroad for less than one year. Because only a portion of all remittances flow through official channels, and not all countries are reflected in the IMF balance of payments statistics, the figures based upon IMF data are "lower bound" estimates.

[33] Sharon Stanton Russell, "Migrant Remittances and Development,"*International Migration*, Vol. XXX, Nos. 3/4, (1992) p. 269; and Russell and Teitelbaum, op. cit., p. 1. Net transfers to developing countries were $36.7 billion in 1990, but this figure may be skewed by incomplete recording of debits; hence, the more complete figure for 1989 is used here.

[34] Russell and Teitelbaum, op. cit., Tables 4-6.

[35] For a fuller discussion of this debate, see Sharon Stanton Russell, "Remittances from International Migration: A Review in Perspective," *World Development*, Vol. 14, No. 6 (1986), pp. 677-696; and Charles B. Keely and Bao Nga Tran, "Remittances from Labor Migration: Evaluation, Performance, and Implications," *International Migration Review*, Vol. 23, No. 3 (Fall 1989), pp. 500-525.

[36] For evidence on land and housing prices, see Ismail Serageldin, James Socknat, Stace Birks, Bob Li, and Clive Sinclair, *Manpower and International Labor Migration in the Middle East and North Africa* (Washington, DC: World Bank, Technical Assistance

and Special Studies Division, June 30, 1981); and Richard H. Adams, Jr., *The Effects of International Remittances on Poverty, Inequality, and Development in Rural Egypt*, Research Report 86 (Washington, DC: International Food Policy Research Institute, 1991). For construction materials, see Demitrios G. Papademetriou and Ira Emke-Poulopoulos in Papademetriou and Martin, op. cit., p. 102.

[37] See, for example, Philip L. Martin, *The Unfinished Story: Turkish Labour Migration to Western Europe* (Geneva: International Labour Organization, 1991); and Papademetriou and Martin, op. cit.

[38] See Nicholas Glytsos, "Measuring the Income Effects of Migrant Remittances: A Methodological Approach Applied to Greece," *Economic Development and Cultural Change*, Vol. 42, (October 1993), pp. 131-168; and Julien Conde, Pap Syr Diagne, and N.G. Ouaidou, *South-North International Migrations, a Case Study: Malian, Mauritanian and Senegalese Migrants from Senegal River Valley to France* (Paris: Organisation for Economic Co-operation and Development, 1986).

[39] Martin, *The Unfinished Story*, op. cit., p. 57.

[40] Ibrahim A. Elbadawi and Roberto Rocha, "Determinants of Expatriate Workers' Remittances in North Africa and Europe," Policy Research Working Papers, WPS 1038 (Washington, DC: World Bank, November 1992), p. 17.

[41] For reviews of the remittance literature, see Russell, "Migrant Remittances and Development," op. cit.; and Russell, "Remittances from International Migration," op. cit.

[42] For example, investment of remittances in agriculture can be affected by factors such as land tenure patterns, producer pricing policies, rates of return to alternative investments, and sexual division of labor in agriculture.

[43] Shahid Javed Burki, "International Migration: Implications for Labor Exporting Countries," *The Middle East Journal*, Vol. 38, No. 4 (1984), pp. 680-682; and Frank Eelens, Toon Schampers, and Johan Dirk Speckmann (eds.), *Labour Migration to the Middle East: From Sri Lanka to the Gulf* (London and New York: Kegan Paul International, 1992), p. 31.

[44] On Egypt, see Adams, op. cit.; on Pakistan, see Richard H. Adams, Jr., "The Effects of Internal and International Migration and Remittances on Income Distribution in Rural Pakistan," report prepared for the U.S. Agency for International Development (Washington, DC: International Food Policy Research Institute, June 1992).

[45] Robert E.B. Lucas, "International Migration: Economic Opportunities, Development Strategies, and World Trade," report submitted to United Nations Development Programme, September 1991, p. 11.

[46] Reginald T. Appleyard, "Migration and Development: Myths and Reality," *International Migration Review*, Vol. 23, No. 3 (Fall 1989), p. 488; and Galal A. Amin and Elizabeth Awny, manuscript report, *International Migration of Egyptian Labor: A Review of the State of the Art* (Ottawa: International Development Research Centre, 1984), p. 96.

[47] Martin, *The Unfinished Story*, op. cit., pp. 29-30.

[48] Charles W. Stahl, "Labor Emigration and Economic Development," *International Migration Review*, Vol. 16, No. 4 (1983), pp. 887-889.

[49] For a review of African evidence on this point, see Sharon Stanton Russell, Karen Jacobsen, and William Deane Stanley, *International Migration and Development in Sub-Saharan Africa*, World Bank Discussion Paper No. 101, Vol. 1, Overview (Washington, DC: World Bank, 1990), pp. 63-65.

[50] On Sri Lanka, see Eelens, Schampers, and Speckmann, op. cit., p. 179; on Mali, see Nancy Birdsall, Jere Behrman, and Punam Chuhan, "Client Choice of Health Care Treatment in Rural Mali," paper presented at the Annual Meeting of the Population Association of America, New Orleans, LA, April 1988.

[51] See Philip L. Martin, *Trade and Migration: NAFTA and Agriculture*, Policy Analyses in International Economics No. 38 (Washington, DC: Institute for International Economics, October 1993).

[52] On intermediaries, see Graeme J. Hugo, paper prepared for the U.N. Expert Group Meeting on Population Distribution and Migration, Santa Cruz, Bolivia, 18-22 January 1993, p. 11; Eelens, Schampers, and Speckmann, op. cit., p. 44, and Ernst Spaan, "Taikongs and Calos: The Role of Middlemen and Brokers in Javanese International Migration," *International Migration Review*, Vol. 28, No. 1 (1994), pp. 93-113.

Chapter Nine

Government, Population, and Poverty: A Win-Win Tale

Nancy Birdsall

Traditional concern that rapid population growth slows development in poor countries has been reinforced in recent years by growing awareness of the fragility of the natural environment in poor countries and its apparent vulnerability to the stresses associated with increasing population size, whether the economy is growing or stagnating. But reinforced concern has not led to a consensus about whether governments should intervene actively to reduce population growth rates. At least some analysts remain skeptical that rapid population growth itself is a fundamental cause of either slower economic growth or of natural resource problems in developing countries. Others worry that government intervention will threaten the sanctity of individual and family decisionmaking in the sensitive arena of reproduction, and question whether the future and uncertain benefits of a smaller population would outweigh immediate social costs—in terms of human pain and suffering—of strong policies to reduce fertility. This sentiment is behind the international opprobrium China has suffered because of its extreme birth control policies.

This chapter first summarizes the three principal concerns raised by rapid population growth in developing countries: slower economic development, greater environmental damage, and greater poverty and income inequality. It then links these concerns to specific rationales for government intervention to reduce rates of fertility, demonstrating the basis for these rationales in simple welfare theory (i.e., economic theory which starts from the notion that the objective of economic arrangements is to maximize human happiness). Finally, the chapter discusses the kinds of public policy interventions that these rationales justify. (Note that not all "interventions" need imply more government-funded programs or more government involvement in the economy; some might consist of policies permitting or encouraging market-led outcomes, for example reducing regulations that stifle private sector supply of contraception.)[1]

The chapter does not review the empirical evidence linking rapid population growth to economic performance, the environment, and poverty (though such evidence exists). The issue here is not to assess the merits of the evidence but to determine whether, if correct, the evidence justifies government intervention (governments after all may better leave problems alone rather than intervene and make matters worse); and if so, what kinds of interventions. As should become clear, this approach of not assessing the merits of the evidence is more sensible than it may seem—because the kinds of interventions that are justified turn out to be justified independently of the population question.

The key reason for this convenient result is the link between high fertility and poverty. Poverty is both a root cause and a common outcome of high fertility. A massive literature amply documents the many specific characteristics of poor households that contribute to high fertility—high infant mortality, lack of education for women, too little family income to "invest" in children, leading to parents' having many children rather than concentrating investments in a few, and finally, for many poor couples, poor access to contraception of reasonable cost and quality.[2] The generalized effect of poverty on fertility is demonstrated in almost every developing country in the form of large differentials in the average family size of households, depending on income, education, and other variables that measure or reflect poverty. At the same time, poverty is often an outcome of high fertility; large family size strains family budgets and reduces the ability of families to invest in their children's health and education.

In short, many developing countries experience a vicious circle of high fertility and poverty. So reducing fertility levels in poor countries requires change in the conditions of poverty that cause high fertility in the first place. Thus, interventions are required that not only reduce the fertility of the poor, but do so by making the poor better off. Such interventions may well be justified independent of their effect on fertility. They need not pass as strict a test of justification and acceptability as "population" interventions which involve a possible trade-off between the welfare of the poor and less rapid population growth, or between the welfare of the poor now and the welfare of future generations.

Interventions that both contribute to reduced fertility and improve human welfare have another advantage. Institutional constraints (including political, administrative, and social constraints) sometimes make it difficult to initiate and implement non-population policies that would mitigate or even eliminate the worst effects of population growth. An example is better pricing of such common property resources as forests, which would greatly reduce logging and burning independent of rapid population growth. The institutional constraints to ideal non-population policies make recourse to fertility reduction policies, especially if they are win-win, easier to justify.

THREE PROMINENT CONCERNS ABOUT RAPID POPULATION GROWTH

Before examining the most frequently cited concerns about rapid population growth, it is useful to first discuss the concept of externality. Negative and positive "externalities" occur, respectively, whenever the costs and benefits of an activity are not fully internalized by the actor. For example, externalities result when my activity imposes costs on my neighbor that I do not bear (I emit smoke or noise and pay no fees) or provides benefits I cannot fully capture (immunizing my child prevents another child's sickness). When an activity has a negative externality, if many people engage in that activity, the results for the group as a whole may be unsatisfactory. The externality signals a failure in the way markets are working, and justifies some collective or government intervention—in the case of pollution, a tax on emissions to impose on each polluter the full social costs of his pollution; and in the case of immunizations, a subsidy to encourage more parents to obtain immunizations.

Concern about population growth is often based, implicitly or explicitly, on the idea that childbearing has negative externalities.[3] Yet there has been relatively little theoretical work,[4] and almost no empirical work, describing the nature and magnitude of externalities.[5]

Conceptually, the potential for externalities to arise is clear. When there is public national wealth (for example, state-owned lands or mineral deposits), the birth of a new citizen dilutes everyone else's claim on this jointly owned property. Similarly, an additional birth reduces per capita consumption of nonprivatizable, congestible common property resources such as fisheries and airsheds. If the resource is not properly managed, as in the classic "tragedy of the commons" scenario, in which access to the resource is unlimited, then population growth exacerbates the losses due to mismanagement.

A similar situation occurs when citizens are entitled to public transfer payments (social security) or subsidized services (education, health), consume public goods, and are obligated to pay taxes. In such situations, the birth of an additional citizen adds to both public revenue and expenditure, resulting in positive and negative externalities to other taxpayers. Depending on the amounts and life-cycle timing of tax payments and receipt of benefits, net externalities could be positive or negative. In societies with high rates of fertility, the assumption is that the externalities are negative—that the social costs of educating more and more children will not be recouped eventually in higher taxes.

A pecuniary externality to childbearing can occur in the labor market. As population, especially rural population, increases, the wages of labor go down, and rents increase. For individual landless or land-poor laborers, it may be rational to have many children as a strategy for maximizing old-age income. However, when all pursue this strategy, wages are depressed, and living standards of both the parents and their children are reduced below their expectations. Hence, one poor family's decision to have children imposes costs on its peers; if all joined in a labor-supply cartel and agreed to have fewer children, the group's income would increase.

This is not a "true" externality because it operates through the market. Although wages are depressed by population growth, rents and profits are boosted; high fertility could potentially create more wealth than low fertility, and make everyone better off, if landlords redistributed some of their increased rents. In practice, however, the landlords or capitalists are unlikely to redistribute their rents and profits. So where income inequality and absolute poverty are already high, population growth is likely to compound these problems.[6]

A final source of childbearing externalities occurs when couples care about their relative—rather than absolute—family size. A family's voice in the village council, prestige, physical security, or claim to the use of common property may depend on its size relative to the group.[7] When a couple has more children, they slightly increase the average family size in their group, making others relatively worse off. Attempts by each couple to have more children than the average family size are mutually frustrating: average family size increases, and no couple achieves the sought-after advantage, although all now have larger families to support.

Childbearing-related externalities underlie the concern about rapid population growth in developing countries. The most frequently cited concerns involve the effect of population growth on economic growth, the environment, and income distribution. They can be summarized as follows:[8]

1) Rapid population growth reduces the rate of growth of per capita income by reducing investments in human capital, investments that have powerful effects on economic growth because of positive externalities;

2) Rapid population growth itself has negative externalities for the environment, leading in some scenarios to degradation of natural resources at the local and national level and contributing to such global problems as loss of biodiversity and the possibility of global warming; and

3) Rapid population growth has negative "pecuniary" externalities, i.e., it reduces the incomes of some groups, particularly the poor, compared to other groups, and therefore exacerbates the problems of poverty and income inequality in developing countries.

Negative Growth Effects

Many people argue that rapid population growth reduces economic growth by reducing investment in physical and human capital.[9] This broad growth concern has been amply explored for at least two decades; its merits are difficult to address empirically. In the absence of compelling evidence it remains a matter of controversy.[10] On the one hand, economists have noted that in the absence of externalities, a negative effect of rapid population growth on economic growth need not in itself be of great concern. Parents may fully realize that children are costly to them (and to society), and yet prefer to have more children rather than higher consumption of other costly things.[11] In that case, rapid population growth may be socially optimal even if it impedes economic growth.

However, a countervailing argument can be made. Recent approaches to growth theory emphasize that investments in human resources may have important positive externalities for economic growth.[12] Cross-national empirical studies of growth have demonstrated that educational attainment measures of populations are consistent and important explanators of growth success. Moreover, education matters over and above its effect as an additional input to production; at the country and the firm level, it is also associated with higher total factor productivity, i.e., with higher product for given inputs.[13] Any persistent effect of education on economy-wide productivity would suggest that a more educated work force has a positive social externality; thus to the extent that rapid population growth inhibits public and family investments in education, its effects on growth would be negative.

At the family level, there is evidence that high fertility inhibits investments in children's education. A study of families with twins in India found that the additional unexpected child represented by twins reduced enrollment levels of all children in the household.[14] Estimates based on Malaysian data show that the children of couples with a higher biological propensity to have births (higher fecundity) tend to remain in school fewer years than those from families with fewer children.[15] At the economy-wide level, there is no simple evidence that rapid population growth reduces overall investment in children, measured, for example, by proportion of GDP spent on education (which falls between 2 and 4 percent of GDP in almost all developing countries). However, it is obvious that the same level of effort has different results depending on the proportion of children in a population and the extent to which the rate of enrollment is increasing. A society with a growing proportion of children of school age, and with a growing proportion attending school, must spend more of its GDP or achieve greater efficiency in its education spending. The declining quality of education in Africa and Latin America suggests increasing difficulties in doing so. For example, between 1970 and 1989, the absolute size of the school-age population in Mexico increased by 60 percent, and enrollment rates went up. Education expenditures increased as well—but by 60 percent, enough to maintain *per child* spending, but not *per student* spending.[16]

In short, high fertility seems to be associated with lower educational attainment per child; at the economy-wide level, less education has a social cost—lower economic growth. Rapid population growth thus implies the loss of a potential positive externality of education for economic growth.[17] Put another way, parents who have many children, and educate them less, in effect deprive society of the potential positive effect (in terms of increased productivity) of a more educated population.

Negative Environmental Externalities

The environmental concern about rapid population growth is straightforward. For given levels of consumption, more people put more stress on natural resources, including both sources (forests, water) and sinks (the air which receives pollution). In the absence of prices that reflect the true scarcity value of these sources and sinks, there is likely to be excessive consumption of these "goods" from society's point of view. Excessive consumption is multiplied the more people there are.

These potential negative environmental externalities, at both the local and the global levels, are increasingly invoked as a rationale for efforts to reduce population growth in developing countries.[18] At the local level, the combination of poverty and rapid population growth is often cited as contributing to environmental degradation, for example because population pressure leads to farming of hillsides and other marginal areas (causing soil erosion) or heavy cutting of forests for fuel (causing damage to watersheds, and thus to agriculture, and contributing to possibly irreversible reductions in biodiversity).[19] At the global level, although the fossil fuel emissions that currently contribute to possible global warming are much greater in industrialized countries on a per capita basis, future rates of income and population growth in developing countries could increase the contribution of these countries to global emissions from about 20 percent today to 50 percent by the middle of the next century.[20]

Concern about the effects of rapid population growth on global food supplies arises now not because of absolute food shortages in the near term, but because necessary increases in agricultural production are likely to impose unsustainable stress on the natural resource base, whether achieved through interior or exterior means. In relatively poor settings, increased demand for food (and for farm income) with rising population has contributed to the extension of farming to less productive and usually more environmentally fragile areas (as in the case of clearing of forests and of hillsides)[21] or to unsustainable recourse to chemical fertilizers.

Some analysts now believe that the problem is not just a local one, but that in the future sustaining food availability at acceptable environmental and economic cost will also be an issue at the global level. One estimate is that by the year 2030 demand for cereals will nearly double, from 2 to 3.6 billion tons, and that 90 percent of this projected demand increase will be due to rising population, and only 10 percent to rising incomes.[22] In a thorough analysis of prospects, Crosson and Anderson conclude that this demand cannot be met on the basis of existing knowledge and available technologies without considerable environmental damage.[23] New knowledge as well as greater use of existing technologies and best practice is therefore critical. In developing areas, the critical constraint is likely to be water, for which there is increasing competition from nonagricultural sources.

Worsening Income Distribution and Poverty

Even if rapid population growth does not create negative externalities for society as a whole, it may systematically lead to lower levels of income for the poor compared to the rich. At the aggregate level, rapid population growth increases the availability of labor in an economy relative to land and physical capital, reducing wages.[24] This is likely to worsen inequality and hurt the poor, who are more reliant on labor income. In most economies today, the distribution of income is in fact more closely linked to differential returns to varying levels of skills among labor, than to differences between labor and capital. For this reason, the effect of population growth on differences in income by education level provides insight into the effect rapid population growth will have on income distribution. From this point of view, it is indicative that evidence from Brazil shows that unskilled laborers suffer a relative decline in wages if they are members of a large age cohort, while skilled laborers do not. The size of cohort (and implicitly the rate of population growth at the time a worker was born) makes a greater negative impact on the income of the less educated than on that of the more educated.[25]

The probable deleterious effect of rapid population growth on the distribution of income has not been given the attention it deserves. However, there seems little doubt that the sustainability of the economic and political reforms of the last decade is in part a function of the extent to which societies succeed in ensuring that the costs of reform are not unduly borne by the poor, and that the benefits of growth, when it returns, are widely shared.[26] The high-growth countries of East Asia provide an example; in these countries, both the gains from growth and the hardships resulting from brief periods of adjustment and austerity were widely shared.[27] Other cross-national studies suggest that the distribution of income affects growth, presumably via its effect on the capacity of governments to implement and sustain economic policies that are costly to at least some groups in the short run. To the extent that rapid population growth exacerbates income inequality, it may thus contribute to the difficulty of sustaining growth, and in particular to the difficulty of sustaining a process of economic reform to ensure growth.

The effect of high fertility (the underlying cause of rapid population growth) on poverty, independent of effects on aggregate income distribution, is easier to document. High fertility contributes to poverty at the family level by straining the budgets of poor families, reducing available resources to feed, educate, and provide health care to children. The evidence cited above regarding the effects of twins on family spending per child for education speaks to this effect.[28]

High fertility in poor families need not reflect irrational decisions on the part of poor parents, even though it reduces family resources per capita in the short run. On the contrary, it can reflect reasonable decisions on their part—to ensure greater future family income once children start working, or to ensure their own security in old age via support from their children. As noted, it may also reflect parents' decisions to enjoy additional children rather than other forms of consumption. In both cases, however, children themselves are likely to receive less health and education—implying a negative intergenerational externality, i.e., a situation in which the parents do not incur the full costs of high fertility but pass some of those costs on to their children. In some cases, parents also may end up worse off—if more children than hoped are girls (who will provide less support in old age), or if children turn out to be less helpful, less capable, or less pleasant than anticipated. This only implies that some parents lose what are reasonable gambles. It is, of course, also possible that poor families have more children than they want, because they have poor access to modern contraception; or they have more children than they might have chosen, because they had poor access to information about the increasing probability that their children would survive, or the increasing opportunities for and returns to education.

RATIONALES FOR GOVERNMENT INTERVENTION

Do the specific concerns about the effect of rapid population growth on economic growth, the environment, and income distribution justify government efforts to reduce fertility? Let us examine the benefits of government intervention in each area of concern separately.

Should governments encourage lower fertility in order to capture positive externalities for economic growth from resulting higher private and public investments in education? A purist would argue that, rather than rely on lower fertility, governments should subsidize education directly (along with other investments in human capital, including health). The subsidy should be large enough to raise private consumption (which, in the case of education, is also private investment) to the socially optimal level.

But there are practical problems with this response. Virtually all governments subsidize education already, and current subsidies are limited not by some notion of an optimal ceiling that has been reached, but by fiscal constraints and the administrative difficulty of subsidizing any service efficiently (whether subsidies are provided directly or through private providers). In some settings, even large subsidies might be insufficient to induce socially optimal private investments in education, since parents may need some commitment of children's time. In other settings, higher subsidies to education might actually induce higher fertility by reducing the cost of children to parents without altering the benefits, thus creating another round of need for new subsidies!

In short, it is usually less costly and more efficient for societies to encourage education by combining direct subsidies to education with separate measures to reduce family size, rather than relying on the former alone.

Should governments encourage lower fertility in order to reduce negative environmental externalities? Here, too, a purist might argue that the appropriate way for government to reduce environmental threats from rapid population growth is to impose higher prices on environmental goods, charging, for example, for burning tree cover, for fishing licenses, and for pollution via chemical fertilizers. However, adequate pricing of environmental goods is politically and administratively difficult, even in rich countries. While pricing should be tried, the magnitude of the problem also justifies collective efforts to reduce fertility. If a country can, through some policy change or program, induce parents to have fewer children voluntarily, then environmental degradation can be slowed and food production per person maintained, and the country as a whole made better off. Analogously, in a global society, if developing countries reduce their fertility level voluntarily, then global welfare can increase.

Do negative effects of high fertility on income distribution and on poverty justify government intervention? In theory, the answer depends on whether a particular society cares about the existence of poverty among some of its members, and about the distribution of income. In fact, most societies do seem to care. First, the well-being of the rich may be affected by knowledge that the poor are vastly worse off than they are—as demonstrated in almost all societies by at least some measure of charitable giving. In addition, the political sustainability of economic reforms and thus of economic growth may be jeopardized where income inequality is great, harming everyone. Finally, democracy, a political arrangement which probably improves human welfare relative to other arrangements (because such freedoms as those of speech, religion, and association make people better off), may be difficult to sustain where income inequality is high and social mobility low.

Consider a typical developing country in which the poor have higher fertility than the rich. Suppose a social program (e.g., education or family planning) could reduce the number of children born to the poor while making them no worse off. The social program is financed by taxing the rich. Through such a program, both the rich and the poor can enjoy an unambiguous increase in welfare—the rich because they prefer the poor to have smaller families, the poor because they benefit from the social program.

In summary, the three concerns all justify in principle government intervention because each concern is rooted in a market failure which collective action through government could correct. Interventions specifically aimed at reducing fertility are among those that can be justified, as long as they enhance rather than reduce the welfare of the poor. (See Box 1.)

WHAT KINDS OF INTERVENTIONS?

The solution to externalities involves ensuring that actors internalize fully the social costs of their actions—in the case of fertility, that the poor who have high fertility bear the full social costs of their choice. At the same time, the poor have many children in part because they are poor, so reducing this fertility requires a change in the conditions of poverty itself—it requires that the poor be made better off. In short, what is needed are interventions that simultaneously 1) increase the cost of children to the poor, inducing lower fertility, and 2) improve the welfare of the poor.[29]

Consider five types of interventions. Except for the first, each does meet the criterion.

Taxes on Children and Incentives to Reduce Fertility

If childbearing imposes external costs, the standard economic remedy would be to impose a tax on children equivalent to the external costs. Then, assuming that couples have perfect control over their fertility, a child would be born only if its value to its parents exceeded its total cost to society.

Although China and Singapore have used taxes to control fertility, they are problematic from a welfare point of view because they are likely to hurt the poor. For the poor much more than for the rich, children are likely to be an important source of income and security in old age. Yet in no society—developed or developing—is it easy to borrow against the future earnings of one's children. Because of this failure of

Dasgupta has pointed out a connection between the population problem and the underpricing of firewood.[1] Firewood in developing countries is underpriced because it is a common property resource, available at no direct cost from local forests. Its underpricing (it is free except for the opportunity cost of the labor in collecting it) reflects the lack of a market in common property resources. Collecting firewood is a usual task for children in poor families; the low price of firewood, and its increasing scarcity (in part because of its low price) make children more valuable to parents than they would otherwise be. This "wrong price" of firewood in fact reflects a market failure (or externality problem)—which contributes to high fertility, and makes high fertility in turn a contributing factor to the worsening of the original environmental problem of underpriced firewood. In this way, rapid population growth results from and compounds a "wrong price."

Other wrong prices also can increase fertility and population growth. In west Africa, the full costs of children are not borne by their parents. Other relatives are expected to provide support, including through extensive fostering out;[2] because parents can capture many of the benefits of children, but need not bear all the costs, there is a kind of externality. The same problem arises wherever the husband is the principal decisionmaker and can capture many of the benefits of children yet pass on many of the costs to his wife. Finally, wherever social norms (what Dasgupta refers to as "diffuse externalities") or local conditions mean that families with more children than average capture some benefits but can pass on to society some costs, there is a wrong price for children rooted in an externality. All these cases of wrong prices in fact justify public policy interventions designed to reduce fertility.

. . . .

[1]Partha Dasgupta, *An Inquiry into Well-Being and Destitution* (Oxford: Oxford University Press, 1993).

[2]See Caroline Bledsoe, "Children Are Like Young Bamboo Trees: Potentiality and Reproduction in Sub-Saharan Africa," paper for Population-Environment Development Seminar, Royal Swedish Academy of Sciences, Stockholm, October 14, 1993.

capital markets, it is easy to imagine a tax forcing a peasant to forgo the birth of a child whose financial security value alone is much greater than the tax. Even if capital markets posed no problem, an administratively simple tax would probably be highly regressive, and it might be difficult to guarantee that the tax revenues would be progressively distributed. There is a particular danger that a tax would penalize, by accident or design, the children born into large poor families.

A tax-financed incentive for not bearing children would have the same effect as a tax, without apparently hurting the poor, since it would add to, rather than reduce, income. However, incentives for not bearing children, though also used in China as well as India and Bangladesh, are politically unpalatable in many countries[30]—in part because they could pose a "tragic choice" for the poor leading to entrapment, that is, inducing decisions which might later be regretted. Entrapment occurs if an individual is induced, for example due to myopia or desperate poverty, to take an irreversible step he or she later regrets. It has been discussed in the context of cash payments to persons who are sterilized.[31]

Education and Other Social Programs to Raise the Cost of Children

Social programs that promote investments in the human capital of the poor are consistently associated with reduced fertility among the poor. Probably the single most important social investment is expanded educational opportunities for girls. Once educated females reach childbearing age, the value of alternative uses of their time rises, both in the labor market and in other activities. Educating girls both raises the cost of children to future mothers, thereby reducing fertility (Figure 1), and enhances their income and other prospects.

Education (of girls as well as boys) can also have an immediate effect on current and potential parents. Where schools are inaccessible or of low quality, they do not affect the "cost" of children to parents. However, accessible schools of reasonable quality that provide good educational opportunity in a village or neighborhood, can raise the cost of children by reducing the relative value of children's potential time spent on household and family chores.[32] By reducing the cost of education and thus the cost of producing an educated child, schools can actually raise the relative cost to parents of having many children. Adding a school to a village is obviously also consistent with improving the welfare of the poor in that village.

Once a village has a school, raising tuition fees or other direct costs (for uniforms, books, equipment) would further raise the cost of children to parents; it is also clearly consistent with the notion of ensuring that parents bear more of the social costs of their children. However, without other changes, such as compensatory changes in the quality of the school, or the redistribution of the resulting resources in the form of transfers back to the poor, raising fees could reduce the welfare of the poor—either by reducing consumption or, perversely, by resulting in children's withdrawal from school (Figure 2).

Pension and other programs that provide some form of security in old age, or that otherwise improve access of parents to capital markets, reduce the benefits of children as providers of old-age security and, if all other things remain the same, raise their relative costs. Like many social programs, pensions are also generally associated with increases in the welfare of the poor.

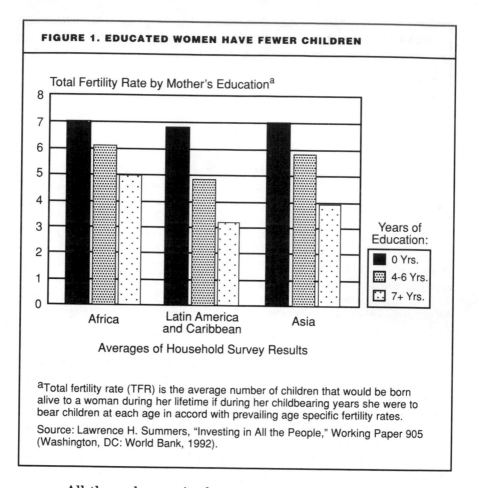

FIGURE 1. EDUCATED WOMEN HAVE FEWER CHILDREN

Total Fertility Rate by Mother's Education[a]

Years of Education:
- 0 Yrs.
- 4-6 Yrs.
- 7+ Yrs.

Averages of Household Survey Results

[a]Total fertility rate (TFR) is the average number of children that would be born alive to a woman during her lifetime if during her childbearing years she were to bear children at each age in accord with prevailing age specific fertility rates.

Source: Lawrence H. Summers, "Investing in All the People," Working Paper 905 (Washington, DC: World Bank, 1992).

All these changes in the parents' situation affect demand for children by raising the "price" of children to parents.[33] These programs tend to have the same effect as taxes on children, but they work indirectly and have the desirable characteristic of succeeding by raising the "quality" of children, and raising rather than reducing the welfare of the poor.

Adjusting the Price of Contraception

If high fertility has negative externalities for societies and economies as a whole, then it makes sense to ensure that unwanted fertility (of the rich and poor alike) is minimized.

Is there unwanted fertility in developing countries? In many countries significant proportions of women say that they would like to

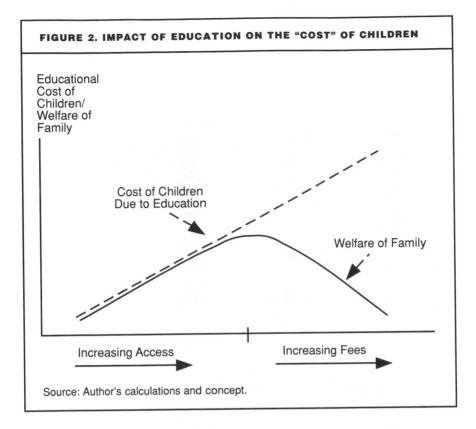

FIGURE 2. IMPACT OF EDUCATION ON THE "COST" OF CHILDREN

Educational
Cost of
Children/
Welfare of
Family

Cost of Children
Due to Education

Welfare of Family

Increasing Access

Increasing Fees

Source: Author's calculations and concept.

limit their fertility, yet do not do so. This condition of "unmet need"—a term used by demographers to signify would-be demand for contraception were the price of contraception zero, including psychic as well as monetary costs—characterizes a quarter of married fecund women in Egypt, one fifth in Tunisia, one eighth in Brazil.[34] A good reason for "unmet need" may be the high price, in one form or another, of contraception. A number of market failures raise the "price" of contraception and may explain why individuals fail to use contraception even when they want no more children.[35]

FAILURE IN THE INFORMATION MARKET. If information (e.g., about the possibility of controlling fertility) cannot easily be tied to a specific marketable product, the market may not provide it. This is one reason governments often finance agricultural extension services. Similarly, information about rhythm and withdrawal has no private market; nor does information about the pill in rural areas where there is no real market for private medical services. Moreover, consumers may not seek new but costly information, especially on contraception, since the product is a complex set of ideas and procedures whose perceived risks are high.

HIGH COSTS OF EARLY ADOPTION OF CONTRACEPTION. It is easy to imagine a situation in which each family would find fertility limitation advantageous, if they did not fear violating social norms and incurring social sanctions. In such a situation, publicly provided information or subsidies could help change norms.[36]

Similarly, early adopters of contraception lower the costs of subsequent adoption for others by providing reliable and specific information about the risks and benefits of contraception. To the extent that family planning is regarded as particularly risky, the demonstration effect, once pioneers verify the innovation's efficacy and safety, could be particularly important.

FAILURE OF CREDIT AND INSURANCE MARKETS. If the benefits to a couple of a smaller family—reduced expenditure on food, more time to devote to work or leisure, increased maternal attention per child, reduced health risks—substantially outweigh the costs of adoption of contraception (and the pleasures associated with a larger but poorer family), why doesn't the couple itself finance the costs of contraception? There are two possible reasons. First, many poor couples, lacking collateral, are not creditworthy. Second, couples may be able to finance the average cost of adopting contraception, but cannot afford, and in the absence of insurance markets, cannot insure against, the possibility of medical complications from procedures that could result in several days of lost wages.[37]

These credit, information, and other constraints that raise the "price" of contraception tend to affect the poor more than the rich; moreover, the direct costs of contraception for the poor represent a larger fraction of the total resources, both human and financial, available to them. In the face of these costs, the most direct way for government to encourage use of contraception is to subsidize family planning services for the poor, as in fact many countries do. Subsidized family planning services targeted to the poor can, if there is any unwanted fertility or unmet need for contraception, both reduce fertility and, by increasing choices for poor couples (especially for women), improve their welfare.[38]

Policy or government failures may also explain some of the unmet need for contraception. All countries regulate access to modern contraception. Some forms of chemical and hormonal contraceptives, as well as some abortifacients are banned; many others are available only through a medical prescription (despite good evidence that trained paramedics can, for example, screen effectively for medical

contraindications to use of the birth control pill). Advertising is often restricted. Although some of these restrictions represent efforts to ensure safe use, others arise from long traditions of medical control or from incorporation into government regulations of religious or cultural views that not all of the population necessarily shares. In some settings, therefore, governments need not positively subsidize contraception, but only reduce current restrictions to its use through appropriate deregulation. The widespread use of modern contraception by the poor in many countries of Latin America is an example of successful market supply without large public subsidies.

Improving Information

Information is costly, particularly to the less educated. Poor couples in developing countries may be unaware of changes in factors that are critical to their fertility decisions. Higher returns to education in a rapidly growing economy might mean that it makes sense to have fewer children in order to educate them better. Declines in child mortality might mean fewer pregnancies are needed to ensure a certain family size. Greater mobility of children as urbanization proceeds may mean parents may not benefit from additional children as security in old age. Government policies to educate and inform the poor about changes such as these could reduce fertility and would, in any event, make the poor better off.

Economic Management for Broad-Based Growth

The most important government activity in reducing fertility is good public management of the economy. Good management includes implementing policies and programs which ensure broad-based growth, that is, growth which benefits all groups, including the poor. As noted, poverty is a root cause of high fertility. Growth which raises incomes of the poor will lower fertility.

Poor economic policies penalize the poor and encourage high fertility in many ways: poorly functioning capital markets, inflation, and other sources of household economic insecurity make children one of the few viable assets a poor couple can count on; overvalued exchange rates reduce the local currency value of farmers' exports, import substitution policies penalize labor; restrictions on access to foreign exchange penalize small entrepreneurs; public monopolies of industries and banking mean higher prices for poor consumers, and so on. Broad-based growth has reduced poverty dramatically in such economies as Indonesia, Thailand, Botswana, Chile, and Costa Rica. The keys to broad-based growth, based on the success of East Asian econ-

omies, include universal access to basic education (which not only reduces fertility but enhances productivity in the workplace and at home); avoidance of undue taxes on the agricultural sector, including overvalued exchange rates and other trade restrictions which burden agricultural exports; and emphasis on non-traditional exports, which encourage productive adaptation and innovation and tend to be labor-demanding.[39]

Outside of East Asia, only a few developing countries have consistently adhered to policies of broad-based growth; many have instead implicitly or explicitly managed the economy for the benefit of various interest and elite groups: urban consumers, organized workers in the formal sector, civil servants, users of subsidies to capital, etc. Broad-based growth which enlarges the economic opportunities of the poor is an essential complement to programs directly aimed at reducing fertility. The fundamental reality is that adequate management of the economy is an appropriate role for government and will help reduce fertility as the welfare of the bottom income groups grows.

CONCLUSIONS

The latter four of the five types of interventions discussed above meet the critical criterion set out: they increase the cost of children to the poor, so that the poor are forced to internalize more fully the social costs of having children, at the same time that they improve the welfare of the poor. They are all win-win policies, in two senses:

■ By addressing one or more of the externalities to childbearing, they make society better off as a whole; the non-poor gain as well as the poor;

■ They can be justified anyway, as sound social programs with high social and economic returns, independent of population concerns.

Whether the consequences of rapid population growth for economic growth and development are large or small, whether the threat to the environment of a growing population is central or tangential, these interventions can be justified by their high economic and social returns, and their effectiveness in improving the choices and welfare of people. Public policies and programs to raise human welfare and reduce population growth are fully consistent, even in the short run. It is a win-win tale.

Notes

This paper draws in part from co-authored papers cited in the bibliography: Birdsall and Griffin; and Chomitz and Birdsall. I am grateful to Robert Cassen for good ideas and general encouragement.

[1] An even broader approach would encompass economic reforms that open up economies to domestic and international competition and reduce public subsidies that penalize agriculture and labor-intensive industries; these subsidies tend to penalize the poor, and as discussed later in this chapter, the resulting reduced income of the poor probably induces high fertility.

[2] Studies on the determinants of fertility are reviewed in Nancy Birdsall, "Economic Approaches to Population Growth," in H. Chenery and T.N. Srinivasan (eds.), *Handbook of Development Economics*, Vol. 1 (North Holland: Elsevier Science Publishers, 1988), pp. 477-542. See also World Bank, *World Development Report: Population Change and Economic Development* (New York: Oxford University Press, 1984). Another study reviews the evidence that reduced fertility, including among the poor, is associated with lower infant mortality, more educated mothers, better educational opportunities for children, and better access to family planning services. See Nancy Birdsall and Charles C. Griffin, "Fertility and Poverty in Developing Countries," *Journal of Policy Modeling*, Vol. 10, No. 1 (1988), pp. 29-56.

[3] See Julian L. Simon, *The Economics of Population Growth* (Princeton, NJ: Princeton University Press, 1977), for a discussion of positive as well as negative externalities to childbearing. While not dismissing the possibility of positive externalities in some situations, in this paper I am concerned with the implications of possible negative externalities.

[4] See Robert J. Willis, "Externalities and Population," in D. Gale Johnson and Ronald D. Lee (eds.), *Population Growth and Economic Development: Issues and Evidence* (Madison, WI: University of Wisconsin Press); and Marc Nerlove, Assal Razin, and Effraim Sadka, *Household and Economy: Welfare Economics of Endogenous Fertility* (New York: Academic Press, 1987).

[5] An exception is a study by Lee and Miller, who describe a number of externalities related to common property and such public services as education. They conclude (with great caution, they note that the numbers are rough and the exercise is experimental) that externalities are not so great nor always in the expected direction and they are not always negative for developing countries. However, as the authors point out, they do not include any estimate to account for externalities arising from renewable common property resources—the environmental externalities discussed below. Ronald D. Lee and Timothy Miller, "Population Growth, Externalities to Childbearing, and Fertility Policy in Developing Countries," *Proceedings of the World Bank Annual Conference on Developing Economics* (Washington, DC: World Bank, 1990).

[6] Evenson provides estimates of the effect of population on wages and rents in North India. He estimates that a 10 percent relative decline in population would boost overall per capita income by 8 percent, boost per capita income of rural landless households by 15 percent, and reduce land rents by 25 percent, ignoring scale economies and induced investments associated with population density. If scale economies are taken into account, a relative reduction in population actually boosts land rents. Robert E. Evenson, "Population Growth, Infrastructure, and Real Incomes in North India, in Ronald D. Lee et al. (eds.), *Population, Food, and Rural Development* (New York: Oxford University Press, 1988).

[7] Nigel R. Crook, "On Social Norms and Fertility Decline," in G. Hawthorne (ed.), *Population and Development* (London: Frank Cass, 1978).

[8] Portions of the discussion of population concerns are based on Nancy Birdsall and Charles C. Griffin, "Population Growth, Externalities, and Poverty," in Michael Lipton and Jaques van der Gaag (eds.), *Including the Poor* (Washington, DC: World Bank, 1993). The discussion of childbearing externalities is based on Kenneth M. Chomitz and Nancy Birdsall, "Incentives to Reduce Fertility: Concepts and Policy Issues," *World Bank Economic Review and Research Observer* (1991).

⁹ A.J. Coale and E.M. Hoover, *Population Growth and Economic Development in Low-Income Countries* (Princeton, NJ: Princeton University Press, 1958). For reviews of the literature on the economic consequences of rapid population growth in developing countries, see Allen C. Kelley, "Economic Consequences of Population Change in the Third World," *Journal of Economic Literature*, Vol. 26, No. 4, pp. 1685-1728; and Birdsall, "Economic Approaches to Population Growth," op. cit.

¹⁰ The best-known skeptic is Julian Simon. (See Simon, op. cit.) A 1986 National Academy of Sciences study concluded that the empirical evidence linking rapid population growth to slower economic growth in developing countries was surprisingly limited, and that what limited evidence there was suggested that any negative effects were relatively small. See National Research Council, *Population Growth and Economic Development: Policy Questions* (Washington, DC: National Academy Press, 1986). For cites of earlier studies and reviews, see Birdsall, "Economic Approaches to Population Growth," op. cit., and Kelley, op. cit.

¹¹ Ronald Lee, "Evaluating Externalities to Childbearing in Developing Countries: The Case of India," *World Bank Economic Review and Research Observer* (Washington, DC: World Bank, 1991). He notes that Demeny, in 1972, pointed out that to decry such a decision on parents' part would be like decrying people's decision not to work on Sundays on the grounds that it reduces their incomes.

¹² For sources of growth including such externalities to human resource investments, see P.M. Romer, "Increasing Returns and Long-Run Growth," *Journal of Political Economy*, Vol. 94, No. 5, pp. 1002-1037; C. Azariadis and A. Drazen, "Threshold Externalities in Economic Development," *Quarterly Journal of Economics* (1990).

¹³ See, for example, Howard Pack and John Page, "Accumulation, Exports, and Growth in the High Performing Asian Economies," paper presented at the Carnegie-Rochester Conference on Public Policy (April 1993).

¹⁴ See M.R. Rosenzweig and Kenneth Wolpin, "Testing the Quantity-Quality Fertility Model: The Use of Twins As A Natural Experiment," *Econometrica*, Vol. 48 (1980), pp. 227-240. This study is useful because parents of twins are not likely to have made a simultaneous or joint decision to have more children and less education, so that lower enrollment rates are more likely due to a causal effect of high fertility. See also Chapter 6 in this volume.

¹⁵ M.R. Rosenzweig and T. Paul Schultz, "The Demand for and Supply of Births: Fertility and Its Life-Cycle Consequences," *American Economic Review*, Vol. 75 (1985), pp. 992-1015.

¹⁶ See Nancy Birdsall and Richard Sabot, "Virtuous Circles: Human Capital, Growth and Equity in East Asia," Policy Research Department, World Bank, unpublished book manuscript. They also quantify the effect of larger families on the "hothouse" effect, i.e., on the extent to which mother's inputs of time per child are affected by the number of children in the home. (Mother's education is also an input to the hothouse effect.)

¹⁷ It is important to emphasize that this goes beyond the usual conclusion that rapid population growth reduces education to show a negative externality to rapid population growth through its effect on education. It is the negative externality, as discussed later in this chapter, that can justify government intervention.

¹⁸ See, for example, Andrew Revkin, *Forum on Population, Environment, and Development—A Bridge Between Rio and Cairo*, unpublished report prepared for The Rene Dubos Center for Human Environments, New York, 1993. In Nancy Birdsall, "Another Look at Population and Global Warming," Policy Research Working Paper Series No. 1020 (November 1992), I compare the costs of reducing greenhouse gas emissions in the United States via a carbon tax to the costs of reducing greenhouse gas emissions in developing countries through family planning and education programs that would reduce population growth; I conclude that the latter is as cost-effective as the former and that therefore the developed countries should include, as part of any optimal carbon strategy, transfers to poor countries to finance family planning and education programs to reduce fertility.

¹⁹ On the former case for the Philippines, see Maria Concepcion J. Cruz, *Population Growth, Poverty, and Environmental Stress: Frontier Migration in the Philippines and*

Costa Rica (Washington, DC: World Resources Institute, 1992). Chapter 5 in this volume rightly questions whether population is really to blame, as opposed to poor policies and failing markets. But if policies and markets do not adjust as population grows, some causal effect must be attributed to population.

[20] John Bongaarts, "Population Growth and Global Warming," *Population and Development Review*, James C. White (ed.), Vol. 18, No. 2 (New York: Elsevier Science Publishing Co., Inc., 1992); and Nancy Birdsall and John A. Dixon, "Some Economics of Global Climate Change: The View from the Developing Countries," in *Global Climate Change: The Economic Costs of Mitigation and Adaptation* (1991).

[21] The case of the Philippines is a good one. On the other hand, a good part of forest clearing, particularly of tropical forests in Brazil, Indonesia, and parts of Africa, has not been due to population growth so much as to road-building and fiscal and pricing policies that made logging commercially attractive.

[22] R.H. Cassen, "Economic Implications of Demographic Change," *Transactions of the Royal Society of Tropical Medicine and Hygiene* (London: Royal Society of Tropical Medicine and Hygiene, 1993).

[23] Pierre Crosson and Jock R. Anderson, "Resources and Global Food Prospects: Supply and Demand for Cereals to 2030," World Bank Technical Paper No. 184 (Washington, DC: World Bank, 1991).

[24] Note that although wages are depressed in the scenario, rents and profits are boosted. High fertility is therefore potentially Pareto superior to low fertility, assuming that there were a mechanism for redistribution of some of the rents of landlords and capitalists. See Yew-Kwang Ng, "On the Welfare Economics of Population Control," *Population and Development Review*, Vol. 12, No. 2 (1986), pp. 247-66; and Robert J. Willis, "Externalities and Population," in Johnson and Lee, op. cit.

[25] For data for males in Brazil, see Jere R. Behrman and Nancy Birdsall, "The Reward for Good Timing: Cohort Effects and Earning Functions for Brazilian Males," *Review of Economics and Statistics*, Vol. 70, No. 1 (1988).

[26] For a relatively pessimistic prognosis for consolidation of reform in Latin America, in part due to the neglect of social issues and the dire situation of the poor, see Moises Naim, "Latin America: Post-Adjustment Blues," *Foreign Policy*, No. 92 (1993).

[27] This is a central message of the World Bank report on East Asia. World Bank, *The East Asian Miracle: Economic Growth and Public Policy* (New York: Oxford University Press, 1993). For the "virtuous circle" of human capital accumulation, improving income equality and rising income in East Asia, see Birdsall and Sabot, op. cit. For a study of the effects of income distribution on growth at the country level, see Nancy Birdsall, David Ross, and Richard Sabot, "Inequality and Growth Reconsidered," paper presented at the annual meetings of the American Economic Association, Boston, January 1994. They attribute the success of East Asian economies in sustaining high growth in part to their low levels of income inequality and policies of "shared growth."

[28] For other evidence on the effect of high fertility on poverty, see Birdsall and Griffin, op. cit.

[29] Only if a change in their situation makes the poor at least as well off as they are now should we expect them to choose fewer children voluntarily. Otherwise there would have to be an element of coercion—which would clearly not increase the welfare of the poor.

[30] Subsidies or positive incentives to encourage high fertility are more common than negative incentives, having been used in France and parts of Eastern Europe, and are obviously a form of incentive that is politically acceptable. For a discussion of the justification for and welfare implications of incentives to reduce fertility, as well as of child taxes and child quotas, see Chomitz and Birdsall, op. cit.

[31] Incentives to correct for failures in the market for information about contraception do have potential in many developing countries, but incentives to correct for externalities are harder to justify; they would probably involve larger financial amounts and raise a number of difficult ethical issues. See Chomitz and Birdsall, op. cit.

[32] More formally, note that the appearance of a school reduces the relative cost to parents of ensuring higher "quality" children vs. ensuring a higher "quantity" of children. For a presentation of the formal argument for the interactive effects of changing

the price of quality on the price of quantity and thus on the demand for different relative amounts of these in the total bundle of "child services," see Gary S. Becker and H. Gregg Lewis, "Interaction Between the Quantity and Quality of Children," in T.W. Schultz (ed.), *Economics of the Family* (Chicago: University of Chicago Press, 1974).

[33] Though counter-intuitive it is easily demonstrated that interventions that would improve the lives of people, such as education and lower mortality, will increase the "price" of the quantity of children by raising the cost of inputs required to rear children, such as the opportunity cost of parents' time; ibid.

[34] See Charles F. Westoff and Luis Hernando Ochoa, "Unmet Need and the Demand for Family Planning," Demographic and Health Surveys Comparative Studies No. 5 (Columbia, MD: Institute for Resource Development/Macro International, Inc., 1991).

[35] The discussion of market failures that raise the price of contraception is drawn from Chomitz and Birdsall, op. cit.

[36] See Crook, op. cit. In this situation, while initial innovators would encounter social resistance, we would expect a "tipping" effect. See Thomas C. Schelling, *Micromotives and Macrobehavior* (New York: W.W. Norton, 1978). Once a critical percentage of families had adopted family planning, the old social norm would be undercut, and the other families would follow suit.

[37] A 1984 study of acceptors of sterilization in Bangladesh indicated that for tubectomy and vasectomy acceptors, out-of-pocket transportation and food costs averaged almost twice the average daily male wage. More than one-third of acceptors spent more than three times the average daily male wage. More than one-third of acceptors eventually faced additional medical complications, and 11 percent eventually spent a total of almost ten times the average daily male wage. Recuperation time averaged four days for men and ten for women, but was also subject to considerable variation. Some 8 percent of men and 37 percent of women needed more than fifteen days to recuperate. Thus, although mean acceptance costs are relatively low, there is a substantial risk of relatively high costs. See John Cleland and W. Parker Mauldin, "Study of Compensation Payments and Family Planning in Bangladesh" (Dhaka: National Institute of Population and Training, 1987).

[38] Family planning services, if of reasonable quality, have certainly contributed to lower fertility, though they are most effective in settings where women are reasonably well educated. In Bangladesh, where women's education is low, contraceptive use rose from 14 to 31 percent in the 1980s, and the total fertility rate fell from 6.3 to 4.6. See Bashir Ahmed, "Determinants of Contraceptive Use in Rural Bangladesh: The Demand for Children, Supply of Children, and Costs of Fertility Regulation," *Demography*, Vol. 24, No. 3 (1987), pp. 361-373; and Charles Griffin, "Bangladesh Public Expenditure Review: Public Resources Management During the 4th 5-Year Plan, FY91-95," World Bank Report 7545 (Washington, DC: World Bank, 1989).

[39] For discussion of these and other aspects of "shared growth," see World Bank, *The East Asian Miracle*, op. cit. and Birdsall and Sabot, op. cit.

About the ODC

ODC fosters an understanding of how development relates to a much changed U.S. domestic and international policy agenda and helps shape the new course of global development cooperation.

ODC's programs focus on three main issues: the challenge of political and economic transitions and the reform of development assistance programs; the development dimensions of international responses to global problems; and the implications of development for U.S. economic security.

In pursuing these themes, ODC functions as:

- *A center for policy analysis.* Bridging the worlds of ideas and actions, ODC translates the best academic research and analysis on selected issues of policy importance into information and recommendations for policymakers in the public and private sectors.

- *A forum for the exchange of ideas.* ODC's conferences, seminars, workshops, and briefings bring together legislators, business executives, scholars, and representatives of international financial institutions and nongovernmental groups.

- *A resource for public education.* Through its publications, meetings, testimony, lectures, and formal and informal networking, ODC makes timely, objective, nonpartisan information available to an audience that includes but reaches far beyond the Washington policy-making community.

ODC is a private, nonprofit organization funded by foundations, corporations, governments, and private individuals.

Stephen J. Friedman is the Chairman of the Overseas Development Council, and John W. Sewell is the Council's President.

276

About the Authors

Project Director

ROBERT CASSEN is a professor of development economics at the International Development Centre, Oxford University. Previously he held academic posts at the Institute of Development Studies, Sussex University; the Centre for Population Studies, London School of Hygiene and Tropical Medicine; and the London School of Economics. He has also been an economic advisor to the British aid program in New Delhi, India, and served on the staff of the World Bank and the Brandt Commission Secretariat in Geneva. His publications in the population field include *Population Policy: A New Consensus* (ODC, July 1994); *India: Population, Economy, Society* (Macmillan). He also directed and coauthored the study *Does Aid Work?* (second edition, Oxford University Press, 1994).

Contributing Authors

DENNIS A. AHLBURG is a professor in the Industrial Relations Center, Carlson School of Management, and a senior fellow in the Center for Population Analysis and Policy, both at the University of Minnesota. He has been a visiting fellow at the East-West Center, Honolulu, and the National Centre for Development Studies, Australian National University. His work focuses on the interactions between population change and economic development, population forecasting, and determinants and impacts of international migration and remittance payments. He has a particular interest in the South Pacific region. Ahlburg has written numerous journal articles and two monographs on Pacific Islander migration and remittances. He is the author of the chapter on "The Impact of Population Growth on Economic Growth in Developing Nations" in the 1986 U.S. National Academy of Sciences study of population growth and economic development.

LISA M. BATES is the assistant director of ODC's Population and Development Project and research/administrative assistant to the vice president for studies of ODC. Ms. Bates previously worked for the Center for Women Policy Studies.

NANCY BIRDSALL is the executive vice president of the Inter-American Development Bank. She has held various policy and management positions at the World Bank, where most recently she served as director of the Policy Research Department. Between 1987 and 1991, Birdsall served as chief of the World Bank's Environment Division for the Latin American Region, and from 1984 to 1987, she served as chief of the World Bank's Policy and Research Division for the Population, Health, and Nutrition Department. Birdsall has been a senior adviser to The Rockefeller Foundation and has served on several committees of the National Academy of Sciences, including the Committee on the Human Dimensions of Global Change. She currently chairs the board of directors of the International Center for Research on Women. She has authored numerous publications analyzing human resource issues in developing countries, including population growth, poverty, education, and health, as well as labor market and environmental issues.

SCHUYLER FRAUTSCHI is a graduate research assistant at the Prevention of Maternal Mortality Program at Columbia University's Center for Population and Family Health. He recently completed a client-based needs assessment at the Queen's Park Counselling Centre and Clinic, the largest public sexually transmitted disease and HIV facility in Trinidad and Tobago. From 1989 to 1992, he worked with the national AIDS prevention program in Honduras as a Peace Corps volunteer.

LYNN FREEDMAN is assistant professor of Clinical Public Health at the Columbia University School of Public Health and staff attorney of the Development Law and Policy Program of Columbia's Center for Population and Family Health. Her work has focused on the relationship between women's legal status and reproductive health, with particular attention to human rights and reproductive rights. Recent publications include "Human Rights and Reproductive Choice," in *Studies in Family Planning* (co-authored with Stephen Isaacs), "Women's Mortality: A Legacy of Neglect," in *The Health of Women: A Global Perspective* (co-authored with Deborah Maine), and "Law and Reproductive Health" in *Beyond the Numbers: A Reader in Population, Consumption, and the Environment* (Island Press, 1994).

KAVAL GULHATI, currently a senior fellow at the Centre for Policy Research in New Delhi and honorary president of UNNITI Foundation, has had an international career spanning nearly three decades. She was the founding director of the Center for Development and Population Activities (CEDPA) as well as a member of several boards including the Global Fund for Women, Population Action International, and the Indian Institute of Health Management, Jaipur. She is the author of many publications and consultant to international organizations.

ALLEN C. KELLEY is James B. Duke professor of economics and associate director of the Center for Demographic Studies at Duke University. Prior to coming to Duke, he was on the faculty of the University of Wisconsin-Madison. He has also held visiting positions at Stanford, Harvard, Monash and Melbourne Universities in Melbourne, Australia, and the International Institute for Applied Systems Analysis in Vienna, Austria. Themes of his several books include Japanese economic and demographic history, Third World urban growth, Egyptian population and development, the economics of disease eradication, and theories of economic development. Representative articles relating to his continuing interest in the consequences of population growth include "Economic Consequences of Population Change in the Third World," *Journal of Economic Literature* (December 1988); "Kenya at the Turning Point," with C. Nobbe (World Bank 1991); and "Revisionism Revisited: An Essay on the Population Debate in Historical Perspective," in *Population, Development, and Welfare; the Nobel Jubilee Symposium in Economics* (Springer-Verlag, 1993).

CYNTHIA B. LLOYD is an economist who currently works as deputy director of the Research Division of The Population Council. Her research focuses on family and gender issues in population and development studies and on the consequences of family size and structure for children's development. Formerly, she worked at the United Nations Population Division, serving for six years as the Chief of the Fertility and Family Planning Studies Section. During the 1970s, she was a member of the economics faculty at Barnard College as well as a research associate at the Columbia University Center for Social Sciences. She is the author of many books and articles on a range of topics including women in the labor market, child survival and fertility, children's living arrangements, and female-headed households.

DEBORAH MAINE is an epidemiologist and program director of the Prevention of Maternal Mortality Program at Columbia University's Center for Population and Family Health (CPFH). She has been consultant to various United Nations Agencies (including UNICEF, United Nations Development Programme, United Nations Fund Population Activities, and World Health Organization), the World Bank, and the Institut National de la Sante et de la Recherche Medicale in France. Prior to joining Columbia, Maine was assistant editor at the Alan Guttmacher Institute and publications assistant to Margaret

Mead. Her publications include three chartbooks on maternal and child health, the most recent of which is *Safe Motherhood Programs: Options and Issues* (CPFH, 1991), as well as *Guidelines for Monitoring Progress in the Reduction of Maternal Mortality*, with J. McCarthy and V. Ward (UNICEF, 1992), and *Safe Motherhood: Priorities and Next Steps*, with M. Law and M.T. Feuerstein (UNDP, 1991), among others.

WILLIAM PAUL McGREEVEY is principal population specialist of the World Bank's Population, Health, and Nutrition Department. Since joining the World Bank in 1980, he has worked in several departments on issues including health sector finance in Latin America, financing of social services, and provision of adequate services to poverty groups. Previously, he taught at the University of Oregon and the University of California, Berkeley, where he also headed the Center for Latin American Studies. His writings include *An Economic History of Colombia 1845–1930* (Cambridge, 1971); *Third World Poverty* (ed.), (Lexington Books, 1980); and *Social Security in Latin America* (World Bank, 1990). He was also a member of the team that produced the *World Development Report* (World Bank, 1984) on population.

THOMAS W. MERRICK is senior population adviser of the Population, Health, and Nutrition Department of the World Bank. Prior to joining the World Bank in 1992, he served as president of the Population Reference Bureau for eight years. From 1976 to 1984, he directed the Center for Population Research and chaired the Department of Demography at Georgetown University, where he was also associate professor of demography. He has held positions with The Ford Foundation in Brazil, the U.S. Agency for International Development, and the Population Studies Center at the University of Pennsylvania. He also leads the World Bank's Population Policy and Advisory Services (PPAS) group, which was formed to strengthen the World Bank's capacity and effectiveness in addressing population, family planning, and related reproductive health concerns.

THEODORE PANAYOTOU is a fellow at the Harvard Institute for International Development, Director of the Institute's International Environment Program, and a lecturer in the Department of Economics at Harvard University. A specialist in environmental and resource economics, environmental policy analysis, and development economics, he has advised governments and institutes in Asia, Africa, and Eastern Europe, as well as numerous other national and international institutions, on the interactions between the natural resource base and economic development. Panayotou served for a decade as visiting professor and resident adviser in Southeast Asia, and recently co-authored a multi-volume environmental policy study at the Thailand Development Research Institute in Bangkok. Other publications include *Green Markets: The Economics of Sustainable Development* (ICS Press, 1992) and *Not by Timber Alone: Economics and Ecology for Sustaining Tropical Forests* (with Peter S. Ashton, Island Press, 1992). He is currently at work on another book, *Natural Resources, Environment, and Development: Economics, Policy, and Management.* Dr. Panayotou received the 1991 Distinguished Achievement Award of the Society for Conservation Biology for his wide-ranging efforts to use economic analysis as a tool for conservation.

SHARON STANTON RUSSELL is a research scholar at the Center for International Studies, Massachusetts Institute of Technology, where she is a member of the Inter-University Committee on International Migration. Russell has also been a consultant on population and human resource development issues with the United Nations Development Programme, the Economic Commission for Europe, several private foundations, and the World Bank, where she is currently a visiting scholar. She served as a member of the 1993 United Nations Expert Group on Population Distribution and Migration, preparatory to the 1994 International Conference on Population and Development, and the 1990 United Nations Expert Group on International Migration Policies and the Status of Female Migrants. She has written extensively on international migration trends and policies and the relationship of migration to economic and social development. Her recent publications include *International Migration in North America, Europe, Central Asia, the Middle East and North Africa: Research and Research Related Activities*; *International Migration in Europe, Central Asia, The Middle East and North Africa: Issues for the World Bank*; and *International Migration and International Trade* (with Michael S. Teitelbaum).

FARIDA SHAHEED is a sociologist based in Lahore, Pakistan, where she is a member of Shirkat Gah, Women's Resource Center. She has written extensively on the status of women in Pakistan, including an award-winning book on the country's women's movement, *Women of Pakistan: Two Steps Forward, One Step Back?* (co-authored with Khawar Mumtaz). She is editor of *The Women of Pakistan*, an annotated bibliography of published and unpublished material on women in Pakistan, and is the author of numerous studies and publications on various aspects of women's employment and economic participation, and on the effects of Islamization of law and the rise of the religious right on women in Pakistan. She has served as consultant to various United Nations agencies (United Nations Development Fund for Women, UNICEF, International Labor Organization, United Nations Research Institute for Social Development, Food and Agriculture Organization), bilateral development agencies, the World Bank, Asia Pacific Development Centre, and the Government of Pakistan.

MICHAEL S. TEITELBAUM is a demographer at the Alfred P. Sloan Foundation in New York. Presently, he serves (via appointment by the Congressional leadership) as one of eight Commissioners of the U.S. Commission on Immigration Reform. In April 1993, he was elected a Vice Chair of the Commission. Prior to joining the Alfred P. Sloan Foundation, he served as a member of the faculties of Oxford University and Princeton University; staff director of the Select Committee on Population, U.S. House of Representatives; and member of the professional staffs of The Ford Foundation and the Carnegie Endowment for International Peace. A regular speaker on demography and international migration, he has also written many articles and books, which include *The Fear of Population Decline* (1985); *Population and Resources in Western Intellectual Traditions* (Cambridge University Press, 1989, co-editor); *The British Fertility Decline: Demographic Transition in the Crucible of the Industrial Revolution* (1984); and *Latin Migration North: The Problem for U.S. Foreign Policy* (1985).